EARLY INTERVENTION II
Working with Parents and Families

Katharine G. Butler, PhD
Editor, *Topics in Language Disorders*
Syracuse University
Syracuse, New York

TOPICS IN LANGUAGE DISORDERS SERIES

AN ASPEN PUBLICATION®
Aspen Publishers, Inc.
Gaithersburg, Maryland
1994

Library of Congress Cataloging-in-Publication Data

Early intervention / Katharine G. Butler, editor.
p. cm.
Compilations from Topics in language disorders.
Includes bibliographical references and index.
Contents: 1. Working with infants and toddlers—2. Working with
families and parents.
ISBN: 0-8342-0584-x (v. 1)—ISBN: 0-8342-0585-8 (v. 2)
1. Communicative disorders in children—Treatment. 2. Communicative
disorders in infants—Treatment 3. Language disorders in children—Treatment.
I. Butler, Katharine G.
II. Topics in language disorders
RJ496.C67E38 1994
618.92'85506—dc20
93-36266
CIP

Editorial Resources: Ruth Bloom

Library of Congress Catalog Card Number: 93-36266
ISBN: 0-8342-0585-8
Series ISBN: 0-8342-0590-4

Printed in the United States

1 2 3 4 5

Table of Contents

Preface

Topics in Language Disorders is a transdisciplinary journal that is devoted to discussion of issues surrounding language acquisition and its disorders. *TLD* has the following major purposes: (1) providing relevant information to practicing professionals who provide services to those who are at-risk or have language disabilities; (2) clarifying the application of theory and research to practice; (3) bringing together professionals across disciplines, who are researchers and clinicians from the health education arenas both as authors and as readers; (4) clarifying the application of theory to practice among professionals and students-in-training; and (5) contributing to the scientific literature while making each issue accessible and relevant to an interdisciplinary readership.

Typically, each *TLD* journal is devoted to a single topic, although the constellation of articles may vary. A few may be wholly clinical in nature, while most blend practice and research. In the *TLD* book series, each book provides a critical but highly sensitive evaluation of current research and translates that analysis into a framework for service delivery. Hence, in this *TLD* book, the reader will find a distillation of the best of the journal's current offerings as well as some seminal articles that may enhance the readers' conceptual knowledge. Offerings are provided from a variety of disciplines: speech-language pathology, audiology, child development, psychology, medicine (including neonatology, pediatrics, psychiatry, etc.) and education (including special and regular education and its myriad of sub-fields).

The authors represented within the covers of *Early Intervention II: Working with Parents and Families* include speech-language pathologists, early childhood special educators, occupational therapists, teachers of the hearing-impaired, administrators, linguists, psychologists, and child psychiatrists. Their accumulated wisdom is reflected in these pages.

PART I. IMPLICATIONS FROM THE EARLY LANGUAGE DEVELOPMENT AND DISORDERS LITERATURE FOR WORKING WITH PARENTS AND FAMILIES

Early intervention services have blossomed recently, following federal funding of services for children zero to three years old. Traditional service patterns have been deemed inappropriate, and early interventionists now emphasize family-centered approaches. We have come to recognize the social nature of the infants' and toddlers' interactions with caregivers and realize the centrality of the family. This has led to a significant shift in models of service delivery in communication disorders (Butler, 1992). Infants in both functional and dysfunctional families are oriented toward their families' social world. The consequences of both the children's dependency and the social nature of caretaker/child interaction are two themes that run throughout this text.

Another theme is the need to bring professionals together as early interventionists and to broaden their focus from evaluating young children's cognitive and motor skills to viewing the whole child in the family context (Gebbs & Teti, 1990). Family-centered intervention requires that professionals from a variety of disciplines come together to develop new ways of assessing the strengths of families and their at-risk or language-disabled young children.

A fourth theme relates to the recent explosion of information concerning "early psychosocial development, parent-child interactions, infant/toddler communication, changing family structure and function and the interaction of all of these factors" (Donahue-Kilburg, 1992, p. xv), and its usefulness in working with parents and families.

Van Kleeck's "Issues in Adult-Child Interaction: Six Philosophical Orientations" sets the stage for all that follows by noting the multiplicity of perspectives that have stemmed from social interaction research, which, in turn, has served as undergirding for assumptions made by early interventionists on the overriding significance of adult-child interactions. After surveying the contributions and the shortcomings of numerous philosophical orientations, she recommends that readers consider both ecological and ethnographic approaches. The former is a systems approach, while the latter uses participant observers and "thick" descriptions. Van Kleeck suggests that since "each approach has its own limiting assumptions, corroboration using a mix of philosophical orientations and their methodologies should yield the most valid and complete results." Readers may find her analyses and interpretations to be of assistance as they build their own philosophical framework.

Foster, a linguist, provides practitioners with possible patterns for the development of discourse in normal and language-disordered infants and toddlers. In "The Development of Discourse Topic Skills by Infants and Young Children," Foster points out that very young children do not have "true competence" in the early stages of the development of topic initiation and maintenance, but there is a relationship between topic type and cognitive development. She provides exemplars and recommends that caregivers be taught to recognize interactional pragmatic behaviors that are very subtly demonstrated by the infant. Foster cites convincing evidence that children develop greater coherence in their conversations when caregivers engage the infants and toddlers in play routines. This suggestion is one that will resurface in the work of other authors in this text.

Crais' "World Knowledge to Word Knowledge" complements Foster's work by tracing the acquisition of word knowledge and the factors that influence vocabulary acquisition. Using the Chapman Child Talk model, Crais helps readers appreciate the shifts in the real-world experiences that young children experi-

ence as well as the sematic processing that occurs over the preschool years. Practitioners will find her descriptions of various assessment procedures to be helpful, as she contrasts definition tasks, work association tasks, and others and provides a number of avenues for making judgments about children's lexical abilities/disabilities. She also discusses in detail intervention with "words," i.e., how to teach new words, using naturalistic and real-word experiences. She suggests that if contextual presentations are not successful, the creative clinician can use some of the many informal or experimental tasks described in this artcle.

Coster and Cicchetti, in "Research on the Communicative Development of Maltreated Children," provide health and education professionals, who encounter, as most will, both dysfunctional and highly motivated functional families, with new information regarding abused children's language acquisition. They cite evidence supporting the notion that maltreated children are found to be at increased risk for communication disorders. Current research attempts to understand the sequelae of maltreatment within a dynamic systems framework, one in which child abuse and maltreatment are viewed within the family's social and physical context. As noted earlier, language development is embedded within children's social-emotional and cognitive development. The authors explain how social class and cultural influences become intertwined with maltreatment. They note that longitudinal studies are not only limited but have been undertaken with only particular racial or cultural groups. Not surprisingly, they find that a family system that provides a "consistent, warm, sensitive and contingent parent-child interaction style is optimal for early communication development." The few existing studies of the language of abused children compared with normal children and matched for socioeconomic status reveal significant language performance deficits. In summarizing those studies, the authors caution that it is difficult to sort out cognitive from language deficits, given the importance of verbal tasks in most intelligence tests. Some researchers have reported that maltreated children's typical pattern for coping within the family context is to monitor the nonverbal rather than the verbal cues in the environment. It may be that such children fail to attend to the examiner's questions during cognitive evaluations due to their anxiety or uncertainty, and as a consequence they fail to reveal their abilities. The authors conclude that interventionists must move beyond "global measures" of linguistic competence to more fine-grained assessment in multiple contexts. Readers will be able to garner a number of suggested directions for such assessment and intervention from comments by Coster and Cicchetti and their expertise in dealing with these children.

Turning to a discussion of toddlers who are not talking at two, Paul concludes this section on early language development and disorders with "Profiles of Toddlers with Slow Expressive Language Development." She discusses her longitudinal study and assists practitioners in dealing with service delivery issues stemming from whether or not intervention is warranted at this age. Paul recognizes that (1) parents often receive conflicting opinions from a variety of professionals, and (2) predictions about who will "outgrow" a language deficit and who will not may make decisions difficult for families and professionals. She also reviews the current status of research and practice. In so doing, she suggests that intervenors might focus first on helping caregivers provide pragmatic and socialization experiences. She also concludes that evidence suggests 40% to 50% of two year olds with expressive language deficits will continue to reveal abbreviated sentence length and syntactical deficits at age three and narrative (e.g., story-retelling) difficulties at age four. Noting that narrative skill is one of the best predicters for later

school-aged achievement and academic success, Paul concludes with a thoughtful discussion of how and when practitioners might undertake clinic-based intervention.

PART II. FAMILY, CAREGIVER, AND PEER INTERACTIONS WITH VERY YOUNG COMMUNICATIVELY IMPAIRED CHILDREN

Part II of the text reviews how families and caregivers can be productively involved as communication intervention agents. This section explores models of intervention that may be fruitfully employed by a coalition of parents, caregivers, and professionals to increase the child's communication abilities.

Conti-Ramsden begins the section with "Mothers in Dialogue with Language-Impaired Children." She provides evidence that earlier researchers tended to focus on only one half of the dyad, i.e., the mother. While this garnered increased understanding of mothers' speech to young children, it failed to capture many aspects of the dyadic nature of conversational interaction itself and of the role played by the child. Noting how it is that mothers modify their own speech as their children's communicative abilities undergo change, Conti-Ramsden analyzes child dialogue characteristics between mothers and their normally developing children and mothers and their language-impaired children. As she illustrates, it is no easy task to untangle the bi-directional aspects of mother-child discourse. Yet, early interventionists must identify these aspects in order to assist mothers and other caregivers in shaping their interactions with their communicatively impaired youngsters. Conti-Ramsden concludes that both interventionists and researchers need to more clearly understand the interactive environment in which communication does (or does not) take place prior to attempting intervention.

Fitzgerald and Fischer in "A Family Involvement Model for Hearing-Impaired Infants" continue the theme of earlier authors in Parts I and II. However, they focus on hearing-impaired infants as the recipients of a family-focused, integrated, ecologically valid approach to early intervention. They, too, report that intervention efforts must be directed at the "systems level" rather than exclusively at either the parents or the infant. They provide evidence of the success of this model through a practical presentation. Both authors have been extensively involved for a number of years with the Mama Lere Parent Infant Training Program at the Bill Wilkerson Hearing and Speech Center. They provide readers with a view of a successful model for assessing family needs and strengths, followed by a discussion of the four service delivery components that comprise the ecological framework of the program (supportive counseling, information exchange, facilitation of child communicative competence, and educational advocacy and team decision making). Readers will find a host of suggested strategies, a decision-making model, and case studies designed to illuminate the basic premises which underlie the Mama Lere program.

In "Peers As Communication Intervention Agents: Some New Strategies and Research Findings," Goldstein and Strain pick up the thread of intervention by significant others through their descriptions of two peer intervention strategies carried out by classmates in developmentally integrated settings. They describe how the literature on social interaction may be utilized to show (1) that peers can be trained to be intervention agents during structured or free play periods and (2) how peers, even at three years old, can interact during sociodramatic play. Specific suggestions for sociodramatic script training and how teachers/clinicians may observe and prompt free play are provided. The authors conclude by summarizing the potency and cost-effectiveness of their suggestions for in-class communication training in integrated settings.

Kenworthy's "Caregiver-Child Interaction and Language Acquisition of Hearing-Impaired Children" completes Part II. He returns to a consideration of preschoolers who have significant hearing impairments requiring early intervention within a synergistic or interactional context. In so doing, he steps away from traditional clinical intervention that frequently addresses speech discrimination and other specific speech skills without regard to facilitation of communicative interactions. When normal-hearing caregivers attempt to provide child-focused, linguistically contingent interactions with hearing-impaired children, it is important that neither interactant places too heavy a conversational burden on the other, since that can lead to communicative breakdowns. Rather, Kenworthy describes how such conversational interaction can be modified by normal-hearing caregivers to support, rather than defeat, hearing-impaired preschoolers' utterances. Two case studies illustrate how interventionists can capitalize on seizing teaching opportunities within natural language sequences.

PART III. CAREGIVERS AND CLINICIANS: LANGUAGE ASSESSMENT AND INTERVENTION

For well over a decade, the precepts of language intervention for preschool language-disordered children have focused on providing for naturally occurring conversational interactions. Friel-Patti and Lougeay-Mottinger's "Preschool Language Intervention: Some Key Concerns" describes the role of clinicians as facilitators of children's language through manipulating the environment, much as previous authors in Parts I and II have identified. The difficulties of this approach are documented by Friel-Patti and her colleague, particularly when interventionists work individually with a child. The authors provide a sound rationale for instituting group-based pragmatic therapy, although they note that heterogeneous groups of language-impaired children require careful planning so that individual children's needs are also met. They address this issue by providing readers with systems for setting goals and measuring student progress. They conclude that pragmatic intervention has become a reality but that there is still much to learn about its implementation. So say we all.

McDade and Varnedoe, in "Training Parents To Be Language Facilitators," describe their experiences at the University of South Carolina in training parents to become primary interventionists. They also summarize the literature and note that it is compelling in its support for programs that involve parents producing greater gains as opposed to programs that do not. As with the other authors in this text, McDade and Varnedoe reflect on how it is that carefully designed studies can lead to a paradigm shift, e.g., parents assuming a central role in their child's intervention, and yet practitioners frequently seem to resist experimentation and change. The authors note that since the 1960s, model programs have existed that involve parents and their hearing-impaired children (see Fitzgerald and Fisher, Part II). And yet, even as the millenium approaches, family-focused intervention is seen as something quite new and untried. McDade and Varnedoe provide exemplars for how parents may learn such language facilitative techniques as providing expansion and commentary, as well as positive feedback. And like Friel-Patti and Lougeay-Mottinger, these authors suggest a large number of implementation strategies. Finally, the authors share with readers both the limitations and successes of various training models.

Another model is offered by Fitzgerald and Karnes in "A Parent-Implemented Language Model for At-Risk and Developmentally Delayed Preschool Children." This model, Regional Intervention Programs for Parent and Preschools (RIP), differs from some others by drawing upon both behavioral and pragmatic frameworks. Thus, both operant and naturalistic strategies are combined to facilitate communication skills in multiple contexts. This model casts families in a greater number of capacities than most models. For example, parents serve as language trainers for other parents; as language interventionists in the classroom with all children, including doing baseline observations and collecting evaluation data and performance feedback; and as interactants with their own at-risk or developmentally delayed preschoolers. This carefully designed model program goes well beyond typical programs in sharing with parents important roles in assessment and intervention through a series of modules. Readers will appreciate the clarity with which the program implementation is described.

So-called dysfunctional families have been discussed by some previous authors in this text; however, Trout and Foley provide a new perspective in "Working with Families of Handicapped Infants and Toddlers." These authors view the family as an ecosystem, a system which requires that interventionists see the family as capable of supporting the infant's optimal development. Professionals who widen their perspectives on family function can form an alliance with the family on behalf of the infant. Trout and Foley discuss some of the parenting responses which may be less than optimal, but they point out that such responses may not signify inadequacy or psychopathology. Rather, inappropriate parenting responses may reflect parental confusion, guilt, mourning, or even simple information overload or anxiety. Working with families in an early intervention context requires great skill; intervention teams reflecting multiple disciplines can and do provide ecologically valid support. Trout and Foley urge readers to become more effectively attuned to families and to understand diverse and unique family styles and values.

Sparks' "Assessment and Intervention with At-Risk Infants and Toddlers: Guidelines for the Speech-Language Pathologist" encapsulates the procedures that a language specialist must know prior to entering the arena of family-centered evaluation and treatment. First, guidelines are provided for neonatal screening and in-depth assessment of preterm infants and include evaluating the infant's hospital environment. For somewhat older infants, event sampling of communicative interactions with caregivers is recommended. At the same time, assessment of multiple caregivers through a number of observational instruments as well as assessment of familial strengths and needs as part of the individual family service plan (IFSP) is required. Secondly, intervention guidelines are provided. In addition, readers are warned to take into account the interactions which may occur in the Neonatal Intensive Care Unit (NICU) between the infant, parents, and other caregivers and to attend to the family's needs during the transition period from hospital to home. Sparks concludes by noting that communication can be integrated into almost every IFSP goal.

Part III closes with a look at "The First Three Years: Special Education Perspectives on Assessment and Intervention" by Ensher. She provides information on current and emerging assessment and intervention procedures, and she makes a plea for programmatic evaluations of ongoing interactions within the context of the home and family. She notes that biomedical studies may offer evidence of significant relationships between environmental and physiological factors, since such factors may be implicated in reducing stress through proper handling and positioning of critically ill infants. Ensher reports that child abuse of infants with handicapping conditions is prevalent, stemming perhaps from the frequently reported irritability and temperamental difficulties manifested by preterm infants. She, too, urges parent-centered intervention in both the NICU and in the home.

And thus comes to a close *Early Intervention II: Working with Parents and Families.* Evidence provided by many of the authors indicates that a paradigm shift is in the making. As the year 2000 approaches, remarkable changes in service delivery patterns to children, zero to three, and their families are occurring. We shall soon have answers to today's questions. What will be the new questions for the new century? Whatever they may be, parents and professionals will asking them together.

REFERENCES

Butler, K.G. (1992). "It's just talking, isn't it?" In G. Donahue-Kilburg *Family-centered early intervention for communication disorders: Prevention and Treatment,* (pp. xi-xiii). Gaithersburg, MD: Aspen Publishers.

Donahue-Kilburg, G. (1992). *Family-centered early intervention for communication disorders: Pre-vention and treatment.* Gaithersburg, MD: Aspen Publishers.

Gebbs, E.D. & Teti, D.M. (1990). *Interdisciplinary assessment of infants: A Guide for early intervention professionals.* Baltimore, MD: Paul H. Brooks.

—*Katharine G. Butler, PhD*
Editor, *Topics in Language Disorders*

Part I
Implications from the Early Language Development and Disorders Literature for Working with Parents and Families

Issues in adult–child interaction: six philosophical orientations

Anne van Kleeck, PhD
Associate Professor
Department of Speech Communication
The University of Texas at Austin
Austin, Texas

PERHAPS MORE than any other area of social interaction research, the study of adult–child interaction freely borrows and, more importantly, mixes paradigms from numerous disciplines. Such rampant cross-disciplinary fertilization, though undoubtedly enriching, requires "a clearer notion of who is buying what from whom than seems to be present" (Brazil, 1981, p. 59). This challenge to understand the contributions of various disciplines is one of the central issues facing the study of adult–child interaction and the related areas of pragmatics and discourse analysis.

Different disciplines have entered the study of social interaction with different philosophical and concomitant theoretical and methodological baggage. Six different philosophical orientations underly various approaches to social interaction research. This article considers the methodologies inspired by each of the six philosophies: rationalism, empiricism, pragmatism, social constructivism, phe-

Top Lang Disord, 5(2), 1-15
© 1985 Aspen Publishers, Inc.

nomenology, and systems theory. Of course, each philosophy's influence is not clear cut. Often, more than one orientation may be influential in a particular approach to social interaction research. Sometimes the notions dovetail in a complementary fashion; at other times, they may cause contradictions within a particular research paradigm.

Both clinicians and researchers interested in understanding adult–child interaction and the related areas of pragmatics and discourse need to become more aware of the philosophical bases and attendant biases of the research, and how these philosophies may distort the picture. Certainly, a combination of research paradigms incorporating numerous philosophical orientations, such as those advocated by ethnographic and ecological approaches, may best illuminate the evanescent, complex set of phenomena that constitute human interaction.

RATIONALISM

"According to rationalist philosophy, reason is the only source of human knowledge" (Brugger & Baker, 1972, p. 339). In focusing on the intellect exclusively, rationalist philosophy ignores any contribution of the senses, will, or emotion to knowledge. Rationalist philosophy has a long legacy in the history of science. "In the study of language and meaning, a persistently anti-empirical logic-bound tradition has plagued Western epistemology for over two millenia" (Givón, 1982, p. 81). The influence of this rationalist, deductive approach is clearly evident in Chomskyan linguistics, where the goal is

to formalize linguistic knowledge in the form of autonomous rules of an ideal speaker-hearer (Chomsky, 1957, 1965). The terms *structuralism* and *formalism* are often associated with this approach.

Gardner (1972) notes that structuralism represents the "conviction that there is structure underlying all human behavior and mental functioning . . . and that structures have generality" (p. 10). Furthermore, "A 'determination of basic structures' will result in simplification of a mass of data as well as confirmation of the existence of laws governing that domain" (pp. 170–171).

Related to the spirit of rationalism is another underlying philosophical notion that Harré (1984) refers to as cognitivism. It is the belief that human action is the "product of individual mental processes" (p. 8)—a monadic rather than dyadic view of the motivation for social action.

In the rationalist orientation, the study of language focuses on determining the unobservable rules that govern language behavior, that is, the logical processes that go on in the mind. This focus is evident in much of the study of syntax, but it is also found in what Givón (1982) refers to as the pseudoformalism of some work in pragmatics. He states,

Grice's observations were automatically couched in terms of Logic of Conversation (Grice, 1975), and soon pressed into Gordon and Lakoff's forbidding Conversational Postulates (Gordon and Lakoff, 1971). . . . It would be of interest some day to speculate why the sweet siren song of formal, deductive logics recurrently proves so irresistible to linguists investigating pragmatics, who then proceed to force the subject matter into a mould which robs it of its very meaning (p. 83).

The interface between rationalism and pragmatism is one that Givón clearly rejects.

Rationalism has also influenced studies that address the ways in which rule systems (both linguistic and social) create expectancies that guide actual interactive behavior. Such studies are another example of the interface between rationalism and the seemingly opposite philosophy of pragmatism. Studies in this genre have considered expectancies regarding objects, events (Schank & Abelson, 1977; Tannen,

---

In general, the influence of rationalism on such studies lies in the emphasis on "what's in a person's head" as opposed to "what's out there" as the primary determinant of language behavior and use.

1979), scripts for talk in specific situations (e.g., Nelson & Gruendel, 1979; Schank & Abelson, 1977), role characteristics and relationships (e.g., Andersen, 1977; Snow, Shonkoff, & Levin, 1981), and the self (Bandura, 1982). In general, the influence of rationalism on such studies lies in the emphasis on "what's in a person's head" as opposed to "what's out there" as the primary determinant of language behavior and use.

Implicit in this type of research is a belief that internal knowledge about the communication process influences the act of communication itself. Since expectancies shape behavior in ongoing interactions to some extent, they are a viable focus for interactional study. In mother–

child interaction, it is sometimes suggested that a mother's expectancies about her child may be a more powerful determinant of the ways in which she interacts with the child than the child's actual behavior. Such an effect may be even more pronounced in mothers' interactions with communicatively handicapped children. Studies regarding expectancies may have a rationalist focus without using the traditional rationalist methodology of introspection. Instead, actual interactions are studied to determine the influence of expectancies on language use.

In traditional rationalist inquiry, on the other hand, the focus is on determining autonomous, logical rule systems. Verification often consists of introspection and native intuition about knowledge, giving rise to two additional terms—*introspectionism* and *mentalism*. The use of these techniques is widespread in linguistics. Mentalistic methodologies have also affected various types of psychological studies that have a bearing on social interaction.

Introspective methods that require subjects to report their internal knowledge, attitudes, and beliefs are found in psychological research in the form of questionnaire studies and inventories. Subjects respond on the basis of what they think they do, or think they should do, neither of

---

Subjects respond on the basis of what they think they do, or think they should do, neither of which is necessarily what they do in actual interactions.

---

which is necessarily what they do in actual interactions. In contrast to the qualitative nature of linguistic study, psychologists often obtain introspective data from many subjects so that the data can be quantified and subjected to statistical analysis. With this combination of rationalism and empiricism, the goal, as in other rationalist inquiry, is to determine universals by considering the most frequently occurring responses. This goal contrasts with that of phenomenology, in which researchers use the technique of informant interviewing to determine the ways in which individual perspectives differ rather than how they are alike. For this reason, the data obtained using this technique do not submit easily to statistical analysis.

Other studies rely on subjects' "native intuition" regarding utterances that are presented out of context. Here, subjects' judgments are a means of inferring their knowledge, attitudes, and beliefs. This method is favored in the study of children's social interactional skills because it is easier to get children to make judgments than to have them answer questionnaires. For example, Edelsky (1977) asked children to judge whether sentences presented out of context were produced by a male or female.

While the influence of rationalism on current social interaction research methodology is apparent in some restricted uses of introspection, its influence is even more apparent in the frequently monadic, rather than dyadic, approach to social interaction. As Hartup (1979) notes, "Most studies are centered on the actions of individuals who are engaged in social interaction, not on social interactions per se" (p. 27). Perhaps the greatest influence

of rationalism on social interaction research lies in the opposing philosophies that it, for different reasons, inspired empiricism and pragmatism.

EMPIRICISM

"Empiricism or the philosophy of experience is the view that recognizes experience as the only source of knowledge" (Brugger & Baker, 1972, p. 108). Extreme empiricists purport that humans acquire knowledge only through sensory data. Whereas the rationalist approach relies on deductive reasoning, empiricist philosophy requires that beliefs be tested using external measurements. To the empiricist, the rationalist tool of logicodeductive reasoning is far too subjective. The empiricist uses inductive reasoning to draw conclusions from externally gathered data. Similarly, behaviorism, led by Watson and Skinner, was a revolt against introspection. Behaviorists use only observable antecedents and consequences to explain behavior.

Empirical social interaction research can study any aspect of interaction that has measurable correlates. Methodologically, such research seeks to control some variables in order to determine the influence of others on actual language use in social interactions. In adult–child interaction research, studies have determined the influence of variables such as characteristics of the adult (e.g., being familiar or unfamiliar with the child; or whether the adult is a clinician or the child's mother); the child (e.g., younger or older; normal or communicatively handicapped; talkative or reticent); the situation (e.g., clinic or home); and the topics or materials (e.g., toys or pictures).

Other empirical social interaction research simply attempts to describe aspects of the interaction rather than compare the effects of different variables. Data are most frequently collected by audio- or videotaping a naturalistic interaction. The influence of the pragmatic movement (stressing the study of language in context) is evident in the methodology. Naturalistic interactions are observed, recorded, and then coded according to a particular taxonomy of behavior, such as a taxonomy of grammatical forms, communicative intents, turn-taking devices, semantic notions, relationship dynamics, and so forth.

Most social interaction research consists of a combination of experimental and observational techniques. For example, certain variables may be controlled, but then the interaction that naturally occurs in the "controlled" situation is coded according to a taxonomy. The goal is to create taxonomies that code discrete units of behavior into categories that are mutually exclusive, so that each behavior can be assigned to only one category and all inclusive, so that all behavior is accounted for. Furthermore, the categories must specify observable behaviors and must not rely on subjective interpretation, thereby ensuring results that are both reliable and replicable. Since these empirical goals often conflict with the actual nature of social interaction, designing valid empirical research is difficult at best.

An attempt to remain faithful to these empirical goals is embodied in the behaviorally inspired work of ethology. The method used in ethology is to create exhaustive catalogues, called ethograms,

of all human behaviors occurring in a particular environmental setting. These ethograms contain descriptions of observable aspects of behavior, again so that coding is not dependent on interpretation. Categories of human behavior that are often explored in human ethology include facial patterns, head patterns, gestures, postures, leg patterns, gross body patterns, and locomotion (McGrew, 1972). Examples of some of the 101 behaviors devised by Blurton Jones and Woodson (1979) to study children under 12 months of age, include (a) put hand on breast or bottle; (b) remove object from mouth; (c) cough, choke, hiccough, burp; and (d) touch object.

The goal of ethology is to determine patterns of observable antecedents and consequences of observable behaviors. The notion of "meaning" is carried no further than what is observable. As Blurton Jones and Woodson (1979) state, "We can see no defense for putting concepts above the data" (p. 105). Such researchers think it inappropriate to go beyond the very molecular descriptions characteristic of ethology, and that to do so is to enter the murky swamp of subjective interpretation. On the other hand, it is important to question the usefulness of molecular descriptions in practical applications and to social interaction theory in general.

PRAGMATISM

Pragmatism is the philosophical orientation that seeks "to reinterpret knowledge as function" (Prutting, 1982, p. 47). Some of its major proponents include the philosophers Peirce, Mead, and James. Prutting (1982) explains that Peirce's term "pragmatism" was adopted from Kant's term *Pragmatisch*, which was used to express "a relation to some purpose." Peirce "used the pragmatic criterion of consequence to define concepts or meanings" (Brugger & Baker, 1972, p. 318). Pragmatics, the study of language use that has been influenced by the philosophy of pragmatism, is concerned with practical aspects of interaction, with functions of language, and with the consequences of linguistic acts.

The philosophy of pragmatism has fostered at least three major focuses in child language pragmatics research: (a) understanding how children learn to adapt their language to various linguistic and nonlinguistic contexts; (b) charting development in terms of the increasing repertoire of language functions and the forms for conveying those functions; and (c) determining the role of social context in fostering various aspects of language development.

Most research in pragmatic development has used naturalistic data in the form of spontaneous language samples. The vast majority of these data involve adult–child interaction, and usually the adult has been the child's mother. Indeed, adult–child interaction is a focus of study in its own right as well as a data collection methodology for the study of a variety of aspects of child language development. For example, studies of children's developing ability to deal with linguistic contexts, (that is, the study of discourse) have most often used the adult–child dyad for data. The same is true of studies investigating children's communicative functions.

Pragmatism also fostered a data collection methodology that has become prevalent in child language research—the spontaneous language sample. While Bates (1976) is often credited with introducing pragmatics as a topic of study to child language research, it was Bloom (1970) who introduced the spontaneous language sample methodology that is essential to work in pragmatics. The naturalistic observations characteristic of spontaneous language samples are usually made under either everyday, real-life, or quasi-experimental conditions. As work has progressed, researchers are becoming more sensitive to the fact that different natural contexts are themselves important variables that need in a sense to be "con-

As work has progressed, researchers are becoming more sensitive to the fact that different natural contexts are themselves important variables that need in a sense to be "controlled" if replicable and comparable research is to be generated.

trolled" if replicable and comparable research is to be generated.

The influence of pragmatism is also seen in data analysis procedures. Two scholars inspired by pragmatism, Austin (1962) and Searle (1969), both speech act theorists, represent the underpinnings of an entire approach to coding natural conversation that has come to be known as discourse analysis. This methodology analyzes ongoing interaction according to categories of speech acts, often called illocutions. The speaker's intention or purpose for saying each utterance is the object of study.

As Corsaro (1979) notes, the analytic schemes in discourse analysis are "deduced from theoretical notions concerning the functions of speech" (p. 375). Although speech act theory has influenced the nature of these schemes, actual coding procedures have been profoundly influenced by empiricism, with resulting conflicts for discourse analysis. The major goals of empiricism as applied to analyzing interaction are to (a) segment the flow of interaction into discrete, measurable units; (b) provide operational definitions of categories of behavior; (c) create categories that are mutually exclusive; and (d) create an exhaustive list of categories so that the code is all-inclusive, that is, all behaviors presented can be coded. Due to the nature of social interaction, each of these goals presents major, if not insurmountable, problems for the researcher or clinician attempting to conduct discourse analysis. Such problems are treated in great detail in a methodological study by van Kleeck, Maxwell, and Gunter (in press) and in discussions by Chapman (1981) and Reeder (in press).

The first problem lies in determining the unit of analysis. Because of the widespread influence of linguistics, the sentence or utterance has often been used as the basic unit of analysis. However, many other equally viable units, both larger and smaller, can be used. A speaker's intent, for example, may span several utterances or perhaps an entire conversation. That is, a person's overall agenda may be to persuade, or perhaps to comfort. On the other hand, one utterance may contain several functions. Chapman (1981) provides the

example of *Hey, Jim, find the ball, ok?*, which is a single sentence but functions as a request for attention, a request for action, and a request for acknowledgment.

Which unit of analysis is most valid is an open question. Perhaps the critical unit does not remain constant throughout a conversation or from one conversation to the next. Furthermore, functions operating over smaller and larger chunks of conversation may interact with each other in complex ways.

Related to the unit-of-analysis problem is the issue of attaining a clear focus of analysis. Not only do utterances have illocutionary functions, they simultaneously function as elements of the ongoing conversation, for example, by answering a question (a discourse function), and as clues concerning feelings and attitudes about oneself, the listener, the topic, and so forth (relationship functions). As van Kleeck et al. (in press) note, "All of these various aspects of communicative function operate simultaneously in any given utterance, and undoubtedly interact in complex ways."

While most researchers provide definitions of the categories of communicative function they have used, such "definitions" usually consist merely of two or three prototypical examples of utterances for each particular category. This approach is understandable, as it would be impossible to describe all of the necessary and sufficient observable conditions that must be met in order to classify any utterance in a particular category. For one thing, "extraordinarily diverse actions share common functions" (Hartup, 1979, p. 22) and, conversely, the same action may serve quite different functions in different contexts. Also, as mentioned earlier, numerous types of functions—illocutionary, discourse, and relationship—undoubtedly interact to complicate coding. Thus, not only are communicative intentions themselves impossible to observe, but a complete list of the behaviors that would signal a particular function is impossible to create.

The coding process, then, is inferential, violating the empirical goal of using as data only what is objectively observable and measurable. It relies heavily on the subjective judgments of the coder, most often without the researcher acknowledging this subjectivity. Garfinkel (1967) calls this phenomenon "ad hocing," when rather than following coding rules or definitions, coders rely on their own practical knowledge. Garfinkel suggests that since ad hocing usually attains priority over the actual coding rules, it would perhaps be better to rely more on the subjective experience of the participants than on the data resulting from coding.

Indeed, while it may be an admirable empirical goal to create categories so that only one function is coded per utterance, this process violates the very nature of language. It assumes that each utterance fulfills only one function, that each function is determinable, and that each function is independent of others and therefore isolable.

Contrary to these assumptions, utterances may be multifunctional. Even if they are unifunctional, the specific function may be ambiguous. Such ambiguity may exist not only for the coder, but also for the listener in the actual interaction and perhaps even for the speaker. Leech (1977) suggests that a speaker may even intend such ambiguity, or "strategic indeterminancy," leaving the interpretation open to negotiation. Regarding the isolability of functions, van Kleeck et al. (in press), with examples from their methodological study, argue that many kinds of communicative functions have a strong tendency to co-occur and therefore may not be either independent of one another or empirically isolable.

The final empirical goal in discourse analysis is to create an exhaustive list of speech acts to account for all behavior. Such a list may also be small enough to be useful. That is, a list of 100 functions would be so long that a researcher would be unable to discern patterns in a conversation containing only 50 utterances. On the other hand, a parsimonious list of functions would violate the nature of actual interaction. Indeed, Austin himself (1962) noted that an exhaustive list of speech acts is probably impossible to create.

SOCIAL CONSTRUCTIVISM

Social constructivism contrasts with the cognitivist orientation by viewing human action as being collectively, rather than individually, motivated. Social constructivists conceive of human action as "the joint intentional actions of minded creatures whose minds are structured and stocked from an interpersonal reality" (Harré, 1984, p. 8). Constructivism considers meaning to be socially created. It focuses on dyadic interrelationships and mutual influences rather than on the contributions of individuals to interactions. Harré links social constructivism closely with pragmatism, suggesting that the famous pragmatic philosophers Peirce, Wittgenstein, and Mead are proponents of the collectivist notion. In addition, he cites the Russian psychologist, Vygotsky, as a constructivist.

Some sociological and anthropological approaches to social interaction embrace the collectivist view of human action and interaction. For example, ethnographies of speaking (e.g., Gumperz, 1983; Hymes, 1974) consider the ways in which contexts are socially created and negotiated as part of the ongoing interaction through contextualization cues. The emphasis in this approach is on the joint creation of social meaning. These researchers focus on all aspects of interaction—linguistic (phonetic, syntactic, and semantic); paralinguistic (pitch, stress, and prosody); and nonverbal (gestural, proxemic, and the manipulation of physical objects) (Corsaro, 1981). Contexts, or as Goffman (1974) calls them, frames, such as fantasy, argument, and so on, are mutually signaled, maintained, and terminated by the participants' constant monitoring of the interaction using such cues.

The notion of framing has its roots in the work of Gregory Bateson (1972). He observed that zoo animals frequently engage in play behavior that is seemingly modeled on combat. The human observer cannot tell immediately which acts are playful and which are true combat, but the animals rarely appear confused about this distinction. The animals must share some form of a "this is play" message in order for them to coordinate playful behavior and know that they are not really fighting.

Goffman (1974) attempts to form a set of analyses based on Bateson's notion of frame. Goffman notes numerous examples of frame-like communication in everyday affairs, including use of direct quotes, use of vocal intonations to indicate kidding, and many others. He uses the term key to refer to messages that signal the presence of a frame that tells participants in interactions how to interpret and hence contribute to what's going on.

Analogous to the zoo animal's ability to communicate the distinction between mock and real combat, young children often frame play to distinguish it from nonplay. As Garvey (1976) notes, "The reality-play distinction appears to be essential in interpreting the partner's gesture in terms of its primary meaning or its non-literal meaning. Both partners must recognize that the state of play obtains in order to interpret and correctly respond to the other's behaviour" (p. 576). This work on framing, although not labeled as such by Garvey, both assumes and demonstrates collectivism in creating meaning in context. During a play episode, the children in Garvey's study were periodically tested to determine whether the play frame was still operating. As Garvey explains, testing the maintenance of the play orientation "appeared to be a relevant factor in the attitude or alignment taken, not only to objects, but to the behaviour of the partner, whose definition of the situation is critical to the continuing interchange" (pp. 576–577).

Another type of social interaction research inspired by the constructivist notions of ethnographic work is called conversational analysis. Researchers make a clear distinction between it and discourse analysis (see French & MacLure,

1981; Levinson, 1981, 1984). While philosophically similar to the ethnography of speaking, proponents of conversational analysis are less interested in inferring the broader social contexts being created than in studying the local management of interaction. They focus on the contingency of one speaker's utterance to the contributions of another, or on how participants coordinate their speaking turns at an immediate, local level.

The focus of such research with adults is on issues such as turn-taking, adjacency pairs (e.g., question-answer, request-grant, challenge-response), repairs, side sequences, presequences, and openings and closings (see Jefferson, 1972; Sacks, Schegloff, & Jefferson, 1974; Schegloff, 1968).

Proponents of conversational analysis distrust the coding process used in discourse analysis. "In general, they argue that no exhaustive account can be given, in terms of the features of the categories, as to how instances of such categories are recognized, that such practices, as ends in themselves, always leave open the question of what methods are used to render instances into instances of X or Y" (Wootton, 1981, p. 100). Instead, conversational analysis is concerned with tracing that which is systematic in the management of interaction rather than locating, as discourse analysis does, instances of categories of acts that have been established a priori.

In child language research, studies that have focused on the relationship of one utterance to the immediately preceding utterance seem to fit the spirit of conversational analysis. Some examples include studies of repairs (Keenan & Schieffelin,

1976; Ochs, Schieffelin, & Platt, 1979); revisions (Gallagher, 1977); remedies and turn-taking (Ervin-Tripp, 1979); back-channel responses (Dittman, 1972); and contingent queries (Garvey, 1977).

Children's methods of creating coherence with an immediately preceding utterance may often differ from adults', reflecting their more limited interactional abilities. For example, they may create contingency through imitation, by retaining the clausal structure (e.g., Bloom, Rocissano, & Hood, 1976), or by retaining a syntactic frame and substituting lexical items (Keenan, 1974, 1975; Benoit, 1982). In peer interactions, children may create cohesion simply by retaining the phonetic aspects of each other's utterances (e.g., Keenan, 1975).

While conversational analysis has avoided some of the pitfalls of discourse analysis, the method is not without problems. Levinson (1981) claims that much of what goes on in conversation is not accounted for by adjacency pairs. Indeed, as Wootton (1981) notes, conversational analysts are more interested in how problems such as misunderstandings and lack of coherence are displayed and resolved. Edmondson (1981) complains that definitions of adjacency pairs are inadequate, arguing furthermore that functionally linked pairs are not necessarily adjacent. In general, conversational analysis is not a cure-all for the problems besetting discourse analysis.

PHENOMENOLOGY

Bronfenbrenner (1979) states, "What matters for behavior and development is the environment as it is perceived rather than as it may exist in 'objective' reality" (p. 4). This phenomenological approach asserts that a person's perception of an interaction, rather than the objectively observable data, determines both action and interpretation.

Phenomenology does not offer a research focus per se, but a radically different methodology than that offered by the behavioral, empiricist orientation. If indeed individual perceptions of interaction are more important than the objective reality in determining social action and interpretation, then far more emphasis should be placed on uncovering the subjective reality of the participants. "The shortcoming of traditional observation systems is that they quantify, through the screen of the observer, and they do not qualify, through the screen of the participants. Systematic observations have chosen to ignore the internal states of the participants" (Sevigny, 1981, p. 68).

Two aspects of ethnographic methodology, participant observation and informant interviews, provide ways of probing the participants' perception of an interaction under study. In participant observation, the researcher begins the research process by spending time actually becoming a part of the culture he or she wishes to study—be it a classroom, a family, or a tribal village. The theater metaphor clarifies the role: "The researcher, rather than appearing in the audience watching the drama unfold on stage, is himself on the stage, acting a role in the production and interaction with the other actors" (Sevigny, 1981, p. 69). Sevigny suggests that the researcher is thus enabled to determine some of the subjective aspects of events that would not otherwise be easy to infer,

since many features, such as the motives, intentions, interests, and perceptions of participants, "are only imperfectly inferable by direct observation" (1981, p. 69).

In addition to direct participation, researchers can use the technique of informant interviewing. Since the researcher's subjective experience may not represent that of all the participants, the interview broadens the base of subjective data. In this way, varied perspectives can be acknowledged and documented, and their effects can be integrated in social organization studies.

Both of these phenomenologically inspired methodologies assume that participants have better access to their own internal states—states that are important to a scientific understanding of social interaction—than the objective, outside, systematic observer. The implications of a phenomenological perspective for the study of adult–child interaction, especially when the focus is communicative intentions, are obvious. "We cannot assume that procedures for interpreting communicative intent are shared. Children, teacher, and outside observers may reach different understandings depending on their social presuppositions and their knowledge of relevant signaling conventions" (Gum-

> *Both methodologies assume that participants have better access to their own internal states—states that are important to a scientific understanding of social interaction—than the objective, outside, systematic observer.*

perz, 1981, p. 8). The techniques discussed here have been adopted by researchers interested in communication in the classroom to study teacher–child and peer interaction (see Green & Wallat, 1981; and Wilkinson, 1982). The techniques may be profitably introduced to the study of mother–child interaction as well.

SYSTEMS THEORY

Much research in the empiricist tradition attempts to break down behavior into discrete, measurable parts. Any such attempt is problematic. As Lutz (1981) noted, "The question of focus is always arbitrary—for the photographer, the biologist, or the social scientist. What brings one thing into clearly observable focus distorts another thing" (p. 54). In a similar vein, Watzlawick, Beavin, and Jackson (1967), in applying systems theory to the study of the pragmatics of communication, discuss the notion of wholeness: "Every part of a system is so related to its fellow parts that a change in one part will cause a change in all of them and in the total system. That is, a system behaves not as a simple composite of independent elements, but coherently and as an inseparable whole" (p. 123). Later they add, "indeed, formal analysis of artificially isolated segments would destroy the very object of interest" (p. 125).

These gestaltist notions argue against research that attempts to focus on subparts of the interactive process. And yet, how can researchers be expected to study the multiple simultaneous channels for messages (linguistic, paralinguistic, nonverbal, and artifactual) and a potential of multiple simultaneously conveyed messages (semantic intent, various levels of communicative intent such as agendas and illocutions, relationship dynamics such as power and affect, and discourse functions)? Furthermore, in interpreting messages, not only do speakers take into account all of the simultaneous messages that occur at one time, but also what has happened previously in the conversation and in the entire shared history of the participants. Sometimes a past event is reinterpreted on the basis of a later event. Is it possible to consider a "whole" of such complexity? Systems theory itself seems to offer little in the way of concrete methodologies. However, some research programs seem to capture the spirit of systems theory by combining numerous philosophies and research paradigms in an effort to get a glimpse of the whole.

•   •   •

This article has discussed the contributions as well as the shortcomings of numerous philosophical orientations to social interaction research. The researcher and clinician may deal with the shortcomings by considering two approaches that combine numerous philosophies in the effort to gain the most complete picture of the phenomenon under study. The first, the ecological approach, has its roots in psychology. The second, ethnography, is used primarily in sociology and anthropology.

Ecologists view psychological processes as properties of systems of which the individual is but one element (Cole, 1979). The individual is "embedded" in a culture, which is seen as a crucial aspect of the environment of human behavior. The ecological environment thus extends far beyond the immediate situation. This view of the individual as part of a larger system contrasts with monadic approaches to the study of interaction, and incorporates a systems theory approach. In addition to an interest in broader, more remote environments, ecologists assert the primacy of the phenomenological aspect of experience.

Bronfenbrenner (1979) proposes combining experimental with descriptive methodologies, including ethnographic data, naturalistic observation, case studies, and field surveys. He adds, "It is neither necessary nor possible to meet all the criteria for ecological research within a single investigation" (p. 14).

Ethnography shares much in common with ecology, although ethnographers profess no interest in experimental and statistical treatments (Lutz, 1981). Lutz describes ethnography as "the development of as complete as possible a body of data that describes the phenomenon being studied" (p. 55), or what Geertz (1973) calls "thick" description. The empirical tools include "participant observation, interview, mapping and charting, interaction analysis, study of historical records and current public documents and the use of demographic data, etc." (Lutz, 1981, p. 52).

Ethnography embraces both mentalistic data, such as the introspections of native informants, and social constructivist procedures, such as actual interaction analysis. Furthermore, the phenomenological nature of experience is acknowledged through the use of participant observers rather than the removed, objective observers more characteristic of behaviorist traditions. An excellent ethnographic study of children's developing communicative competence is provided by Schieffelin (1979).

Of the two orientations, Bronfenbrenner's (1979) ecological approach is perhaps the more encompassing, since it includes ethnographic and other techniques as well as the rigors of empiricism. The philosophy rejects the idea of being trained to think in terms of one particular approach to scientific inquiry. Instead, it urges the scientist to approach an area of interest from as many different perspectives as possible. Since each approach has its own limiting assumptions, corroboration using a mix of philosophical orientations and their methodologies should yield the most valid and complete results.

REFERENCES

Andersen, E. (1977). Young children's knowledge of role-related speech differences: A mommy is not a daddy is not a baby. *Papers and Reports on Child Language Development*, 13, 83–90.

Austin, J.L. (1962). *How to do things with words.* Cambridge: Oxford University Press.

Bandura, A. (1982). Self-efficacy mechanism in human agency. *American Psychologist*, 37, 122–147.

Bates, E. (1976). *Language and context: The acquisition of pragmatics.* New York: Academic Press.

Bateson, G. (1972). *Steps to an ecology of mind.* New York: Ballantine Books.

Benoit, P.J. (1982). Formal coherence production in children's discourse. *First Language*, 3, 161–179.

Bloom, L. (1970). *Language development: Form and function in emerging grammars.* Cambridge, MA: MIT Press.

Bloom, L., Rocissano, L., & Hood, L. (1976). Adult-child discourse: Developmental interaction between information processing and linguistic knowledge. *Cognitive Psychology*, 8, 521–552.

Blurton Jones, N., & Woodson, R. (1979). Describing

behavior: The ethologists' perspective. In M. Lamb, S. Soumi, & G. Stephenson (Eds.), *Social interaction analysis*. Madison, WI: The University of Wisconsin Press.

Brazil, D. (1981). Discourse analysis as linguistics: A response to Hammersley. In P. French & M. MaClure (Eds.), *Adult-Child Conversation*, London: Croom-Helm.

Bronfenbrenner, U. (1979). *The ecology of human development*. Cambridge, MA: Harvard University Press.

Brugger, W., & Baker, K. (1972). *Philosophical dictionary*. Spokane, WA: Gonzaga University Press.

Chapman, R. (1981). Exploring children's communicative attempts. In J. Miller (Ed.), *Assessing language production in children*. Baltimore, MD: University Park Press.

Chomsky, N. (1957). *Syntactic structures*. The Hague: Mouton.

Chomsky, N. (1965). *Aspects of a theory of syntax*. Cambridge, MA: MIT Press.

Cole, M. (1979). In U. Bronfenbrenner (Ed.), *The ecology of human development* (Foreword). Cambridge, MA: Harvard University Press.

Corsaro, W. (1981). Entering the child's world: Research strategies for field entry and data collection in a preschool setting. In J. Green & C. Wallat (Eds.), *Ethnography and language in educational settings*. Norwood, NJ: Ablex.

Corsaro, W. (1979). Sociolinguistic patterns in adult-child interaction. In E. Ochs & B. Schieffelin (Eds.), *Developmental pragmatics*. New York: Academic Press.

Dittman, A.T. (1972). Developmental factors in conversational behavior. *Journal of Communication, 22*, 404–423.

Edelsky, C. (1977). Acquisition of an aspect of communicative competence: Learning what it means to talk like a lady. In S. Ervin-Tripp & C. Mitchell-Kernan (Eds.), *Child discourse*. New York: Academic Press.

Edmondson, W. (1981). *Spoken discourse: A model for analysis*. London: Longman.

Ervin-Tripp, S. (1979). Children's verbal turn-taking. In E. Ochs & B. Schieffelin (Eds.), *Developmental pragmatics*. New York: Academic Press.

French, P., & MaClure, M. (Eds.). (1981). *Adult-child conversation*. London: Croom-Helm.

Gallagher, T. (1977). Revision behaviors in the speech of normal children developing language. *Journal of Speech and Hearing Research, 2*, 303–318.

Gardner, H. (1972). *The quest for mind: Piaget, Levi-Strauss, and the structuralist movement*. Chicago: University of Chicago Press.

Garfinkel, H. (1967). *Studies in ethnomethodology*. Englewood Cliffs, NJ: Prentice-Hall.

Garvey, C. (1976). Some properties of social play. In J. Bruner, A. Jolly, and K. Sylva (Eds.), *Play: Its role in development and evaluation*. New York: Basic Books, 570–583.

Garvey, C. (1977). The contingent query: A dependent act in conversation. In M. Lewis & L. Rosenblum (Eds.), *Interaction, conversation and the development of language*. New York: Wiley.

Geertz, C. (1973). *The interpretation of cultures*. New York: Basic Books.

Givón, T. (1982). Logic vs. pragmatics, with human language as the referee: Toward an empirically viable epistemology. *Journal of Pragmatics, 6*, 81–133.

Goffman, E. (1974). *Frame analysis*. New York: Harper & Row.

Gordon, D., & Lakoff, G. (1971). Conversational postulates. Papers from the Seventh Regional Meeting, Chicago Linguistics Society, University of Chicago.

Green, J., & Wallat, C. (Eds.). (1981). *Ethnography and language in educational settings*. Norwood, NJ: Ablex.

Grice, H. (1975). Logic and conversation. In P. Cole and J. Morgan (Eds.), *Syntax and semantics*, Vol. 3, *Speech Acts*. New York: Academic Press.

Gumperz, J. (1981). Conversational inference and classroom learning. In J. Green & C. Wallat (Eds.), *Ethnography and language in educational settings*. Norwood NJ: Ablex.

Gumperz, J. (1983). *Discourse strategies*. Cambridge, England: Cambridge University Press.

Harré, R. (1984). *Personal being*. Cambridge, MA: Harvard University Press.

Hartup, W. (1979). Levels of analysis in the study of social interaction: An historical perspective. In M. Lamb, S. Soumi, & G. Stephenson (Eds.), *Social interaction analysis: Methodological issues*. Madison, WI: The University of Wisconsin Press.

Hymes, D. (1974). Ways of speaking. In R. Bauman & J. Sherzer (Eds.), *Explorations in the ethnography of speaking*. London: Cambridge University Press.

Jefferson, G. (1972). Side sequences. In D. Sudnow (Ed.), *Studies in social interaction*. New York: Free press.

Keenan, E. (1974). Conversational competence in children. *Journal of Child Language, 1*, 163–183.

Keenan, E. (1975). Evolving discourse: The next step. *Papers and Reports on Child Language Development, 10*, 80–87.

Keenan, E., & Schieffelin, B. (1976). Topic as a discourse notion: A study of topic in the conversations of children and adults. In C. Li (Ed.), *Subject and topic*. New York: Academic Press.

Leech, G. (1977). *Language and tact*. (Paper No. 46). Trier, Germany: University of Trier, Linguistic Agency.

Levinson, S. (1981). Some preobservations on the modelling of dialogue. *Discourse Processes, 4*, 93–116.

Levinson, S. (1984). *Pragmatics*. Cambridge, England: Cambridge University Press.

Lutz, F. (1981). Ethnography—The holistic approach to understanding schooling. In J. Green & C. Wallat (Eds.), *Ethnography and language in educational settings*. Norwood, NJ: Ablex.

McGrew, W. (1972). *An ethological study of children's behavior*. New York: Academic Press.

Nelson, K., & Gruendel, J. (1979). At morning it's lunchtime: A scriptal view of children's dialogues. *Discourse Processes, 2*, 73–94.

Ochs, E., Schieffelin, B., & Platt, M. (1979). Propositions across utterances and speakers. In E. Ochs & B. Schieffelin (Eds.), *Developmental pragmatics*. New York: Academic Press.

Prutting, C. (1982). Pragmatics and social competence. *Journal of Speech and Hearing Disorders, 2*, 123–134.

Reeder, K. (in press). Classifications of children's speech acts: A consumer's guide. *Journal of Pragmatics*.

Sacks, H., Schegloff, E., & Jefferson, G. (1974). A simplest systematics for the organization of turn-taking for conversation. *Language, 50*, 696–735.

Schank, R., & Abelson, R. (1977). *Scripts, plans, goals and understandings*. Hillsdale, NJ: Erlbaum.

Schieffelin, B. (1979). Getting it together: An ethnographic approach to the study of the development of communicative competence. In E. Ochs & B. Schieffelin (Eds.), *Developmental pragmatics*. New York: Academic Press.

Schegloff, E. (1968). Sequencing in conversational openings. *American Anthropologist, 70*, 1075–1095.

Searle, J. (1969). *Speech acts: An essay in the philosophy of language*. Cambridge, England: Cambridge University Press.

Sevigny, M. (1981). Triangulated inquiry—A methodology for the analysis of classroom interaction. In J. Green & C. Wallat (Eds.), *Ethnography and language in educational contexts*. Norwood, NJ: Ablex.

Snow, C., Shonkoff, F., & Levin, H. (1981, August). *The acquisition of sociolinguistic skills: How do children learn the sick-room register*. Paper presented at the Second International Congress for the Study of Child Language, Vancouver, British Columbia.

Tannen, D. (1979). What's in a frame? Surface evidence for underlying expectations. In R.O. Freedle (Ed.), *New directions in discourse processing: Vol. 2*. Norwood, NJ: Ablex.

van Kleeck, A., Maxwell, M., & Gunter, C. (in press). A methodological study of coding adult-child interaction. *Journal of Pragmatics*.

Watzlawick, P., Beavin, J., & Jackson, D. (1967). *The pragmatics of human communication*. New York: W.W. Norton.

Wilkinson, L.C. (Ed.). (1982). *Communicating in the classroom*. New York: Academic Press.

Wootton, A.J. (1981). Conversation analysis. In P. French & M. MaClure (Eds.), *Adult-child conversation*. London: Croom-Helm.

The development of discourse topic skills by infants and young children

Susan Foster, PhD
Post-Doctoral Fellow
Freshman Writing Program and
  Department of Linguistics
University of Southern California
Los Angeles, California

IN TWO RECENT publications Chomsky (1980) and Fodor (1983) explored the idea that the linguistic system is best understood as a set of interconnecting cognitive modules that exist alongside other modules that constitute the visual system, the aural system, and so on. The integrated functioning of all the modules is achieved through a central processor. If the modularity thesis is correct, it has important implications for the understanding of language disorders.

The present focus is on the development by young children of one aspect of linguistic functioning—the use of both verbal and nonverbal behavior to express discourse topics. Topic development is one part of the more general area of pragmatics, involving the way the central processor interacts with the grammar module. It is shown here that young children's ability to handle topics of conversation involves an interplay of linguistic, general cognitive, and social factors.

Communicative competence can be di-

Top Lang Disord, 5(2), 31-45
© 1985 Aspen Publishers, Inc.

vided into two main components: grammatical competence and pragmatic competence. The former consists of rules that define possible structures of a given language, and the latter consists of rules for implementing these structures in communication—rules of turn-taking; rules of topic initiation and maintenance; rules of politeness; rules for organizing information within sentences; and so on.

Grammar rules are discrete (i.e., sentences are either grammatically well formed or grammatically ill formed), they are defined over linguistic units (syntactic rules over sentences, morphological rules over words, etc.), and they appear to be specific to language. Nothing in other areas of human functioning appears to be isomorphic with the rules of grammar.

Pragmatic rules, on the other hand, operate according to degree (i.e., utterances are more or less relevant, polite, informative and so on). They are defined over messages—verbal or nonverbal. For example, requests can be made with sentences, single words, or facial expressions. Pragmatic rules are not specifically linguistic. Rather, they are the same kinds of rules that can be seen in other areas of human functioning, reflecting the application of the central processor or general cognition to communicative messages.

Since pragmatics and grammar are different in kind (see Foster [1984] for further discussion of this issue), they may have different developmental stories. Furthermore, the development of discourse topics involves various aspects of general cognitive development, with communicative behaviors being learned through the child's interaction experience.

TOPIC AND TOPIC DEVELOPMENT

Among the key skills of a communicatively competent speaker are the ability to make clear what he or she is interested in talking about, the ability to produce a series of relevant propositions and the ability to express ideas in a way that is sensitive to what the speaker knows about the hearer. In other words, the competent speaker is able to initiate and maintain a topic of conversation.

The emergence of the ability to initiate topics was the focus of a study carried out with a group of 5 children aged between 1 month and $2^{1}/_{2}$ years (Foster 1979, 1981b, 1982). The children (all middle class, Western, white first borns) were observed and videotaped in their homes interacting with their mothers in everyday situations over a period of 6 months. The resulting data were transcribed and analyzed in detail in order to determine: (a) the kinds of topics young children initiate and develop; (b) the kinds of behaviors they use to do it; and (c) how these topic types and behaviors change as children mature.

A topic was defined as anything that mother and child communicated jointly about as a result of specific attention-getting and attention-directing activities by one of the participants. Using this definition, it became obvious that long before children are able to use their language in any even vaguely sophisticated way, they are able to engage in topics of conversation through the use of gesture, vocalization, and eye gaze.

Well before their first birthdays these children were able to gain their mother's attention and direct it to an object in the immediate physical environment as the object of interest. By their second birthdays they used language to achieve these results and, in addition, had acquired the ability to attract their hearer's attention to objects not in the immediate environment, either to displaced objects or to abstract ideas such as past events. In addition, the data showed that the ability to maintain topics, once initiated, also developed. In the early stages, the coherence of the children's conversation depended, to a large extent, on the adults engaging them in play routine. But with development, the children gradually took over responsibility for topic maintenance and became able to produce extended sequences of propositions unaided.

TOPIC INITIATION

Keenan and Schieffelin (1976) have proposed that the initiation of a topic involves four basic components, the first of which is the speaker's ability to get the attention of the hearer. As any caretaker knows, even the youngest child is quite proficient at getting attention. However, in the arena of communicative development, a distinction must be made between occasions when the child *deliberately* attracts attention and those when something he or she does *just happens* to attract attention. This distinction is not always easy to make. However various clues are available, most notably if a cry or other attention-getting behavior (such as prodding or pulling) is combined with a gaze at the adult, or if the behavior continues until attention is secured (Bruner,

1974; Greenfield, 1980). Using these criteria even a 1-month-old is capable of deliberate attention getting.

Self topics

At 1-month, however, attention getting is the limit of infants' communicative ability. Although they can get the adult's attention, they cannot yet direct it to something besides themselves. Therefore, the earliest topics are labeled *self topics* (Foster, 1979). Topics in which the child is in focus include expressions of discomfort, such as wanting a diaper changed; requests for food; and so on. Following is an example of a child initiating a topic by simply attracting attention to himself. (Notice that the mother is well aware of her child's communicative intent.)

Russell at 5 months

Russell is in his high chair. His meal is at an end, and his mother is cleaning the tray attached to the chair. His mother stops cleaning the tray.

```
⎧M.  There + stands⎧up straight
⎩C.                 ⎩gazes at M.
 M.  Oh
 C.  /ə/ + continues to gaze at M. +
     flexes body
⎧M.  Isn't that⎧(super) now?
⎩C.            ⎩/ə:::/
 C.  /ə/
 M.  Yes + moves away
⎧C.  /ə::⎧ə: ə cry _____
⎩M.     ⎩Yes
 C.  Continues cry + continues gaze to M.
     + body flexing
 M.  Laughs
⎧C.  Cry～～～～～～～～～～～～
⎩M.  ⎧He's asking me to come out. I
     hope you're making a note of it.
```

Notes: In all the data samples, braces indicate the simultaneous production of the behaviors transcribed. Prelinguistic vocalizations are indicated in phonetic transcription. Sections of utterances that appear in parentheses are those where the accuracy of the transcript was uncertain.

While self topics are the earliest to emerge, they are present in the data throughout the sample. Thus, it is not to simply the case that such topics are precursors of some other category, disappear-

---

By age five months, children's motor skills are such that they can manipulate toys and other objects of interest, and can attract an adult's attention to such objects.

---

ing when more mature types emerge. They are, though, the ones that make the smallest behavioral demands on the child and can thus be expressed the earliest.

Environmental topics

The next stage in topic development begins around 5 months. By this age, children's motor skills are such that they can manipulate toys and other objects of interest, and can attract an adult's attention to such objects, although the children do not yet use specific gestures. At this point, a second type of topic emerges: *environmental topics*. These occur when children direct adults' attention away from themselves to some object in the immediate physical environment. Toward the end of the first year, with the emergence of recognizable gestures—pointing, reaching, giving, and so on—the category of environmental topics is firmly established. Following are some examples of environmental topics in the early stages.

Lauren at 7 months

Mother and child are playing with toys on the floor. Lauren is gazing at a can. Her mother is gazing at her.

C. /ɛːðe/ + *gaze away. Then: cries + gazes at can + waves arms.*
M. What d'you want then? *Then: lifts Lauren nearer the can and supports her while she reaches for it.*

Note: At this stage of development children cannot yet combine gaze at an object with gaze at an interlocutor in the same communicative act. Therefore, although at a later stage such behavior can be used as an indication of intention to communicate, or lack of it, it cannot be so used here. [See Trevarthen and Hubley (1978) on the development of "secondary intersubjectivity."]

Nicholas at 9 months

Bathtime. The water is draining away. Nicholas is standing up in the bath. His mother is gazing at him.

M. You're a little bit chilly, aren't you, tonight? + *starts to lift him up*
C. *Gazing at drain*
{ M. Mm? Are you coming out? *Then: gazes at C's face*
  C. *Waves at drain* }
M. Are you waving to the water?
C. *Gazes at M.*

Kate at 1 year, 3 months

Mealtime. Mother is gazing at Kate. Kate is gazing around the room.

{
  C. *Gazes ahead. Then: reaches ahead + gazes ahead + /gðe/*
  M. *Gazes where Kate is pointing + what can you see? gazes at C.*
  C. */gðe/ + gazes at M.*
{
  M. Bananas.
  C. *Draws hand back slowly*

Note: By this stage the coordination of gaze at object and at interlocutor has emerged.

The example of Nicholas shows one of the earliest gestures to emerge: a wave. This gesture is interesting because, unlike reaching, pointing and other early gestures, it appears to be learned through explicit teaching rather than developing naturally out of functional (noncommunicative) actions. As such, its use here clearly shows that the child has understood something of the function of his action and can probably use it in an appropriate situation. (This is probably not a routinized use of a wave. See Foster [1979] for further discussion of the origins of early gestures.) The example of Kate shows a child who has acquired, and can use, a pointing gesture to direct the adult's attention.

By this stage of development, young children have clearly mastered the three remaining components of topic initiation detailed by Keenan and Schieffelin (1976). These are that the speaker should identify the objects (real or imagined) included in the discourse topic, identify the semantic relationships among the objects, and articulate the utterance clearly. If the last of these is interpreted to mean simply that the child's communicative intent should be clear to the hearer, then a successful prelinguistic communication of the type exemplified in the preceding data passes the test. Similarly, gestural identification of the object of interest will constitute the fulfillment of the remaining requirements, since a reach not only makes clear what the child is interested in, but also communicates that he or she wants the object. Identifying the semantic relationships among the objects in the topic simply means communicating what it is the speaker wanted to say about them.

Abstract topics and expressive development

Two major steps remain in the child's development toward competent topic initiation. One is the development of the ability to initiate topics about things not in the here and now—*abstract* or *displaced topics*—including reference to objects that are out of sight, past events and abstract attributes of objects (such as who they belong to, where they come from, and so on). The other is the emergence of linguistic expression as children expand their behavioral repertoires to include speech in addition to the vocalizations and gestures of the earlier stages. Following are examples of each of the three topic types from the oldest child in the study.

Ross at 2 years, 6 months
Self topic

Ross is sitting on his mother's knee. Both are gazing at a magazine.

C. *Twists onto his back so that he is lying on his mother's knee looking up at her.*
M. *Gazes at C.*
C. *Vocalizes.*
M. Oh! You being softy, m?

Environmental topic

Mealtime. Mother is cutting up a tomato. Both are looking at what she is doing. (The tomato has peculiar seeds.)

{ M. I don't like funny tomatoes.
{ C. *Gazes at table/tomato*
  C. *Apple + gaze at M.'s hand/tomato + points to apple + other hand reaches out to M. Then:* please *+ points at apple.*
{   *Then:* apple *+ gazes at M. + both hands back.*
{ M. *Gazes at C.*
  M. Please *+ gaze at apple + reach to bowl of apples to get him one.*

Abstract topic

Mealtime. Mother has given Ross a piece of apple.

C. *Gazing at piece of apple he has been given + picks up apple + screams*
M. *Gazes at C.*
C. Hey! Bitten it. *+ offers piece to M.*
M. I haven't bitten it!
C. Daddy bitten it!
Note: "Daddy" is not present.

Examples such as these show that, once they have emerged, all three topic types persist; one type does not replace another. Furthermore, even when children are at the two- and three-word stage, they still use gestural communication, particularly with environmental topics, for which gesture, in combination with language, continues to carry an important part of the message. As is apparent from the last example, however, the ability to initiate a topic entirely through language has emerged by this stage.

The modularity thesis

What are the implications of this pattern of development for the modularity thesis referred to earlier? Clearly, the ability to engage in conversations on a topic of joint interest is to a large degree independent of the acquisition of grammar. The fact that prelinguistic topic initiation is possible, and the fact that the topic types initiated prelinguistically continue to be initiated in the linguistic period, point to this independence. Pragmatic development and grammatical development are not completely separate, however, because the emergence of new types of communicative behavior tends to coincide with that of new types of topic. Clearly children cannot direct attention to things in the environment until they have the behavioral resources to do so. And they cannot talk about things abstracted or displaced from the here and now without a linguistic system. The question remains, therefore, whether children acquire or develop the communicative behaviors as a consequence of developing the new type of communicative intent, or vice versa.

The question remains, therefore, whether children acquire or develop communicative behaviors as a consequence of developing the new type of communicative intent, or vice versa.

It is not entirely true that children cannot initiate abstract topics before the onset of spoken language. With help, they can; for example, if the adult responds appropriately, simple manipulation of an object at the pregestural stage can result in the establishment of an environmental topic. The key to this potentiality is the adult response. If adults use their knowledge of the child and of the situation, and are prepared to *interpret* the child's behavior, successful communication is possible on more complex topics than can be managed unaided (for a related discussion, see Vygotsky's [1962] "Zone of proximal development"). For example, when one mother asked her daughter where a certain toy was, and the child turned toward the door to the next room, the mother was able to interpret the action as a communication to the effect that her child thought the toy was in another room.

Thus, in many instances at least, the cognitive advances that underlie communicative intent may precede the development of the actual communicative behaviors. In other instances, however, the reverse seems to be true: Children sometimes produce behaviors in advance of acquiring either the adult meaning, or even in their own communicative meaning for them. For example, one child announced that she had finished her meal by handing her plate to her mother and saying, "Good girl," appearing not to understand what she had said. She had simply acquired her mother's usual way of marking the end of a meal, and used it to mean that the meal was over. A frequent example of action lacking communicative intent for children is when, at the preges-

tural stage, they reach for objects intending to grasp them, but are understood to be communicating requests for the objects.

Again, such behaviors take on communicative import only because of the adults' interpretations. In all these cases it seems a reasonable hypothesis that such interpretation by adults of children's behavior may aid children's development of the adult forms and meanings (see Foster [1981a] for an extended discussion of this possibility). It is important to remember, however, that such behavior is not found in all cultures (see Ochs' [1982] work on the Samoan language learning experience). Thus, children who have these kinds of experiences may make use of them; children who do not will find other kinds of learning experiences that are equally effective. The Western "interpretive" style helps reveal an aspect of development that may be less open to scrutiny in other cultures; interpretation sheds light on communicative intentions beyond the limits of the communicative system.

TOPIC MAINTENANCE

Once initiated, topics are usually maintained over a sequence of turns by speakers expressing a series of propositions. Each proposition is related both locally to the proposition or propositions that precede it and globally to what van Dijk (1977) has termed "macroproposition" that represents the sequence as a whole. Speakers' ability to maintain topics develops over time and represents a major aspect of pragmatic development. In the following sequence, Ross (aged 2½) demonstrates that, with limited linguistic ability and a supportive conversational partner, he can manage the rudiments of connectedness.

Ross at 2 years, 6 months

C. Ross got breakfast got ⌈break-
M. ⌊Yes, you, you, well, you certainly got your breakfast at the usual time but you were awake long before that.
C. Ross got toast.
M. Toast. Oh yes you were given toast, that's right.
C. Granny give ⌈gr-
M. ⌊Yes granny gave you toast.

Ross clearly wants to contribute a number of related propositions; his mother's sensitivity to his intentions (although sometimes she is oversensitive, often responding before he has finished speaking, though his message is usually complete), and her knowledge of his experience, allow him to be successful. Because the topic is abstract, it is cognitively demanding. With an environmental topic, at the same age, he can achieve an even higher degree of sophistication, as in the next example. (Although claims about cognitive demand ultimately require sophisticated testing, it seems reasonable to suggest that recalling a past event is cognitively more demanding than commenting on something currently present.) In the following example, Ross demonstrates his ability to produce a full hierarchy of propositions unaided:

Ross at 2 years, 6 months

Mother and child are sitting at the table. On each wall, to the child's left and right, are ornamental plates with designs on them.

C. Des dat's flower + *points to plate on his right.*
M. That's not a flower.
C. Plate.
M. It's a plate with a pattern on, but it's not like a flower.
C. It's a flower pattern.
M. Ooh dear (*referring to her sandwich, which has fallen apart*).
C. Dis another plate dere + *points to the other plate.*
M. Mm (*attending to her sandwich*).
C. Dook! Buvvers, buvvers + *points to the two plates at once.*
M. What did you say? What was that word? What did you say?

(It seems clear that the word was "brothers," but the conversation turns to other matters and the problem is not resolved.)

The hierarchy of propositions is depicted in Figure 1.

Not only do adults aid children's topic maintenance by using their background knowledge about the children as input to their interpretations, but they also provide children with interactional frameworks that allow for multiple turns on a single topic at a stage before the children are able to do it by themselves. The data strongly suggest that, at least for these mother–child pairs, the routines that the adult teaches the child act as "carriers" of the propositional relatedness that constitutes a topic. Comparison of the number of turns on the same topic at different ages suggests that events such as book reading or the naming game result in a considerably greater number of turns than occurs in nonroutinized events. The following is a typical example of a routinized interaction in which the child engages in a long

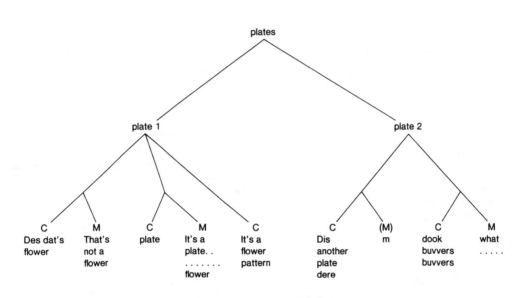

Figure 1. Hierarchical arrangement of propositions. Reprinted with permission from *The Volta Review*, Vol. 85, No. 3, "Topics and the Development of Discourse Structure," p. 49. Copyright ©1983 by The Alexander Graham Bell Association for the Deaf, 3417 Volta Place, NW, Washington, DC 20007.

sequence of topically related turns by simply "playing the game."

Kate at 1 year, 10 months

Mother and child are looking at a book together.

  M. 'n what's that one?
  C. /dðeʰ/
  M. What does that one say?
  C. /dðeʰ/
  M. It's a cat. What does it say?
  C. (/ðg/)
{M. Miaow (   )
{C. /jðe dða²/ + *points to back door to yard.*
  M. Yes, there's a cat outside isn't there?
{C. /gɔ²/
{M. Sometimes. It's gone now, yes. We saw it yesterday, didn't we? And can you see a little pig?
  C. *Snorts.*
  M. *Snorts.* That's what he says.

Note: Empty parentheses indicate that no reliable transcription could be made.

In fact, this example shows a more advanced routine than the simpler (and earliest acquired) ones because, while the supportive effect of the routine is apparent, the beginnings of a manipulation of the routine's structure are also evident. The child's introduction of new material—in this case talking about the cat outside—is the first step toward greater control of the topic by this child. The child's successful reference to the cat outside is another example of the adult's role in supporting the prelinguistic child's use of absent beings as topics.

Routines of this kind can be contrasted with nonroutine interactions such as the following, in which the child does not maintain an interest in a single topic, but moves quickly from one to another.

Kate at 1 year, 10 months

Mealtime.

  M. Would you like an apple?
  C. /ð:/ + *reach to apple.*

M. Yes

C. /xʋ::/

M. Mummy cut it?

⎧C. /aa/ ⎧a/ + *reach to apple.*
⎩M.   ⎩Yes.

    Or do you want it like that?

C. /m/ + *grasps apple.*

M. D'you want Mummy to cut it?

C. /k ∂ (r) l² / + *draws hand away.*

M. Shall I? Look here. I'll give you the stalk, shall I? There's a little stalk. It's only a little one, isn't it?

C. /¹∂ʰm/ + *manipulating stalk.*

⎧C. /mi:g∂e/ + *cry* + *reach to apple M.*
⎨   ⎧ *is cutting.*
⎩M.   ⎩There's er a piece of apple.

C. /g∂e g∂e/

M. 've you drunk your milk yet love? Go on.

C. *Laughs* + *picks up plate.*

M. Oh, Kate, no, put it down, poppet. Put it down.

Although the interaction is coherent, the child makes only simple requests, responds to them, or makes isolated comments. There is no sense of even a partially planned topic. Nor is there continuity of the kind seen in the routine-based sequence. Interestingly enough, what makes the sequence coherent is the situation—the mealtime. The exchanges between adult and child are controlled by what is being *done*—the function of the interaction—in this case, feeding Kate. Moreover, if routines are also functionally defined in that they are sequences of verbal and nonverbal actions designed to establish an interpersonal relationship rather than convey information, then it would seem that, in general, propositional continuity is initially mediated functional-

ly. Thus, skills may be said to come in on the coattails of the functional structuring of discourses.

The development of topic maintenance shares with the development of topic initiation the feature that children perform without true competence in the early stages. They do in collaboration with an adult what they cannot do by themselves. Moreover, performance without competence continues to be apparent well into the linguistic period. By producing an utterance over the course of more than one turn (Ochs, Schieffelin, & Platt, 1979; Scollon, 1976), or by simply repeating a word or phrase from an earlier utterance of the adult, children produce linguistic indicators of topical cohesion before controlling the adult devices.

To summarize, the ability to engage in mature discourse topics in which propositions are expressed in a hierarchically organized way develops during the course of the first 2¹/₂ years of life. During that time, competence and performance develop hand in hand, sometimes with competence ahead of performance, sometimes vice versa. In the study presented, there are strong indications that the adults who interact with children play an important role by allowing them to express their communicative intentions, thus giving the children the valuable experience of participation in more mature discourse than they might experience unaided.

ORIGINS AND IMPLICATIONS FOR DISORDER

The pattern of emergence of topic skills suggests that mature topic management involves the integration of a number of subskills: attention getting, hierarchy building, and so on. What are the possible cognitive, social, and linguistic underpinnings to these subskills? What are the implications for language-disordered populations?

Clearly, to initiate a discourse topic a speaker must recognize that other people's minds are separate and that the communication act mediates between the minds of different speakers. Indeed, to communicate at all, children must realize that they are separate from their environment and from other people. They have to realize what others can and cannot know without being told. In communicating about themselves, the environment, or abstract/displaced ideas, they have to realize that their apprehension of their physical and mental world is fundamentally inaccessible to others without communication. Furthermore, they must be able to distinguish their perceptions of their own state, of the environment, and of their abstract thoughts and ideas. Without such recognition, children would not possible realize that each topic type requires different communicative behaviors for its expression: Abstract topics require language, for example, and environmental topics require language or attention-directing gestures. The development of topic skills thus demands that children be sufficiently advanced in the appropriate aspect of cognitive development to make the necessary distinctions.

The implications of the relationship between topic type and cognitive development for language impairment is that children whose cognitive development is retarded, arrested, or disordered in this respect will probably have specific problems with discourse topics. Children who fail to realize that their perceptions of themselves and the world are often completely inaccessible to others without communication will fail to initiate or maintain topics in ways that make such information accessible. In the extreme case, a child may not communicate at all, but the subtler cases are more interesting. If a child fails to realize that, for example, abstract ideas are inherently less available to others than observations about a shared physical environment, then it would be predicted that, even after developing the grammatical resources to be able to express the relevant information, such a child may not know when it would be necessary to use those resources. In other words, the child will fail to select the appropriate communicative means for each topic type, and experience considerable frustration at being misinterpreted as a consequence. Thus when children seem frustrated in communication, it would be worth trying to determine whether they have problems with understanding the status of different kinds of information or with their perception of themselves and others.

Another aspect of discourse topic management is the requirement of relevance. To produce a relevant next utterance, a speaker must have a sufficiently sophisticated grasp of the kinds of information that the hearer is likely to share, as well as the kinds of propositional connections a hearer can be expected to make among contributions to a topic. Again, such an ability requires an understanding about others' minds and the knowledge they may have. It involves, among other things, a memory for information that is established during a discourse or over the course of a relationship with a hearer, as well as information that is generally known in the culture. Memory problems, therefore, might be expected to have a negative effect on the relevancy of topic contributions. Moreover, if pragmatic rules are not specific to language, then where there are problems with relevancy in discourse, problems may exist with relevancy in other areas, such as relevancy of actions in a planned complex event. Snyder (1975, 1978) suggested that there is at least no *simple* generation of this kind, since the children she studied were able to be informative nonverbally, but not verbally. However, it may be the case that some impaired children have trouble applying this aspect of cognition to the output of the grammar, that is, a problem with the interconnection between modules.

Another related issue is the nature of the hierarchical arrangement of propositions in a discourse topic. Hierarchies are found not only in the organization of propositions in a discourse, but also in various classification systems (Keil, 1981) and in planned behaviors (Miller, Galanter & Pribram, 1960), for example. Therefore, children who fail to produce hierarchies of propositions may also be disordered in some or all of these other areas, depending on the relationship between these various types of hierarchies. Correlational studies would be appropriate. Future researchers should be aware, however, that topic hierarchies are more characteristic of white, middle-class populations where proposi-

tion is more common than of other groups, (Michaels & Cook-Gumperz, 1979). It is important, therefore, to choose an appropriate population with which to test such correlations, and to avoid the claim that certain children are deficient when, in fact, they may simply be conforming to a different norm.

Other relationships can also be studied, as Snyder (1984) advocates in her discussion of a multiple resources model for understanding the pragmatic problems of language-disordered children. Attentional problems, for example, may well be manifested in an inability either to plan or to follow an extended discourse topic. Similarly, perceptual problems may also affect the ability to initiate and maintain topics. Successful topic initiation, for example, requires that the child be able to secure and maintain the attention of the listener. When it is difficult for a child to be sure that attention has been gained—in blind children, for example—an abnormally high proportion of failed initiations may be expected, or such children may seek alternative means of checking their hearer's attention. The latter hypothesis has already received confirmation from the work of Andersen, Dunlea, and Kekelis, (1984), and Kekelis and Andersen, (1984), who found that blind children use what might otherwise be interpreted as irrelevant remarks for precisely this purpose.

The ability to take turns and to respond to both verbal and nonverbal indications of turn transitions between speakers is also a prerequisite for successful topic management. Children who have such difficulty may have corresponding discourse topic problems.

The ability to take turns and to respond to both verbal and nonverbal indications of turn transitions between speakers is also a prerequesite for successful topic management.

The relationship of topic management to grammatical competence should also be explored in further detail. If grammar and pragmatics are indeed fundamentally independent developments, then the emergence of discourse topic skills must involve the connections between these two developments. Therefore, a potential source of language disorder lies in the possibility that children may develop a grammar and the pragmatic skills for topic management, but be unable to use them together appropriately (see Snyder, 1984). Children may be able to engage in prelinguistic topics and produce grammatical sentences, but be unable to engage in linguistically expressed topics.

These predictions and avenues of research are based on the contention that grammar and pragmatics are separate developments, and that pragmatics is dependent on a variety of cognitive and perceptual functions. Also, since young children learn how to make appropriate use of the behavioral repertoire at their disposal through interactional experiences with mature speakers, another dimension of potential language disorder lies in the kind of interaction children experience.

One of the difficulties faced when considering the role of the environment in any aspect of language development is that, as yet, there is no real agreement concerning the limits of normal variation. Because cultures and groups vary considerably in the way they treat children, it is difficult to determine whether the environment could be responsible for various disorders. However, it is clear that some environments are genuinely socially or physically abusive. If the development of topic skills requires support from the environment, it is likely that children who receive insufficient social contact or whose social contact is threatening or uncooperative would have consequent discourse problems. To date there is little research on the pragmatic development of abused children (but see Braunwald, 1983). However, preliminary observations of a group of abused and neglected children suggest that these children are seriously delayed in topic management skills. It remains to be seen whether they are genuinely disordered.

With respect to other populations of language-imparied children, the role of the environment in causing or compounding problems is also an issue. Children who are not communicating normally for any of the reasons discussed earlier may induce an abnormal environment (Johnston, 1980; Wulbert, Inglis, Kriegsmann, & Mills, 1975). It is hard for an adult to react normally to a nonnormal infant or to know how to compensate for the abnormality. This problem is likely to exist for topic management as much as for any other aspect of communicative competence (see Millet & Newhoff, 1978).

The role of the environment in topic skill disorders is affected by the presence or absence of other distorting factors, along with the range of variation found in normal environments. For example, it might be worthwhile to determine whether children who live in a community that characteristically engages in routines of the kind described here, *but* who have difficulties with topic hierarchies are getting as much experience with such routines as their normal counterparts. If not, it would be worth investigating whether increasing such experience would have a remedial benefit. Also, given the suggestion that interpretation by adults of children's early expressions may encourage the development of adult meanings and forms, it could be predicted that increasing the amount of such interpretive feedback in a remedial situation would aid in the disordered child's development. In some cases this may involve teaching caregivers to recognize certain behaviors as potentially communicative to which they might not otherwise attend. For example, mothers of blind children often have to be taught to recognize their children's idiosyncratic requests for attention (Fraiberg, 1979).

•   •   •

The nature and development of discourse topic skills in young children are founded on a number of contributing cognitive developments and certain interactional experiences. Understanding the causes of disorder in this area of pragmatics requires understanding each of these contributing factors. The application of the modularity thesis for understanding the linguistic abilities of both normal and disordered children may indeed prove to be useful should the predictions given here be borne out.

REFERENCES

Andersen, E., Dunlea, A., & Kekelis, L. (1984). Blind children's language: Resolving some difficulties. *Journal of Child Language* 2(3), 645–664.

Braunwald, S. (1983). Why social interaction makes a difference: Insights from abused toddlers. In R.M. Golinkoff (Ed.), *The transition from prelinguistic to linguistic communication*. Hillsdale, NJ: Erlbaum.

Bruner, J.S. (1974). The organization of early skilled action. In M.P.M. Richards (Ed.), *The integration of a child into a social world*. Cambridge, England: Cambridge University Press.

Chomsky, N. (1980). *Rules and representations*. New York: Columbia University Press.

Fodor, J.A. (1983). *The modularity of mind*. Cambridge, MA: MIT Press.

Foster, S.H. (1979). *From nonverbal to verbal communication: A study of the development of topic initiation strategies during the first two-and-a-half years of life*. Unpublished doctoral dissertation, Lancaster University, Lancaster, England.

Foster, S.H. (1981a). Interpretation and the origin of meaning and form. In S. Hutcheson (Ed.), *Work in progress*, (pp. 9–18). Department of Linguistics, University of Edinburgh, Scotland.

Foster, S.H. (1981b). The emergence of topic type in children under 2;6–A chicken and egg problem. *Papers and reports on child language development*, 20, 52–60. Stanford, CA: Department of Linguistics, Stanford University.

Foster, S.H. (1982). Learning to develop a topic. *Papers and reports on child language development*, 21, 63–70. Department of Linguistics, Stanford University.

Foster, S.H. (1984, July). *Modularity and language acquisition: Distinguishing syntax and pragmatics*. Paper presented at the Third International Congress for the Study of Child Language, Austin, TX.

Fraiberg, S. (1979). Blind infants and their mothers: An examination of the sign system. In M. Bullowa (Ed.), *Before speech: The beginning of interpersonal communication*. Cambridge, England: Cambridge University Press.

Greenfield, P.M. (1980). Toward an operational and logical analysis of intentionality: The use of discourse in early child language. In D. Olson (Ed.), *The social foundations of language and thought.* New York: W. W. Norton.

Johnston, J. (1980). The language disordered child. In N. Lass, J. Northern, D. Yoder, & L. McReynolds (Eds.), *Speech, language and hearing.* Philadelphia: W.B. Saunders.

Keenan, E.O., & Schieffelin, B. (1976). Topic as a discourse notion: A study of topic in the conversation of children and adults. In C. Li (Ed.), *Subject and topic.* New York: Academic Press.

Keil, F.C. (1981). Constraints on knowledge and cognitive development. *Psychological Review, 88,*(3), 197–227.

Kekelis, L., & Andersen, E. (1984). Family communication styles. *Journal of Visual Impairment and Blindness, 78*(2) 54–65.

Michaels, S., & Cook-Gumperz, J. (1979). A study of sharing time with first-grade students: Discourse narratives in the classroom. *Proceedings of the Berkeley Linguistic Society, 5,* 647–660.

Miller, G.A., Galanter, E., & Primbram, K.H. (1960). *Plans and the structure of behavior.* New York: Holt, Rinehart and Winston.

Millet, A., & Newhoff, M. (1978). Language disordered children: Language disordered mothers? Paper presented at the meeting of the American Speech and Hearing Association, San Francisco.

Ochs, E. (1982). Talking to children in Western Samoa. *Language in Society, 11,* 77–104.

Ochs, E., Schieffelin, B., & Platt, M. (1979). Propositions across utterances and speakers. In E. Ochs & B. Schieffelin (Eds.), *Developmental Pragmatics.* New York: Academic Press.

Scollon, R. (1976). *Conversations with a one year old: A case study in the developmental foundation of syntax.* Honoluli: University of Hawaii Press.

Snyder, L. (1975). *Pragmatics in language disordered children: Their prelinguistic and early verbal performatives and presuppositions.* Unpublished doctoral dissertation. Boulder: University of Colorado.

Snyder, L. (1978). Communicative and cognitive abilities and disabilities in the sensorimotor period. *Merrill-Palmer Quarterly, 24,* 161–180.

Snyder, L. (1984). Communicative competence in children with delayed language development. In R. Schiefelbusch & J. Pickar (Eds.), *Communicative competence: Acquisition and intervention.* Vol 1. Baltimore, MD: University Park Press.

Trevarthen, C., & Hubley, P. (1978). Secondary intersubjectivity: Confidence, confiding and acts of meaning in the first year. In A. Lock (Ed.), *Action, gesture and symbol: The emergence of language.* London: Academic Press.

van Dijk, T.A. (1977). *Text and context: Explorations in the semantics and pragmatics of discourse.* London: Longman.

Vygotsky, L.S. (1962). *Thought and language.* Cambridge, MA: MIT Press.

Wulbert, M., Inglis, S., Kriegsmann, E., & Mills, B. (1975). Language delay and associated mother-child interactions. *Developmental Psychology, 11,* 61–70.

World knowledge to word knowledge

Elizabeth R. Crais, PhD
Assistant Professor
Division of Speech and Hearing Sciences
University of North Carolina at Chapel Hill
Chapel Hill, North Carolina

THE ABILITY to acquire new vocabulary in a naturalistic context is a major part of early language acquisition, and Sternberg and Powell (1983) suggest it may be the basis of learning in general. Children's acquisition of new vocabulary is said to occur very rapidly, with five word roots added daily for children between 1.5 and 6 years of age (Carey, 1978), and 14,000 words in the comprehension vocabulary of the average 6-year-old (Miller, 1977). Clinicians and researchers examining children's acquisition of words need to discover what children know about the words in their vocabularies and what skills are available to children for word learning. This article focuses on the acquisition of word knowledge from world knowledge, factors affecting the word-learning process, and vocabulary assessment and remediation methods. Issues related to word finding are not directly addressed except where they overlap with general vocabulary development and deficits. Indeed, the findings of Kail and

Top Lang Disord, 1990,10(3),45–62
© 1990 Aspen Publishers, Inc.

Leonard (1986) with language-impaired (LI) children argue for elaboration limitations rather than retrieval deficits in this population. Thus, the focus here will be on the development, elaboration, and measurement of the lexicon.

DEVELOPING WORD KNOWLEDGE FROM WORLD KNOWLEDGE

A child's knowledge of the world and events in the world greatly influences vocabulary acquisition. Early words are first comprehended and then later produced in the context of episodic or event-related experiences (Nelson, 1986; Nelson & Brown, 1979; Nelson & Gruendel, 1979). Nelson and her colleagues argue that all cognitive and linguistic information emanates from event-based episodes and that language is initially bound to these situational contexts. How then does the child learn words from context?

The predictable interaction sequences and routinized language in the play of parents and their children have been reported by many (Bruner, 1978; Ninio & Bruner, 1978; Peters, 1984; Snow, 1977). Parents develop the routines by repeating actions and words, and with these repetitions the child begins to produce the actions and later the words of the routines. Social games like peek-a-boo and book-reading experiences are examples of the episodic nature of these interactions. When peek-a-boo is first initiated around 5 months of age, only certain participants, objects, and actions signal to the child that the game has begun and any alterations to the elements cause the game to cease (Greenfield, 1972). Months later, the child

recognizes and participates in the game with different persons or settings.

Nelson and her colleagues (Nelson & Brown, 1979; Nelson & Gruendel, 1979), following the work of Schank and Abelson (1977), use the term "scripts" to describe these early social routines and argue that scripts include certain actors, actions, objects, contextual circumstances, and relationships of these elements in the event representation. It is clear in these instances that the child has "recorded" the words and actions used in the script, and, in the presence of certain aspects of the script, the original elements are activated in memory. Past experiences are thus used to interpret the immediate experience, to set expectations for what will follow, and to provide dialogue for the interaction. Snow and Goldfield (1983) describe a young child's use of just such a production strategy during book-reading, that is, "say in any particular situation what others have said in previous occurrences of that situation." Thus, embedded within the child's scripts are the words that surround the event, and with repetition, the words themselves become cues for the entire script.

Barrett (1983) provides an example of such a lexical script for a child who only produced the word "off" when removing clothing from either her own or another person's body. Barrett hypothesized that the child's "off" script included, and was restricted to, an actor (the child), an object (clothing), an action (taking off), and a recipient (the child or other person). Barrett proposes that script development involves acquisition, generalization (to other actors, objects, and actions), and eventual decontextualization. Bowerman (1981) provides examples of decontextualization of utterances using the term "combinatorial independence" to refer to the child's ability to use the elements of an utterance in a nonsituation-specific instance or in a recombined new utterance. As children make this shift, for specific words and utterances, from context-bound to decontextualized use, they make a gradual and general shift from processing based on particular events and familiar routines to more abstract, semantically based processing.

Nelson (1977) has suggested that the bases for this shift to semantic processing are cognitive reorganization, the availability of conceptual information, and the child's approach to the task. Cognitive changes can be seen in a child's ability to talk about present versus absent objects. An 18-month-old child is typically tied to the immediate context and talks about what is physically present, whereas older children are more able to comprehend and talk about objects not present.

Bowerman (1981) agrees that changes in nonlinguistic cognitive abilities drive reorganization of the lexicon and the child's productions, but suggests that the growth of knowledge about language is also a significant factor. Bowerman uses as an example of the growth in both knowledge bases her daughter Christy's early correct use of "open," which later shifted to, "Will you unopen this?" Bowerman suggests that achieving productive use of a form and achieving adultlike knowledge of its structure are not necessarily one and the same. As both the child's nonlinguistic cognitive knowledge (i.e., things to be opened) and the knowledge of the language itself (i.e., the meaning of "un") increase, changes in lexical use will result.

Nelson and Brown (1979) cite the syntagmatic-paradigmatic shift seen in children's responses to word association tasks as an example of this general processing shift. Early accounts (Brown & Berko, 1960; Entwisle, 1966) argued that young children (4- to 5-year-olds) respond syntagmatically or syntactically, for example, "dog bites" to the stimulus "dog"; and older children (8- to 10-year-olds) respond paradigmatically or categorically, for example, "cat" for "dog." Nelson (1977), however, argued the younger children's responses, rather than being syntax based, are event related. In support of an event-based to semantically based shift is the work of Petrey (1977), who reanalyzed Entwisle's (1966) word association data to argue that children initially use situation-based responses and only later use semantically organized ones. Petrey argued that the kindergartners' responses such as "Bundle up" or "Get your coat" to the stimulus "cold" were indicative of the episodic nature of their processing. In contrast, the third-graders' responses showed significant decline in the dependence on physical context.

A recent, experience-based account of the reorganization of the child's knowledge and lexicon is provided by Child Talk, a model of children's language production (Chapman, 1988; Chapman et al., in press). The Child Talk model argues for shifts in lexical domains relative to shifts in real-world experiences of the kind noted by Crais (1987a) in a study of children's and adults' comprehension of novel and familiar words in stories. When asked to tell what was remembered about common words from the stories (e.g., "tree"), 4 of 20 third- and 8 of 20 fifth-graders responded with definitions, whereas none of the 20 first-graders or 20 adults did so. Crais hypothesized that the use of definitions by some third- and fifth-graders was prompted by the educational emphasis on definition tasks in these later grades.

Although there is a general shift to semantic processing, children and adults may, at times, use an event-based strategy or a syntactic strategy based on a particular event. An example of this experience-based processing can be seen when trying to recall a stranger's name, where people often report trying to visualize the situation during which they met the person. When adults are asked to define unfamiliar words that cannot be immediately paradigmatically associated, they too exhibit syntagmatic responses based on what was just heard (Crais, 1987a). In Crais's study with novel words presented in stories, the adults, when unable to provide the immediate meaning of a word, often responded with the phrase or sentence surrounding the word from the story. Petrey (1977) suggested a similar occurrence for unusual words such as "hermetically," where most adults respond "sealed," due to the frequent experiential co-occurrence of the words.

Although there is a general shift to semantic processing, children and adults may, at times, use an event-based strategy or a syntactic strategy based on a particular event.

Continued, as well as conventional, organization of the lexicon, according to the Child Talk model (Chapman et al., in press), occurs with a child's introduction to preschool and school-like activities (categorizing, listing, associating words). Social learning also occurs in these school experiences as the child learns to make socially and educationally appropriate responses to various tasks. The child learns to use certain words and inhibit others, to define words in acceptable and conventional ways, to answer questions with only the type of information requested, and to make judgments about individual words. These changes reflect developing word and world knowledge and their interplay in the child's lexicon. To summarize in terms of lexical reorganization, specific words shift from contextualized to decontextualized use as the child is gradually changing from solely event-based processing to multiple processing strategies.

FACTORS AFFECTING THE VOCABULARY ACQUISITION PROCESS

Although much is known about the type of words learned first and the ways children learn to combine words, only recently have researchers begun to look at the acquisition process itself. Carey (1978) suggests two phases of "mapping" information about words into memory. The "fast-mapping" phase refers to the rapid acquisition of information about a word during the first few encounters. During this phase, only a small portion of the information available to the child is actually mapped into memory, and during later encounters, a more gradual phase, the remainder of the information is mapped.

In a study of the fast-mapping skills of 3- to 4-year-old preschool children, Carey and Bartlett (1978) introduced a new word in a naturalistic setting. The teacher, when setting up for snack-time, took each child aside and said, "See those two trays? Bring me the chromium one, not the red one." The contrast with the word "red" indicated chromium as a color-word and allowed the child to identify easily the intended referent (the olive-colored tray). A week later, Carey and Bartlett administered comprehension and production tasks, and found that only one encounter with the word had allowed more than half of the children to map something about the word into memory. The children's partial mappings of chromium were quite variable, and Carey (1982) later argued that the mappings were affected by the properties of each child's preexisting color lexicon and the name the child used for olive during the pretests. Thus, both the previous world and the immediate word knowledge held by each child before the encounter affected what was mapped into memory.

Dollaghan (1985), in a study following Carey and Bartlett's, asked 2- to 5-year-old children to hide three familiar objects and then to hide a "koob" (a novel plastic object). From this single exposure, more than 80% of the children were able to recognize the referent among two familiar and three unfamiliar objects when asked to feed the "koob" to a puppet. In addition, more than half of the children were able to give episodic information about the "koob" by identifying the location (box, bowl, or wrapping paper) where it

was initially hidden. Because more subjects succeeded on the comprehension and identification-of-hiding-place tasks than on the production task, Dollaghan suggested that phonetic production was the most vulnerable aspect of the fast-mapping process. These two studies reveal that with only one exposure, young children were able to (a) choose a referent (olive tray, plastic object), (b) recognize the semantic category (color term, object name), (c) identify the location and actions on the original referent, and (d) store some information about the phonetic shape of the word, at least for recognition.

When Dollaghan (1987) used her "koob" task to contrast the fast-mapping skills of LI versus normally developing 4- and 5-year-olds, she found no differences between the groups in their abilities to choose a referent, to comprehend the word, and to store nonlinguistic information. However, differences were evident when subjects were asked to name the object. Dollaghan was unable to determine conclusively whether the difficulty for the LI subjects was due to storage or retrieval deficits, but suggested that it was more likely retrieval, as four of five children who did not name the object were able to recognize "koob" when given "soob" and "teed" as foils.

Others who have studied the early word-learning process have focused on either the introduction of new words in a naturalistic setting (Bates, Bretherton, & Snyder, 1988; Crais, 1987a; Dickinson, 1984) or the presentation of a number of words in a training session paradigm (Holdgrafer & Sorenson, 1984; Nelson & Bonvillian, 1973; Schwartz & Leonard, 1984). Although these studies suggest the aspects of words that are mapped during early encounters, little information is available regarding the factors that influence the fast-mapping process.

In a study that introduced novel words in stories to first-, third-, and fifth-grade children and adults, Crais (1987a) examined factors hypothesized to affect the fast-mapping process. In the stories, both the distance between the three repetitions of each novel word and the type of propositional information provided for each word were varied. The subjects heard the stories, then retold them and answered questions about familiar and novel words in the stories. Measures of the subjects' abilities to produce the words and the recall of propositional information about the words revealed significant differences between three of the four groups. No differences were found between the third- and fifth-graders. When the repetitions of the words were close together and the information about the words was specific, the listeners had difficulty remembering the phonological form of the new words, although they performed well on the recall of information about the word. Thus, the listeners were more likely to choose a referent for the novel word and were therefore less dependent on the novel word itself. When the words were farther apart and less specific propositional information was provided, the phonological forms were recalled better, and the propositional information was less well recalled. In these cases, the listeners had difficulty figuring out the meaning of the word and choosing a referent, and therefore, the phonological form of the words was more important to retain. Thus, both the distance between the novel words and the type of propositional information affected the fast-mapping process.

The conclusions drawn from these fast-mapping studies are as follows: (a) even one encounter with a new word is sufficient for very young children (2 years old) to map something in memory; (b) as predicted by Carey and Bartlett (1978), the more exposures to a word, the more complete is the map; (c) comprehension and phonetic production of the word are achieved separately, and as noted by Dollaghan (1985), the production of the new word is the most vulnerable aspect; and (d) factors influencing acquisition may be the type of referents available for each word, repetition distance between words, type of propositional information, and as noted by Dickinson (1984), presentation context (conversation, story, definition).

ASSESSMENT OF WORDS AND WORD KNOWLEDGE

Recognizing that a word is linked with a conventional meaning is both a means for communicating knowledge within a culture and a representation of the child's knowledge about the culture (Drum & Konopak, 1987). Sternberg and Powell (1983) argue that vocabulary development, verbal comprehension, and learning from context are integrally related. Accordingly, difficulties in vocabulary development are seen as the consequence of problems in verbal comprehension, and both vocabulary development and verbal comprehension depend on the student's ability to learn from context. Sternberg and Powell contend that the relationship between learning from context and vocabulary development is bidirectional and that growth in either area can facilitate growth in the other. Vocabulary development is then reflective of both learning from context and overall verbal comprehension.

One persistent difficulty in assessing vocabulary knowledge is the differing criteria used to determine that a word is acquired or known. As noted by Drum and Konopak (1987), "access to word knowledge cannot be compared to an on/off toggle switch" (p. 79). The learner's success in lexical comprehension or production tasks may depend on the type of information available to the learner and the type of response required. A second difficulty that occurs when assessing vocabulary knowledge may be the confounding of results with the use of expressive measures to assess children with expressive language deficits. Additionally, a problem may exist when attempting to differentiate between deficits in word knowledge versus word finding. A child suspected of word-finding deficits should be evaluated with a measure that takes this deficit specifically into account, such as the Test of Word Finding (German, 1986).

The following discussion of assessment measures will first focus on more traditional measures, followed by those more recently developed, and will conclude with several experimental techniques.

The most frequently used methods of evaluating vocabulary knowledge continue to be single-word receptive or expressive tests. In single-word comprehension tests, the student is asked to recognize a particular phonetic shape and associate it with one of three to four pictures. The subject's responses are usually only scored as correct or incorrect, with no information gained as to the type and degree of

partial knowledge the student may have used to recognize the word. Examination of the incorrect response choices is only useful if the clinician knows how the foils for each item are systematically varied. In addition, the tasks only assess the student's recognition in one context. In contrast, expressive vocabulary tests assess whether the child recognizes the stimulus picture and can call up a phonetic representation of the item from memory.

The results of receptive and expressive vocabulary tests, although limited, can indicate children's ability to recognize or produce the conventional word used by the immediate culture, reflecting learning from context, and do give an estimate of children's single-word vocabulary level compared to their peers. The clinician, however, knows little about children's routine use or frequency of use of a word. Additionally, rather than focus solely on bipolar decisions of whether or not a word has been acquired, the assessment should highlight a continuum of acquisition by examining various types and levels of word knowledge using tasks such as definition, semantic relation, varied meaning, creation of sentence, and metaphorical understanding. Discussion of such tasks for assessing word knowledge follows.

Definition tasks

Definition tasks can be used to measure aspects of the child's developmental experiences with words, especially when all the information supplied by the child is recorded. As noted by Curtis (1987), the development of word definitions has its own history, with children first giving the use of the item, a description or demonstration of it, or providing its use in context.

Later, children use synonyms or explanations, and only with training do they use the conventional definitions learned in school.

In an effort to characterize students' knowledge about the meanings of words, Dale (1965) used the students' own comments to represent four stages of word learning: stage 1: "I never saw it before" (does not know if it is a real word); stage 2: "I've heard of it, but I don't know what it means" (no definition available); stage 3: "I recognize it in context, it has something to do with . . ." (definition given in specific context); and stage 4: "I know it, it means . . ." (definition given in more general context). Typical multiple-choice vocabulary tests only assess stage 3 knowledge of whether the student recognizes the word in the context provided. Curtis (1987) suggests that definition tasks can provide an estimate of the student's familiarity with word meanings and, therefore, may provide an index of his or her world knowledge.

Although definition tasks can be a positive addition to single-word vocabulary testing, they also have their limitations, particularly when the student is only given credit for complete and conventional definitions. Performance on a definition task is not reflective of the student's ability to use the word productively in oral or written expression unless the task is modified to look at the type of response made by the student.

Word association tasks

Word association tasks have also been used to assess word knowledge by examining the student's ability to use categorical processing versus event-based processing. Although the free association task, "cat-dog" can be useful, the most popular association task involves providing a category and asking the student to name as many elements in the category as possible within a specified time period. Although some standardized psychological tests include such a measure (e.g., McCarthy Scales, McCarthy, 1970), few language tests do so. The Clinical Evaluation of Language Fundamentals-Revised (Semel, Wiig, & Secord, 1987) and the Language Processing Test (Richard & Hanner, 1985) do provide this type of measure.

One difficulty with some word association measures is their inability to differentiate between disordered and normal groups. In a naming-to-category task, Kail and Leonard (1986) reported no significant differences between LI and age-matched normally developing children on "animal" and "furniture" categories, although differences were noted on "occupations." It may be argued that the occupation category differences were related to the likely variability in the groups' levels of world knowledge. Indeed, Kail and Leonard suggest that the "occupation" results may represent the typical word knowledge delay seen in LI children. In terms of comparing the groups' categori-

> *Although definition tasks can be a positive addition to single-word vocabulary testing, they also have their limitations, particularly when the student is only given credit for complete and conventional definitions.*

cal responses, both groups gave prototypical responses first, then provided familiar but not prototypical instances, and finally gave progressively less common items.

Clearly, when assessing word associations, the clinician needs to examine the type and familiarity of category used and the number and prototypicality of responses given. As suggested by Israel (1984), it is also useful to look at the student's responses by subcategories; for example, for "animals," are they farm animals, zoo animals, or pets? Counting the units within a subgroup can also be informative, especially if a child only gives one item per subcategory (e.g., farm: horse; zoo: lion; pet: dog) rather than multiple items from one subcategory (e.g., pets: parakeet, cat, turtle). Richard and Hanner (1985) also suggest asking the student, "What goes with X?" and encouraging the student to think of any words associated with the target word.

Additional tasks

Broader knowledge of words is seen on tasks assessing antonyms, synonyms, word similarities/differences, semantic attributes, semantic absurdities, multiple meanings, ambiguous sentences, and metaphoric understanding. The first three measures, antonyms, synonyms, and word similarities or differences prompt the student to use semantic attributes as a basis for response. Antonyms require the student either to use learned word associations (e.g., hot-cold) or to analyze the characteristics of the stimulus and to choose which characteristic is the critical one to oppose. Jorgensen, Barrett, Huisingh, and Zachman (1981) suggest that failure to produce antonyms may reflect (a) inability to determine the steps necessary for antonymous responses, (b) difficulty in focusing on the critical semantic dimension, (c) vocabulary that does not include an opposite lexical item for each stimulus, (d) inability to retrieve the opposite term, or (e) difficulty understanding the meaning of the stimulus. Jorgensen et al.'s error types and example responses can be useful in determining the type of difficulty exhibited on antonym tasks. A synonym task can also be performed with learned responses (purse = handbag) or by completing the analysis steps to find sufficient similarities of attributes. A related task is that of similarities or differences, where the student is asked to choose which items are either similar or different among three or four items and then may be asked to give a reason for the choice. Like the antonym or synonym tasks, the student must have available the appropriate semantic categories, knowledge of membership attributes, and ability to compare/contrast the items by their attributes, but then also must select the item that does or does not fit. Unlike antonyms/synonyms, the student has the choices already available and does not have to search for a lexical term. Analyzing a student's incorrect responses and the reasons for response selection can reveal the steps taken by the student. Information can also be gained by problem-solving with the student other possible correct or incorrect choices.

Another attribute task is one used by Richard and Hanner (1985) in which the student is asked to tell all that is known about a word, and the clinician prompts the student to use varied attributes (function, size, color, category, etc.). Although little developmental data are available on the number and type of attributes that should be expected, this type of task can be useful for observing how words and attributes are organized by the student and particularly which attributes are limited or entirely omitted.

In semantic absurdities tasks, the student must know each individual lexical item and its semantic features, and must use world knowledge to recognize the probable interrelationships of the words in this context. Finally, the student must be able to express what is wrong with the sentence and why it is absurd. In Jorgensen et al.'s (1981) absurdities subtest, there are three types of possible incongruencies: agent to object of action (e.g., The plumber fixed the lights); cause and effect (e.g., Judy was exhausted from sleeping all night); and lack of semantic redundancy (e.g., The miniature statue was 10 ft tall). As noted by Jorgensen et al., the student may respond by simply negating the statement (e.g., Plumbers don't fix lights), and the clinician must then probe further to find out the student's understanding. Breaking down the task into its separate components (i.e., comprehension of separate words, interpretation of the sentence, etc.) can be useful in determining the focus of difficulty.

In recent years, some researchers and clinicians have begun focusing on metaphorical or figurative interpretations of language (Lakoff & Johnson, 1980; Winner, Rosenstiel, & Gardner, 1976). Typically in these tasks, the student hears or reads a metaphor out of context and is asked to interpret its meaning. In contrast, Wiig and Secord (1985), by providing the student with a context (e.g., two boys talking at a dog show) and an utterance

used in that context (e.g., "He is crazy about that pet"), promote the use of world knowledge in interpreting the meaning. After the student tells what the speaker meant by the utterance, he or she then hears and reads four expressions and is asked to choose the one closest to the original utterance's meaning. Thus, both recall and recognition memory are assessed.

Multiple meaning and ambiguous sentence tasks can also be used and can be viewed as promoting similar processing about words and word meanings, but from opposite directions. For multiple meanings, the student is given a word (e.g., bank), asked to provide a meaning, and then asked to provide an additional meaning. With ambiguous sentences (e.g., The man wiped the glasses), the student is supplied a context and must provide two meanings that are congruent with that context. Wiig and Secord (1985) provide step-by-step guidelines for assessing factors affecting both lexical and structural processing of ambiguities and later for developing these skills.

A measure that assesses, in part, lexical use is to provide the student with one to three words and ask him or her to make up a sentence. In a variation of this task, Wiig and Secord (1985) first provide a pictorial context (e.g., two people near a park bench) and three words (e.g., sit, painted, because), and ask the student to make up a sentence that fits the situation. With the context provided, the student is prompted to use past experiences to create a sentence. Clearly, some students may be disadvantaged if they have not had personal experience with the context. Although the scoring on the task is somewhat confusing (i.e., the clinician needs to identify single or multiple deviations of semantics, syntax, or pragmatics), the idea of providing context and asking for sentence construction is a unique one. Wiig and Secord suggest that the student who fails the task can be tested further with reduced lexical complexity (deletion of one or two words from the stimulus list).

Spontaneous language sampling can be an additional means of assessing the student's use of words and word knowledge. Beyond informal measures such as the Multilevel Informal Language Inventory (Goldsworthy, 1982), several computer programs are available that can analyze the student's word use. Programs such as Systematic Analysis of Language Transcripts (SALT) (Miller & Chapman, 1985), contain several convenient and fairly simple ways to look at word use. After transcription by the clinician, the SALT program automatically gives calculations of total number of words, total number of different words, type–token ratio (different words/total words), and an alphabetical word list of all words said by the child and makes comparisons between the words used by the examiner and those used by the child. Other programs that include lexical or semantic analyses are Lingquest (Mordecai, Palin, & Palmer, 1985) and Computerized Profiling (Long & Fey, 1988).

Crais (1988) used SALT to compare language/learning disabled (LLD) and age-matched and younger comprehension-vocabulary-matched normally developing children's story retelling skills. Because both number of different words and total number of words increase with age from 3 to 8 years (Miller, 1986), no differences between the groups were seen for type-token ratio. Significant differences were seen, however, between the groups on number of words and number of different words, with the comprehension–vocabulary matched and LLD children performing similarly and with both groups differing significantly from the age-matched group. Hence, numbers of total words and different words, at least on a story-retelling task, can be examined when comparing older versus younger children and particularly when looking at disordered versus normally developing children.

The final group of vocabulary measures are those that have been used experimentally with interesting results. Keil (1983) used novel words and the inferences made about them to assess categorical knowledge. The kindergarten, second-grade, and fourth-grade children in Keil's study heard three sentences about an unfamiliar word (i.e., "The hyrax is asleep."). The children were then queried about the word's meaning (i.e., Could a hyrax be hungry?). Keil suggests that a person with mature ontological knowledge will provide information such as, "A hyrax is an animal and like other members of its class can eat, breathe, etc." Keil suggests that children make fewer and less complete inferences in this case due to their limited ontological knowledge. Using novel words to discover the level of children's categorical knowledge and the depth of that knowledge can be useful and fun for the child, as most children enjoy activities with "silly" words. Similarly, syntactic and morphologic information can be tested by using novel words, as Berko (1958) did when she introduced a picture of a bird-like figure and said,

"Here is one wug, and here are two
_____."

Rather than use novel or nonsense words, Werner and Kaplan (1952) looked at 9- to 13-year-old children's abilities to infer the meaning of real, but unfamiliar, words in sentence contexts. The children were presented six different sentences that provided different contexts for each word and were then asked to interpret each sentence in light of the preceding sentences. Werner and Kaplan found developmental differences in the children's abilities to infer meaning from context and noted that correctness of response increased significantly with increasing age. A simplified form of this task, with fewer sentences and more familiar, concrete words, may be used to investigate a child's use of context to interpret word meaning.

Finally, as noted previously, Crais (1987a) in a fast-mapping task used stories with novel words to evaluate the type of information that children and adults could store and recall about new words. Crais found major differences in the groups' abilities to produce the phonological form of the new words. Crais (1987b) noted the importance of distance of the word repetitions and the specificity of the propositions in the acquisition process. Crais suggested that if the intent of instruction with new words is for students to recall the phonological form of a new word, then spaced presentations of the word with less contextual information are useful. If the goal is recall of the propositional information, however, close repetitions that provide very specific information are better.

Using stories to introduce new words and observing which aspects are stored and recalled can illuminate what and how

Using stories to introduce new words and observing which aspects are stored and recalled can illuminate what and how a student learns from context.

a student learns from context. The use of stories to look at fast-mapping skills was informative across a wide developmental range, provided a natural context for word acquisition, motivated the subjects to attend to the task, and permitted the systematic manipulation of variables affecting the fast-mapping process. The clinician can use many variations of the story task by introducing one or more new words; different grammatical categories (noun, verb); more versus less specific propositional information; varied types of contextual cues; or variations in story type and length, or mode of presentation (oral vs. written, or story, conversation, or definition). Information available can be judged for its level of phonetic, syntactic, semantic, pragmatic, morphological, and contextual accuracy.

In conclusion, no one task can be adequate for assessing all types of word knowledge, and, therefore, the clinician needs to choose carefully among those available. Kameenui, Dixon, and Carnine (1987) note the issue is not which test is "best," but which ones are consistent with, and provide the types of knowledge necessary for, specific goals.

INTERVENTION WITH WORDS

Just as vocabulary assessment tasks can be classified by the type of knowledge measured, so too can intervention tasks with the clinician choosing tasks that teach the targeted content and skills. For some words, simply consolidating the meanings and uses of the word will suffice; for other words, expansion is useful. Often, it is necessary to introduce new words, including both their content and labels. The following discussion highlights these methods of consolidating, expanding, and adding to a student's vocabulary knowledge and use.

Elshout-Mohr and van Daalen-Kapteijns (1987) provide suggestions for consolidating the existing meanings of words. They suggest (a) find out what the student knows about a word, (b) try to respect whatever that knowledge is, and (c) build on existing knowledge while breaking down any misconceptions. They recommend discussion of varied experiences with the word, and although conventional information is important, it is also helpful to use idiosyncratic ideas or experiences. Also useful is developing a tree diagram for the word and targeting associated words.

A second choice in vocabulary development is to expand the characteristics that are associated with the word. Johnson and Pearson (1984) describe a technique called semantic feature analysis in which the student is presented a grid containing a set of related words on one axis (e.g., car, motorcycle, bike), a set of attributes on the other axis (e.g., 2-wheeled, motorized), and columns of + and − marks to indicate presence or absence of attributes. The student is shown a completed grid and is encouraged to discuss the words and the attributes. The student is then given an empty grid and asked to fill in the + and − marks. Later, the student can add

words and attributes to the grid and can develop new grids with new words. Becker and Snyder (1982) and Wiig and Becker-Caplan (1984) have implemented similar ideas with LI children in expanding students' linguistic retrieval strategies in relation to word-finding problems.

Another form of vocabulary expansion is the introducing of alternate meanings of words. Graves (1987) suggests there are two groups of polysemous words, those that have a number of common meanings (e.g., run, head) and those with both common and specialized meanings (e.g., product, legend). Graves suggests there are far too many polysemous words to teach them all directly and instead encourages helping the student to recognize instances of multiple word meanings, to realize that some words have specialized word meanings in particular subject areas, and to understand that word meaning varies as a function of context.

A third source of expanding knowledge about words is the use of a root-word strategy whereby the clinician introduces a word-root and helps the student discover possible additions to the word (inflectional suffixes, e.g., ing, es, s; derivational suffixes, e.g., less, ty; prefixes, e.g., un, im). Using concrete and easily definable prefixes such as "un" can be a starting place. Further suggestions for training word elements are found in White and Speidel (in press). These researchers reported that more than half of prefixed words begin with one of four negation prefixes: un, in, dis, and non. The clinician can also use common elements (e.g., ly, ty) to introduce the concept that changes in words often bring about changes in grammatical category.

A final means of expanding existing vocabulary is to introduce semantically related information, such as categories and their members, super- and subordinate items, antonyms, and synonyms. Many basal reading programs can be used to identify appropriate grade-level (and for LI children, language-level) words and their antonyms, synonyms, and so forth. Graves (1987) suggests that although, for example, synonyms have roughly the same meaning, it is also important for students to recognize the small differences in these words and to appreciate the differing conditions for their use (e.g., angry vs. furious).

The last area of vocabulary development is that of introducing new words. Graves (1987) suggests that learning new words that represent known concepts is the largest vocabulary task facing middle-grade students and the most difficult is learning new words for new concepts. As noted by Nagy and Herman (1987), vocabulary instruction has often been used to increase reading comprehension, and the most successful programs usually contain some of the following: multiple exposures to the new words, varied information about each word, exposure in meaningful contexts, established connections between the words and the child's experiences and prior knowledge, and an active role taken by the student in the word-learning process. In contrast, then, if the goal is to add new words to a student's oral vocabulary, how should one do so?

Clearly, from all that has preceded, the initial suggestion for building new vocabulary is merely to expose the child to real-life events as a bridge to developing new information and new words. The caveat comes, however, when considering LI children's impoverished world and word knowledge gained when attempting to learn from events and context that surround them. With normally developing children, Sternberg (1987) suggests using contextual learning to help them acquire new words, but also argues that presenting words in context is not enough. He argues that children need to learn how to learn from context and that they must see the relevance of these efforts to their own lives. With LI children, the need to learn how to learn from context appears all the more necessary.

Sternberg and Powell (1983) have categorized eight cues that a student needs to be aware of to be able to learn from context. The eight cues are temporal, spatial, value, stative descriptive, functional descriptive, causal, class membership, and equivalence. In the sentence, "At dawn, the blen arose on the horizon and shone brightly," four context cues can be used to infer that "blen" means "sun." The cues are as follows: at dawn = temporal; arose, shone = functional descriptive; on the horizon = spatial; and brightly = stative descriptive. Sternberg (1987) used these cues to teach high school students how to learn from written context and found that the cues vary in difficulty. The easiest to recognize are the class membership cues, with functional-descriptive cues next, and stative-descriptive cues the most difficult.

In following Sternberg and Powell's (1983) guidelines for vocabulary learning in oral contexts, the clinician needs to be sensitive to differences in using written versus oral presentations (i.e., the temporality of the message and context). Initially, the clinician may want to use a pictorial or written format to allow the student time to consider the context of the message and to derive meaning. In addition, the clinician can systematically vary the eight contextual cues or several mediating variables (suggested by Sternberg & Powell), such as number of occurrences of the words and importance of the unknown words, to see which ones are the most helpful for particular students. (See Sternberg & Powell, 1983, for further specification.)

Beck, McKeown, and Omanson (1987) use games to help students recognize unfamiliar words. Games include having students bring in new words to "stump" the class or playing a modified "fictionary" game with preselected words. These researchers suggest using an activity called Word Wizard, in which students earn points by reporting their own or others' uses of target words outside of the classroom. In addition, students can be required to teach a lesson on a particular word or word set. Graves (1987) recommends fostering good attitudes about word learning by using word games such as puzzles, Boggle, or Scrabble. Beck et al. (1987) also suggest introducing games to reward students for recognizing unfamiliar words, using initially very obvious and highly unusual words and extending later to words used in the wrong context. Hall (1984) encourages making up words or "sniglets," which are any words that do not exist in the dictionary, but should (e.g., "cinemuck" meaning the goop that covers the floor in movie theaters). Atkinson and Longman (1985) provide a number of ideas for creating sniglets and situations

needing a sniglet or sniglets with common affixes or word-roots.

Crais (1987a) found using stories with novel words to be fun and motivating for first-, third-, and fifth-grade children in a story-retelling task. It was difficult for the children to remember four novel words per story; however, the one novel word in the practice story was recalled quite well. It is suggested that the clinician begin with only one novel (or unfamiliar) word representing a known concept. Later, more words can be introduced, and the familiarity of the concept can shift from known to unknown.

Levin et al. (1984) proposed a mnemonic strategy for teaching new vocabulary words called the "keyword method." The student is first encouraged to link the new word (e.g., persuade) with a familiar, acoustically or visually similar keyword (e.g., purse). The student is then shown a picture of the new word interacting with the keyword (e.g., a woman giving money from her purse to a salesperson), and underneath the picture is written the connection (e.g., persuade = when someone talks you into something). The keyword then becomes a retrieval cue for recalling the meaning of the new word. Later, students are encouraged to develop their own keywords and visual representations for new words. Levin et al. (1984) compared this method with a more traditional contextual method of teaching new words with fourth- and fifth-grade students and discovered that the students using the keyword method were able to recall 50% more definitions. In a recent study with learning-disabled students, Condus, Marshall, and Miller (1986) compared the keyword method to using picture context alone or sentence experiences for teaching word meanings. The keyword students performed better, both immediately and 8 weeks later, than either the students receiving the picture context or sentence experiences.

Once a clinician has chosen to introduce new words into a student's vocabulary, a difficulty arises when deciding which words should be targeted. Graves (1987) suggests considering (a) the frequency with which a student is likely to use a word; (b) how many students at a given grade level know a word (reading comprehension data available in Dale & O'Rourke, 1981); (c) the importance of the word to understanding; and (d) the likelihood a student will learn the word through context alone. Additionally, Kameenui et al. (1987) acknowledge that the goal in vocabulary instruction is often for the student to achieve full knowledge of the new word and to be able to use the word in novel situations. They note, however, that partial knowledge is often adequate for students to achieve some tasks and, therefore, the utility of students possessing varied degrees of knowledge about different words must be recognized.

• • •

The areas of vocabulary assessment and intervention have been broadly expanded within the last several years, and one of the current challenges facing clinicians is how to incorporate the new findings and new ideas into everyday practices. The recent trends in therapy to use naturalistic and real-world experiences are positive ones given the developmental nature of word and world knowledge, and yet, it is clear that LI children have often failed to use available events and contexts for learning. Recent literature on the learning of new words supports the use of alternative means beyond just contextual presentation. In addition, there are growing numbers of standardized assessment instruments, new and exciting experimental approaches, and remediation techniques as varied as the assessment measures. Using new methods to consolidate, expand, and add to a student's word and world knowledge can be an exciting endeavor and awaits the creative clinician.

REFERENCES

Atkinson, R.H., & Longman, D.G. (1985). Sniglets: Give a twist to teenage and adult vocabulary instruction. *Journal of Reading, 29* 103–105.

Barrett, M.D. (1983). The course of early lexical development: A review and an interpretation. *Early Child Development and Care, 11,* 19–32.

Bates, E., Bretherton, I., & Snyder, L. (1988). Study 5: Acquisition of a novel concept at 20 months. *From first words to grammar.* New York, NY: Cambridge University Press.

Beck, I.L., McKeown, M.G., & Omanson, R.C. (1987). The effects and uses of diverse vocabulary instructional techniques. In M.G. McKeown & M.E. Curtis (Eds.),

The nature of vocabulary acquisition. Hillsdale, NJ: Erlbaum.

Becker, L., & Snyder, L. (1982, November). *Word retrieval intervention: Changing the lexicon versus changing the strategy.* Paper presented to the annual convention of the American Speech-Language-Hearing Association, Toronto, Canada.

Berko, J. (1958). The child's learning of English morphology. *Word, 14,* 150–177.

Bowerman, M. (1981). Beyond communicative adequacy: From piecemeal knowledge to an integrated system in the child's acquisition of language. *Papers and Reports on Child Language Development, 20,* 1–24.

Brown, R., & Berko, J. (1960). Word association and the acquisition of grammar. *Child Development, 31,* 1–14.

Bruner, J. (1978). On prelinguistic prerequisites of speech. In R.N. Campbell & P.T. Smith (Eds.), *Recent advances in the psychology of language.* New York, NY: Plenum Press.

Carey, S. (1978). The child as word learner. In M. Halle, J. Bresnan, & G. Miller (Eds.), *Linguistic theory and psychological reality.* Cambridge, MA: MIT Press.

Carey, S. (1982). Semantic development: The state of the art. In E. Wanner & L. Gleitman (Eds.), *Language acquisition: State of the art.* London, England: Cambridge Press.

Carey, S., & Bartlett, E. (1978). Acquiring a single new word. *Papers and Reports in Child Language Development, 15,* 17–29.

Chapman, R.S. (1988). *Child Talk: Assumptions of a developmental process model for early language learning.* Paper presented at the Symposium on Research in Child Language Disorders, University of Wisconsin, Madison, WI.

Chapman, R.S., Streim, N., Crais, E., Salmon, D., Strand, E., & Negri-Shoultz, N. (in press). *Child Talk: Assumptions of a developmental process model for early language learning.* Manuscript submitted for publication.

Condus, M.M., Marshall, K.J., & Miller, S.R. (1986). Effects of the keyword mnemonic strategy of vocabulary acquisition and maintenance by learning disabled children. *Journal of Learning Disabilities, 19,* 609–613.

Crais, E. (1987a). Fast mapping of novel words in oral story context. *Dissertation Abstracts International, 48,* Part 3b, 724. (University Microfilms No. AAC8711019)

Crais, E. (1987b). Fast mapping of novel words in oral story context. *Papers and Reports in Child Language Development, 26,* 40–47.

Crais, E. (1988, November). *Language/learning disabled children's storyretelling compared with same-age and younger peers.* Paper presented at the American Speech-Language-Hearing Association annual convention, Boston, MA.

Curtis, M.E. (1987). Vocabulary testing and vocabulary instruction. In M.G. McKeown & M.E. Curtis (Eds.), *The nature of vocabulary acquisition.* Hillsdale, NJ: Erlbaum.

Dale, E. (1965). Vocabulary measurement: Techniques and major findings. *Elementary English, 42,* 895–901.

Dale, E., & O'Rourke, J. (1981). *The living word vocabulary.* Chicago, IL: World Book-Childcraft.

Dickinson, D. (1984). First impressions: Children's knowledge of words gained from a single exposure. *Applied Psycholinguistics, 5,* 359–373.

Dollaghan, C. (1985). Child meets word: "Fast mapping" in preschool children. *Journal of Speech and Hearing Research, 28,* 449–454.

Dollaghan, C. (1987). Fast mapping in normal and language impaired children. *Journal of Speech and Hearing Disorders, 52,* 218–222.

Drum, P.A., & Konopak, B.C. (1987). Learning word meanings from written context. In M.G. McKeown & M.E. Curtis (Eds.), *The nature of vocabulary acquisition.* Hillsdale, NJ: Erlbaum.

Elshout-Mohr, M., & van Daalen-Kapteijns, M.M. (1987). Cognitive processes in learning word meanings. In M.G. McKeown & M.E. Curtis, (Eds.), *The nature of vocabulary acquisition.* Hillsdale, NJ: Erlbaum.

Entwisle, D.R. (1966). *Word associations in young children.* Baltimore, MD: Johns Hopkins University Press.

German, D. (1986). *Test of word finding.* Allen, TX: Developmental Learning Materials.

Goldsworthy, C. (1982). *Multilevel informal language inventory.* Columbus, OH: Merrill.

Graves, M.F. (1987). The roles of instruction in fostering vocabulary development. In M.G. McKeown & M.E. Curtis (Eds.), *The nature of vocabulary acquisition.* Hillsdale, NJ: Erlbaum.

Greenfield, P. (1972). Playing peek-a-boo with a four month old: A study of the role of speech and nonspeech sounds in the formation of a visual schema. *Journal of Psychology, 82,* 278–298.

Hall, R. (1984). *Sniglets (Snig'lit): Any word that doesn't appear in the dictionary, but should.* New York, NY: Macmillan.

Holdgrafer, G., & Sorenson, P. (1984). Informativeness and lexical learning. *Psychological Reports, 54,* 75–80.

Israel, L.I. (1984). Word knowledge and word retrieval. In G.P. Wallach & K.G. Butler (Eds.), *Language learning disabilities in school-age children.* Baltimore, MD: Williams & Wilkins.

Johnson, D.D., & Pearson, P.D. (1984). *Teaching reading comprehension* (2nd ed.). New York, NY: Holt, Rinehart, & Winston.

Jorgensen, C., Barrett, M., Huisingh, R., & Zachman, L. (1981). *The word test.* East Moline, IL: LinguiSystems.

Kail, R., & Leonard, L. (1986). *Word-finding abilities in language-impaired children (ASHA Monograph 25).* Rockville, MD: ASHA.

Kameenui, E.J., Dixon, R.C., & Carnine, D.W. (1987). Issues in the design of vocabulary instruction. In M.G. McKeown & M.E. Curtis (Eds.), *The nature of vocabulary acquisition.* Hillsdale, NJ: Erlbaum.

Keil, F. (1983). Semantic inferences and the acquisition of word meaning. In T. Seiler & W. Wannenmacher (Eds.), *Concept development and the development of word meaning.* New York, NY: Springer-Verlag.

Lakoff, G., & Johnson, M. (1980). *Metaphors we live by*. Chicago, IL: Chicago University Press.

Levin, J.R., Johnson, D.D., Pittelman, S.D., Hayes, B.L., Levin, K.M., Shriberg, L.K., & Toms-Bronowski, S. (1984). A comparison of semantic- and mnemonic-based vocabulary-learning strategies. *Reading Psychology, 5*, 1-15.

Long, S.H., & Fey, M.E. (1988, November). *A computerized system for multi-level analysis of speech samples*. Paper presented to the American Speech-Language-Hearing Association Annual Convention, Boston, MA.

McCarthy, D. (1970). *McCarthy scales of children's abilities*. New York, NY: Psychological Corporation.

Miller, G.A. (1977). *Spontaneous apprentices: Children and language*. New York, NY: Seabury.

Miller, J. (1986). *Reference data base for SALT*. Madison, WI: Language Analysis Laboratory, Waisman Center on Mental Retardation and Human Development.

Miller, J., & Chapman, R. (1985). *Systematic analysis of language transcripts, SALT* [Computer program and manual]. Madison, WI: Language Analysis Laboratory, Waisman Center on Mental Retardation and Human Development.

Mordecai D., Palin, M., & Palmer, C. (1985). *Linguest 1* [Computer program]. Columbus, OH: Merrill.

Nagy, W.E., & Herman, P.A. (1987). Breadth and depth of vocabulary knowledge: Implications for acquisition and instruction. In M.G. McKeown & M.E. Curtis (Eds.), *The nature of vocabulary acquisition*. Hillsdale, NJ: Erlbaum.

Nelson, K. (1977). The syntagmatic-paradigmatic shift revisited: A review of research and theory. *Psychological Bulletin, 84*, 93-116.

Nelson, K. (1986). *Event knowledge*. New York: Academic Press.

Nelson, K., & Bonvillian, J.D. (1973). Concepts and words in the 18-month-old: Acquiring concept names under controlled conditions. *Cognition, 2*, 435-450.

Nelson, K., & Brown, A. (1979). The semantic-episodic distinction in memory development. In P. Ornstein (Ed.), *Development of memory*. Hillsdale, NJ: Erlbaum.

Nelson, K., & Gruendel, J. (1979). At morning it's lunchtime: A scriptal view of children's dialogues. *Discourse Processes, 2*, 73-94.

Ninio, A., & Bruner, J. (1978). The achievement and antecedents of labeling. *Journal of Child Language, 5*, 1-16.

Peters, A. (1984). *The units of language acquisition*. New York: Cambridge University Press.

Petrey, S. (1977). Word associations and the development of lexical memory. *Cognition, 5*, 55-71.

Richard, G.J., & Hanner, M.A. (1985). *Language processing test*. East Moline, IL: LinguiSystems.

Schank, R.C., & Abelson, R.P. (1977). *Scripts, plans, goals and understanding*. Hillsdale, NJ: Erlbaum.

Schwartz, R., & Leonard, L. (1984). Words, objects, and actions in early lexical acquisition. *Journal of Speech and Hearing Research, 27*, 119-127.

Semel, E., Wiig, E., & Secord, W. (1987). *Clinical evaluation of language fundamentals-revised*. San Antonio, TX: The Psychological Corporation.

Snow, C.E. (1977). The development of conversation between mothers and babies. *Journal of Child Language, 4*, 1-22.

Snow, C.E., & Goldfield, B.A. (1983). Turn the page please: Situation-specific language acquisition. *Journal of Child Language, 10*, 551-569.

Sternberg, R.J. (1987). Most vocabulary is learned from context. In M.G. McKeown & M.E. Curtis (Eds.), *The nature of vocabulary acquisition*. Hillsdale, NJ: Erlbaum.

Sternberg, R.J., & Powell, J.S. (1983). Comprehending verbal comprehension. *American Psychologist, 38*, 878-893.

Werner, H., & Kaplan, E. (1952). The acquisition of word meanings: A developmental study. *Monographs of the Society for Research in Child Development, 15*(51).

White, T.G., & Speidel, G.E. (in press). Children's knowledge of prefixes, suffixes, and word roots. Unpublished manuscript.

Wiig, E.H., & Becker-Caplan, L. (1984). Linguistic retrieval strategies and word-finding difficulties among children with language disabilities. *Topics in Language Disorders, 4*, 1-18.

Wiig, E.H., & Secord, W. (1985). *Test of language competence*. San Antonio, TX: The Psychological Corporation.

Winner, E., Rosenstiel, A.K., & Gardner, H. (1976). The development of metaphoric understanding. *Developmental Psychology, 12*, 289-297.

Research on the communicative development of maltreated children: Clinical implications

Wendy Coster, PhD
Department of Occupational Therapy
Boston University
Boston, Massachusetts

Dante Cicchetti, PhD
Mt. Hope Family Center
University of Rochester
Rochester, New York

RESEARCH during the past two decades has provided increasing evidence of the deleterious effects of a maltreating environment on children's development (Cicchetti & Carlson, 1989). Maltreated children have been found to be at significant risk for the development of insecure attachments and negative self-representations, as well as for difficulties in the regulation of emotion and of emotion-related behavior, development of satisfying peer relations, and achievement of the task-related behaviors required in academic settings (see Cicchetti, Toth, & Hennessey [1989] for summary). In addition, maltreated children have consistently been reported to be at increased risk for difficulties with language and communication skills. The present article will review these data on problems in communicative development and discuss

We wish to thank the William T. Grant Foundation; the John D. and Catherine T. MacArthur Foundation; the National Center on Child Abuse and Neglect; the National Institute of Mental Health; the Smith Richardson Foundation, Inc.; the American Occupational Therapy Foundation; and the Kenworthy Swift Foundation for their support of our work on child maltreatment and the preparation of this article.

Top Lang Disord 1993;13(4):25–38
© 1993 Aspen Publishers, Inc.

their implications for practitioners concerned with communicative development and disorders in children.

In the decades since Kempe and his colleagues first called attention to the "battered child syndrome" (Kempe, Silverman, Steele, Droegemueller, & Silver, 1962), models of the etiology and sequelae of maltreatment have become more complex. As information about maltreating families has grown, earlier models, in which maltreatment was seen as an expression of parental pathology, or a problem of individuals, have given way to more current models in which maltreatment is viewed as an extreme on a continuum of family dysfunction (Cicchetti, 1987; Cicchetti & Rizley, 1981; Salzinger, Feldman, Hammer, & Rosario, 1991). These newer models incorporate a dynamic systems framework in which maltreatment is the end result of a complex interplay of multiple influences within the child and family, as well as in the immediate and broader physical and social environment. Thus, to understand the sequelae of maltreatment, the entire social context in which the child is being raised must be considered (Cicchetti & Lynch, 1993). This broader context may contribute to the occurrence of episodes of maltreatment (as when job loss imposes severe stress on a parent), mediate the negative sequelae (as in the case of neglect, where the overall impoverishment of the social and physical environment may be critical for outcome), exacerbate negative consequences (as when the child witnesses as well as experiences repeated violence [Rosenberg, 1987]), or help ameliorate some of the effects (as when another supportive adult is available to the child [Lynch & Cicchetti, 1991; Masten, Best, & Garmezy, 1990).

Current frameworks also have attempted to integrate a more developmental perspective. A developmental organizational perspective views the child as engaged in addressing a series of tasks or issues in different domains whose mastery or resolution provides a base for the building of successive competencies (Greenspan, 1981; Sroufe, 1979). Competence in one domain affects, and in turn is affected by, competence in other domains; thus development in any given area must be interpreted in relation to the other aspects of the child's functioning. Evaluation of the effects of maltreatment must consider not only the immediate impact on particular skills and behaviors, but also the impact that altered behavior may have on the child's response to new situations and how the acquisition of other competencies that depend on the behavior may be affected (Cicchetti, 1990).

An organizational perspective is especially relevant for thinking about language and maltreatment. The acquisition of communication skills is intricately intertwined with both cognitive and social-emotional development. In turn, because language is the primary medium for social exchange, as well as one of the primary means through which schooling is accomplished, language difficulties have the potential to affect a wide range of developmental tasks, from establishing satisfactory peer relations to acquiring basic literary skills.

Commitment to a developmental model of the effects of maltreatment also requires a conceptual shift in the focus of research. Many earlier studies treated maltreatment as an event that would lead directly to negative psychological sequelae, in the same way that a physical injury would result in direct impairments (Cicchetti & Rizley, 1981).

This approach ignores the multiple contextual influences that also affect child development, as well as the differential impact that specific events may have, depending on the child's current level of development. For example, it is implausible to expect that the impact of an extremely impoverished language environment would be the same on a school-aged child as on an infant who is just beginning the language-learning process. Similarly, it is now recognized that there may be differential effects of particular kinds of maltreatment experiences, depending on whether the maltreatment has been ongoing since infancy or began at some later time (Barnett, Manly, & Cicchetti, 1991). Although this point may appear obvious, the issue has not been examined rigorously in the literature to date.

Given the complexity of current models, it is clear that longitudinal studies are needed to help clarify the processes whereby maltreatment affects developmental outcome. Unfortunately, at present most of our knowledge is derived from studies of children seen at one point in time. Although these studies are increasingly clear in detailing the negative consequences of maltreatment, the longer term effects of these sequelae and the mechanisms that mediate both positive and negative outcomes remain to be delineated.

SOCIAL CLASS AND CULTURAL INFLUENCES

Although maltreatment is not limited to any particular social class, it seems clear that membership in the lower socioeconomic strata (SES) is associated with increased incidence of maltreatment. Studies suggest that many of the factors associated with low SES—including inadequate economic resources, housing, and nutrition; increased health problems; and lower levels of both educational achievement and employment—may constitute either ongoing or situational challenges that increase the risk of maltreatment (Pelton, 1978; Trickett, Aber, Carlson, & Cicchetti, 1991).

The relation between social class and maltreatment is a critical consideration when reviewing evidence on the communicative development of maltreated children. One of the lingering issues in this field is the degree to which the experience of maltreatment exerts additional influence on language development over and above the well-documented impact of growing up in a low-SES environment (Elmer, 1977; Hoff-Ginsberg, 1991). Resolution of this question requires studies that incorporate appropriate comparison groups matched for SES and examine social class status in relation to outcome among different groups of maltreated children. Without such comparisons, there is a significant risk that negative judgments about language competence may be biased by application of inappropriate standards.

In earlier research, comparison groups were often lacking, making interpretation of results difficult. However, more recent studies that have used SES-matched samples suggest that specific differences in interaction patterns and amount of negativity are found in the maltreating family environment (Trickett et al., 1991) and that differences in the complexity and functional use of language remain when SES is controlled through the use of appropriately matched comparison groups (Coster, Gersten, Beeghly, & Cicchetti, 1989).

Issues raised concerning social class effects also apply to cultural or ethnic differences among children included in studies of maltreatment. As always, when minority group children are assessed using tasks and expectations that may differ from their cultural experience, the possibility of biased results or interpretations must be entertained. The inclusion of a comparison sample of nonmaltreated children of the same ethnic or cultural background is essential to enable valid evaluation of the performance of the maltreated group. Recent studies have been more careful in selecting such matched comparison groups. In general, however, children included in samples have been predominantly white. No studies have directly examined the issue of the cultural appropriateness of the typical measures of communication used or the contexts in which language is studied.

In summary, considerable advances have been made in developing conceptual models of maltreatment that more adequately acknowledge the complexity of this phenomenon and the effects it may have on a child's development. However, the translation of these models into appropriate research designs has just begun. Currently available data on the language of maltreated children reflect these limitations, including the lack of longitudinal information, restriction of samples to particular racial or cultural groups, and a tendency to focus on only one domain of function or one context at a time. Nevertheless, as the next sections will illustrate, there are some converging findings suggesting that maltreatment is a significant risk factor affecting communicative development.

INFANTS AND TODDLERS

Infants have received the most attention in the research literature on maltreatment. In part, this focus has resulted from a desire to try to understand the socioemotional context of maltreatment as it evolves after birth and to develop methods for intervening before problems have become well established. These studies of parent-child interaction during infancy provide an important window into the language-learning environment of the infant and the particular kinds of deviant experiences that may shape later communicative behavior.

Studies of normal child language suggest that a consistent, warm, sensitive, and contingent parent-child interaction style is optimal for early communicative development (Barnes, Gutfreund, Satterly, & Wells, 1983; Clarke-Stewart, VanderStoep, & Killian, 1979; Olson, Bates, & Bayles, 1984). During such interactions, even before the onset of language, the infant presumably learns important cause-effect relations between vocal signals and caregiver responses, as well as rudimentary pragmatic skills, including turn-taking, joint attention, and the exchange of different functional messages (Bretherton, Bates, Benigni, Camaioni, and Volterra, 1979). As language begins to develop, the use of communication begins to be shaped by the model provided by the partner, the wider social context, and the supportive interactions provided to help clarify and expand the child's messages.

Given a model that defines maltreatment as an extreme manifestation of dysfunctional interaction, it might be expected that the interactions of maltreating dyads would differ on precisely those dimensions suggested to be relevant for the development of language. For the most part, research has supported this expectation. Information comes from two related bodies of literature: studies of the quality of infant-caregiver attachment, and observational studies of parent-child interaction.

The development of a secure attachment relationship with the caregiver is considered to be a central developmental issue in children between 6 and 12 months of age (Bowlby, 1988; Sroufe, 1979). It is believed that engagement in interactions with a caregiver that are consistent, sensitive, contingent on infant cues, and affectively positive leads to successful socioemotional adaptation at this stage. Furthermore, it is thought that this first model relationship continues to exert a powerful influence on subsequent relationships by setting expectations of efficacy or inefficacy, as well as comfort or anxiety (Lynch & Cicchetti, 1991; Main, Kaplan, & Cassidy, 1985).

Quality of attachment in young children has typically been assessed using Ainsworth's "strange situation" paradigm (Ainsworth, Blehar, Waters, & Wall, 1978). In this procedure the infant is exposed to a series of increasingly stressful episodes that involve an unfamiliar room, an unfamiliar female examiner, and separation from the caregiver. On the basis of the child's responses, the quality of the relation with the caregiver is classified into one of four categories: secure, insecure/avoidant, insecure/resistant, or the more recently identified disorganized/disoriented (Main et al., 1985). A secure attachment relationship is viewed as an optimal pattern for further development (as it reflects an ability to use the caregiver as a "secure base" for exploration and effective engagement with the environment), as well as for comfort and the restoration of a sense of security when distressed.

Studies using this paradigm with maltreated children have consistently found elevated rates of insecure attachment in this population of between 70% and 100%,

compared with a base rate of 30% in comparison samples (Browne & Sagi, 1988; Carlson, Cicchetti, Barnett, & Braunwald, 1989; Crittenden, 1988). The most characteristic patterns tend to be insecure/avoidant or disorganized/disoriented, a pattern in which the infant shows inconsistent and contradictory behaviors characteristic of mutually exclusive attachment categories, as well as signs of apprehension in the presence of the caregiver. These patterns may reflect coping styles that the infant has adopted to deal with the difficulties in his or her environment; for example, a maltreated infant may avoid interactions to minimize the likelihood of producing hostile or frustrating responses on the part of his or her caregiver (Schneider-Rosen, Braunwald, Carlson, & Cicchetti, 1985). In the long term, however, these coping styles may place the child at risk for other developmental difficulties by limiting his or her participation in necessary learning experiences. For example, the child may not participate in social encounters in which communication skills could be elaborated.

Although secure attachment has been viewed as facilitative of optimal language development, the research findings on this question have been inconsistent (e.g. Bretherton et al., 1979; Clarke-Stewart, 1973). However, Bates, Bretherton, Beeghly-Smith, & McNew (1982) suggested that the lack of relationship may reflect the limited range of variability typically seen in the populations studied (mostly mother-child dyads from the middle SES) and that a stronger relationship might be more apparent in populations exposed to more extreme variations in the language-learning environment.

Studies of maltreated and high-risk children suggest that this may be the case. In a study of 24-month-old maltreated and low-SES comparison infants, quality of attachment was significantly related to measures of language development in both groups, while maltreatment did not have a main effect (Gersten, Coster, Schneider-Rosen, Carlson, & Cicchetti, 1986). Morisset, Barnard, Greenberg, Booth, and Spieker (1990), in a study of a sample at high risk from a variety of maternal and environment factors (including maltreatment), found that a secure attachment relationship moderated the negative influence of other risk factors on communicative development.

A second body of literature that complements and extends the findings of attachment research stems from observational studies of parent-child interaction. These studies address the question of what patterns of interaction may underlie the disturbances in relationship suggested by the attachment data.

In a series of studies, Crittenden and her colleagues have examined the interactions of adequate, neglecting, abusing, neglecting-and-abusing, and inept groups of mothers and their infants (Christopoulos, Bonvillian, & Crittenden, 1988; Crittenden, 1981, 1988). Groups were equivalent in terms of SES and racial composition. They found that abusing mothers were the most controlling of infant behavior and neglecting mothers the most unresponsive to their infant's signals, whereas abusing-and-neglecting mothers showed aspects of each of these patterns (Crittenden, 1988). Crittenden interprets these patterns as suggesting that the abusing mothers approached their interactions with the infant according to an internal plan that was imposed on the infant and not adjusted on the basis of the infant's responses. In contrast, the neglecting mothers were withdrawn and appeared to have little expectation that they could influence the infant or could derive satisfaction from their interaction with him or her.

Other studies have generally confirmed these patterns. Although there are variations across studies in the samples used, the groupings adopted, or the methods employed for defining maltreatment, the overall picture is one of interactions that often do not provide the support for building effective social or communication skills (Allen & Wasserman, 1985; Aragona & Eyberg, 1981; Wasserman, Green, & Allen, 1983). While the abused child experiences engagement, the engagement often carries hostile overtones, may be inconsistently responsive or overcontrolling, and often does not provide an experience of self-efficacy in successful communication of wants and needs. At the other extreme, the severely neglected child may not be able to make the necessary cause-effect connection between social cues (including language) and environmental responsiveness and may become increasingly passive.

A few of the studies of interaction have used measures that characterize aspects of the environment specifically relevant to language learning. Crittenden (1981) reported that, relative to matched comparison mothers who were classified as "adequate," neglecting mothers in her sample used less grammatical utterances and a higher proportion of directives. Mothers who had abused their infants were more rejecting and negative in their communications. Wasserman and her colleagues (1983) also reported that abusing mothers showed reduced rates of verbal stimulation relative to comparisons. Very few studies have examined the critical question of whether there is a relation between differences in interaction in maltreating families and early language development in the same children (Gersten et al., 1986). This question ideally should be addressed longitudinally across several stages in the language-learning process, since the strength of the relationship may vary at different stages (Morisset et al., 1990).

A growing body of research evidence suggests that the differences in interaction and the social context in which early language development occurs do have consequences for subsequent communicative development. These consequences appear to extend to almost all aspects of language, at least during the early years. For example, Coster et al. (1989) found a significantly shorter mean length of utterance (MLU) in their sample of maltreated 31-month-olds, compared with a lower-SES matched control group. (Both samples were more than 90% white). The maltreated toddlers also displayed a more limited expressive (but not receptive) vocabulary during play sessions with their mothers. Additional important differences were found in the toddlers' use of language. In particular, a significantly smaller proportion of the maltreated toddlers' communications was directed at exchanging information about their own activities or feelings, when compared with the use of communication for instrumental purposes. They made fewer references to persons or events outside the immediate context (decontextualized utterances) and engaged in shorter bouts of continuous contingent discourse. Although use of more descriptive language was associated with increasing MLU in the comparison children, this relationship between syntactic maturity and functional use did not hold in the maltreated group.

These findings suggest that the maltreated toddlers, along with their mothers, had developed a style in which language served to get tasks accomplished but was used less frequently as a medium for social or affective exchanges. This interpretation is consistent with the mother-child interaction studies that suggested that maltreating mothers, compared with matched comparison mothers, focused more on controlling the child's behavior rather than understanding the child's thoughts, opinions, or feelings. The persistence of such a pattern across the preschool period may place restrictions on the child's ability to utilize language for a variety of other social and emotional tasks, including the following:

- the ability to use language to articulate needs and feelings, which has been suggested as an important step toward development of appropriate cognitive behavioral controls (Santostefano, 1978);
- the ability to use language to convey abstractions, which has been suggested as a critical transition in the acquisition of literacy skills (Donaldson, 1978); and
- the ability to sustain coherent narrative and dialogue, which is a key competence for social exchange with both peers and adult figures (Hemphill, Picardi, & Tager-Flusberg, 1991; McCabe & Peterson, 1991).

Despite acknowledgment of the importance of examining such complex interrelations among domains, little research has addressed these questions to date, and no studies have focused specifically on the relation between language and other cognitive or social competencies in young maltreated children. Furthermore, the question of whether the patterns of language use seen in infants and toddlers are also found in older maltreated children or simply reflect a unique vulnerability evidenced primarily during early language development remains open. Ideally, this question should be addressed via longitudinal data. However, such studies are not yet available, and cross-sectional studies of preschool and older children are the only source of information on this issue.

STUDIES OF PRESCHOOL AND SCHOOL-AGE CHILDREN

The earliest studies of the developmental effects of maltreatment involved heterogeneous samples of predominantly older children; it was in these samples that language difficulties were first identified as a prevalent problem. For example, Blager and Martin (1976) reported that the majority of their sample of 13 physically abused children were at the bottom of the low-normal range on the Illinois Test of Psycholinguistic Abilities and had widely divergent subtest profiles. Furthermore, they noted that even when test scores were adequate, the speech of the children during conversation was impoverished and inadequate for conveying their thoughts and feelings.

The methods for determining the presence of language disorders in other studies have varied. Inferences about deficient language performance often have been based on the finding of large discrepancies between verbal and performance intelligence quotients (IQs), a discrepancy that could have multiple explanations (Martin, Beezeley, Conway, & Kempe, 1974, Martin & Breezely, 1977). Martin et al. (1974) report that poorer outcome was related to docu-

mented head trauma and neurologic sequelae in their sample. However, language deficits were not limited to the group with obvious central nervous system damage, and continued placement in an abusive or otherwise nonsupportive environment was also related to the presence of developmental delays.

Elmer and Gregg (Elmer, 1977; Elmer & Gregg, 1967) also reported a high rate of language difficulties in their follow-up studies comparing abused, neglected, accident, and comparison samples. Based on qualitative ratings by a speech-language pathologist, they concluded that although a number of maltreated children displayed language delays, the percentage did not differ significantly across the groups. The exception was children in the "high certainty" maltreatment group who did perform significantly worse than the other children. Elmer and Gregg concluded that membership in the lower SES was more related to "poor" language outcome than maltreatment. Although these studies have a number of significant methodologic limitations, including questionable selection criteria for comparison subjects and uncertain validity and sensitivity of measures (Aber & Cicchetti, 1984; Cicchetti & Rizley, 1981), this conclusion had the unfortunate effect of discouraging further research into the language development of maltreated children for some time.

In more recent work, Allen and Oliver (1982) compared the language development of abused, neglected and abused-and-neglected children, as well as an SES-matched comparison group of children. The mean chronologic age of each of these groups was four years, and the majority of the subjects were white. Allen and Oliver's primary finding was that neglect significantly contributed to decreased performance on the Preschool Language Scale (PLS), which they interpreted as reflecting the impact of lack of stimulation.

Lynch and Roberts (1982) conducted a follow-up evaluation of a sample of 42 children four years after hospitalization for maltreatment. The children, who were generally between the ages of five and eight years at the time of follow-up, showed a significant decrement in verbal IQ relative to performance IQ. This result is consistent with findings from a follow-up study by Oates, Peacock, & Forrest (1984), who also found significant decreases in verbal language performance and reading achievement in a slightly older sample (mean age, 8.9 years). These differences remained even after controlling for the presence of documented head injury. In one of the few studies specifically addressing receptive language skills, Fox, Long, and Anglois (1988) found significantly decreased performance on both the Peabody Picture Vocabulary Test and Miller-Yoder Language Comprehension Test in their sample of maltreated three- to eight-year-olds. The severely neglected children had the most impaired performance, followed by the abused children. Recently, this finding of decreased receptive skills in neglected children was replicated in a sample of preschool children (Culp, Watkins, Lawrence, Letts, Kelly, & Rice, 1991).

Although the general picture of high risk for language difficulties appears consistent from study to study, from a research standpoint, there are a number of problems affecting interpretation of these results (McCauley & Swisher, 1987). Most of the time, the design of these studies does not permit clear conclusions about the source of the observed deficits. A variety of complex factors are involved in a child's performance by the time he or she has reached school age, only some of which have been considered and included for examination in current research. First, as noted by some of the authors, the maltreatment may have resulted in physical sequelae that themselves are known to be associated with developmental difficulties. These changes include the long-term cognitive and behavioral sequelae of head trauma, as well as the long-term impact of malnourishment. Both of these circumstances were documented in a high proportion of children in several of the samples (Martin et al., 1974; Oates et al., 1984).

Current performance deficits also likely represent the cumulative effects of continuous rearing in nonoptimal environments. As noted by several of the authors of follow-up studies, it cannot be assumed that identification of maltreatment necessarily resulted in delivery of effective social services to the families and children or to substantial improvement in the child rearing context. In fact, in many cases, multiple separations and temporary placements ensued. In cases where children remained with their families, observational studies document persistence of the interaction patterns described earlier in families with younger children (e.g., excessive punitiveness, overt hostility or neglect, and high achievement expectations coupled with inadequate or overly controlling teaching and discipline) (Bousha & Twentyman, 1984; Mash, Johnston, & Kovitz, 1983). Continuous rearing in nonoptimal environments results in maintenance of adverse learning conditions, so that instead of having opportunity for remediation, children continue to fall behind as they attempt each developmental task with inadequate inner resources or social support.

Finally, it is not always clear whether the language deficiencies reported are above and beyond what might be expected, given the child's general cognitive level, which itself is often depressed in maltreated children. The frequent use of decreased verbal IQ test scores as indicators of language deficits in many of the studies of older maltreated children illustrates this problem. Given the heavy dependence of many cognitive tests on verbal responses, future studies will need to use multiple verbal and nonverbal cognitive measures to differentiate specific language effects from other, more general performance deficits.

The functional implications of these language difficulties also remain unclear. As discussed earlier, there are a number of predictions that can be made from developmental organizational theory about the impact of language deficiencies on behavioral self-regulation, peer relations, or school performance; however, few of these predictions have been tested empirically. One area that has received limited attention is the relation between linguistic deficits and aggression. Several studies of older physically abused children have reported a link between violent behavior and deficient verbal and reading skills (Burke, Crenshaw, Green, Schlosser, & Strocchia-Rivera, 1989; Lewis, Shanok, Pincus, & Glaser, 1979; Tarter, Hegedus, Wiastein, & Alterman, 1984). Burke et al. (1989) use these findings to argue for the importance of providing remedial language services for maltreated children during their school years to encour-age the use of verbal problem solving rather than acting-out behavior.

CLINICAL IMPLICATIONS OF RESEARCH

Although much research remains to be done, the overall picture of risk for communication difficulties in children with a history of maltreatment is clear. These findings suggest that a thorough language evaluation should be part of the educational or psychological assessment of children with such a history. Conversely, a language assessment should also be seen as one part of a broader, interdisciplinary assessment of the child and his or her family (Cicchetti & Wagner, 1990). Either component alone may provide an incomplete picture of the child's strengths and weaknesses and, more importantly, may fail to consider the complex interrelationships among cognitive, linguistic, and socioemotional difficulties that often characterize the maltreated child's performance.

The research to date also suggests that evaluation of the child's language should go beyond examination of linguistic aspects to include the pragmatic and narrative functions. Clinical reports and some of the research data from young maltreated children indicate that the ability to utilize language in connected discourse and to convey a variety of functions beyond the strictly instrumental may be particularly affected by growing up in a maltreating environment. The child may have had minimal experience using verbal problem-solving methods and little exposure to adults who encourage the kind of self-reporting of ideas or feelings often expected in a classroom setting (Cicchetti, 1990). The child may also have had limited experience attending to complex communications and may have difficulty extracting key ideas embedded in more lengthy narratives.

The same socioemotional factors associated with less adequate language development also may contribute to performance-related behavior that complicates the language assessment process. Studies have found decreased mastery motivation, patterns of overcompliance or passivity, and decreased frustration tolerance in maltreated children, compared with SES-matched controls (Aber, Allen, Carlson, & Cicchetti, 1989). Other observers have suggested that the maltreated child is preoccupied with monitoring the affective messages from interactions with adults (for example, they may be acutely monitoring the evaluator's nonverbal cues about the adequacy of their performance). Thus, they may not be approaching the requests made of them during assessment in the manner intended (Aber & Allen, 1987). These observations have raised concerns about whether the data obtained in typical assessment situations are accurate representations of the child's competence or more often reflect the maltreated child's typical pattern for coping with uncertain performance expectations. This concern can only be addressed by obtaining assessment information from a variety of contexts and informants and looking for consistent patterns.

The socioemotional and behavioral sequelae of maltreatment also present significant challenges to those involved in language intervention efforts. The research documents increased prevalence of behavior problems—particularly aggression and noncompliance, as well as depression, decreased motivation, and readiness to learn—in children who have experienced abuse and neglect (Aber et al., 1989; Mueller & Silverman, 1989; Toth, Manly, & Cicchetti, 1992). Interventions to address the child's communicative difficulties must incorporate attention to these interpersonal difficulties and to the different forms they may take in one-on-one interaction with an adult, as well as in small groups of peers (see, e.g., Crittenden [1989] for a detailed discussion of these issues). Training and consultation on appropriate methods for structuring the environment and managing disruptive behavior are vital to ensure that the intervention situation supports the overall growth of the child.

CONCLUSION AND DIRECTIONS FOR FUTURE RESEARCH

There is a critical need for more studies of maltreated children to help better understand the nature, sources, and consequences of the communication difficulties that are consistently reported in the literature. In particular, the field would benefit greatly from studies that address specific hypotheses about the expected pattern of strengths and weaknesses that might be predicted from theory and current knowledge of the maltreating environment. We need to move beyond global measure of linguistic competence to examine in greater depth the communicative performance of maltreated children in a variety of social and functional contexts (e.g., during ordinary daily activities at home, in the classroom, with their caregiver, and with other adults and peers) and at different developmental stages. We also need to explore more carefully the social, emotional, and cognitive consequences of communication difficulties to understand the ways in which limitations in this critical functional domain may impose additional constraints on skill development in other domains. In particular, the relationship between language skills and the ability to utilize cognitive controls for problem solving and coping with frustration warrants careful investigation, as behavioral deficits in these areas constitute a significant risk for future maladaptation and social disadvantage. Finally, because much of the existing data are derived from predominantly white, low-

SES samples, there is a significant need to extend research efforts to include a more diverse population. Such efforts will also require the development of culturally appropriate methods to elicit and measure the communicative behavior of children and their families.

We believe that policy-relevant decisions concerning such issues as how to develop and implement developmentally appropriate and sensitive interventions to meet the needs of maltreated children, and how to evaluate these treatment efforts, would all profit immeasurably from a more methodologically sound and comprehensive database on the developmental sequelae of maltreatment.

REFERENCES

Aber, J.L., & Allen, J.P. (1987). Effects of maltreatment on young children's socioemotional development: an attachment theory perspective. *Developmental Psychology, 23,* 406–414.

Aber, J.L., Allen, J., Carlson, V., & Cicchetti, D. (1989). The effects of maltreatment oN development during early childhood: recent studies and their theoretical, clinical, and policy implications. In D. Cicchetti & V. Carlson (Eds.), *Child maltreatment: theory and research on the causes and consequences of child abuse and neglect* (pp. 579–619). Cambridge, England: Cambridge University Press.

Aber, J.L., & Cicchetti, D. (1984). The socioemotional development of maltreated children: an empirical and theoretical analysis. In H. Fitzgerald, B. Lester, & M. Yogman (Eds.), *Theory and research in behavioral pediatrics, Vol. 2* (pp. 147–205). New York, NY: Plenum.

Ainsworth, M., Blehar, M., Waters, E., & Wall, S. (1978). *Patterns of attachment.* Hillsdale, NJ: Erlbaum.

Allen, R.E., & Oliver, J.M. (1982). The effects of child maltreatment on language development. *Child Abuse and Neglect, 6,* 299–305.

Allen, R. & Wasserman, G.A. (1985). Origins of language delay in abused children. *Child Abuse and Neglect, 9,* 333–338.

Aragona, J.A., & Eyberg, S.M. (1981). Neglected children: mother's report of child behavior problems and observed verbal behavior. *Child Development, 52,* 596–602.

Barnes, S., Gutfreund, M., Satterly, D., & Wells, G. (1983). Characteristics of adult speech which predict children's language development. *Child Language, 10,* 65–84.

Barnett, D., Manly, J., & Cicchetti, D. (1991). Continuing toward operational definition of psychological maltreatment. *Development and Psychopathology, 3,* 19–30.

Bates, E., Bretherton, I., Beeghly-Smith, M., & McNew, S. (1982). Social bases of language development: a reassessment. In H. Reese & L. Lipsitt (Eds.), *Advances in child development and behavior, Vol. 16* (pp. 8–75). New York, NY: Academic Press.

Blager, F.B., & Martin, H.P. (1976). Speech and language of abused children. In H.P. Martin (Ed.), *The abused child: a multidisciplinary approach to developmental issues and treatment* (pp. 83–92). Cambridge, MA: Ballinger.

Bousha, D.M., & Twentyman, C.T. (1984). Mother–child interactional style in abuse, neglect, and control groups: naturalistic observations in the home. *Journal of Abnormal Psychology, 93,* 106–114.

Bowlby, J. (1988). Developmental psychiatry comes of age. *American Journal of Psychiatry, 145,* 1–10.

Bretherton, I., Bates, E., Benigni, L., Camaioni, D., &

Volterra, V. (1979). Relationships between cognition, communication, and quality of attachment. In E. Bates, L. Benigni, I. Bretherton, L. Camaioni, & V. Volterra (Eds.), *The emergence of symbols: cognition and communication in infancy* (pp. 223–270). New York, NY: Academic.

Browne, K., & Sagi, S. (1988). Mother–infant interaction and attachment in physically abusing families. *Journal of Reproductive and Infant Psychology, 6,* 163–182.

Burke, A.E., Crenshaw, D.A., Green, J., Schlosser, M.A., & Strocchia-Rivera, L. (1989). Influence of verbal ability on the expression of aggression in physically abused children. *Journal of the American Academy of Child and Adolescent Psychiatry, 28,* 215–218.

Carlson, V., Cicchetti, D., Barnett, D., & Braunwald, K.B. (1989). The development of disorganized/disoriented attachments in maltreated infants. *Developmental Psychology, 25,* 525–531.

Christopoulos, C., Bonvillian, J., & Crittenden, P.M. (1988). Maternal input and children maltreatment. *Infant Mental Health Journal, 9,* 272–286.

Cicchetti, D. (1987). Developmental psychopathology in infancy: illustration from the study of maltreated youngsters. *Journal of Consulting and Clinical Psychology, 55,* 837–845.

Cicchetti, D. (1990). The organization and coherence of socioemotional, cognitive, and representational development: illustrations through a developmental psychopathology perspective on Down Syndrome and child maltreatment. In R. Thompson (Ed.), *Nebraska symposium on motivation. Vol. 36: Socioemotional development* (pp. 250–366). Lincoln, NE: University of Nebraska Press.

Cicchetti, D., & Carlson, V. (Eds.) (1989). *Child maltreatment: theory and research on the causes and consequences of child abuse and neglect.* New York, NY: Cambridge University Press.

Cicchetti, D., & Lynch, M. (1993). Toward an ecological/transactional model of community violence and child maltreatment: consequences for children's development. *Psychiatry, 56.*

Cicchetti, D., & Rizley, R. (1981). Developmental perspectives on the etiology, inter-generational transmission, and sequelae of child maltreatment. *New Directions for Child Development, 11,* 31–55.

Cicchetti, D., Toth, S.L., & Hennessy, K. (1989). Research on the consequences of child maltreatment and its application to educational settings. *Topics in Early Childhood Special Education, 9*(2), 33–55.

Cicchetti, D., & Wagner, S. (1990). Alternative assessment strategies for the evaluation of infants and toddlers: an organizational perspective. In S. Meisels & J. Shonkoff (Eds.), *Handbook of early intervention* (pp. 246–277). New York, NY: Cambridge University Press.

Clarke-Stewart, K.A. (1973). Interactions between mothers and their young children: Characteristics and consequences. *Monographs of the Society for Research in Child Development, 38* (Serial #153).

Clarke-Stewart, K.A., VanderStoep, L.P., & Killian, G.A. (1979). Analysis and replication of mother–child relations at two years of age. *Child Development, 50,* 777–793.

Coster, W.J., Gersten, M.S., Beeghly, M., & Cicchetti, D. (1989). Communicative functioning in maltreated toddlers. *Developmental Psychology, 25,* 1,020–1,029.

Crittenden, P.M. (1981). Abusing, neglecting, problematic, and adequate dyads: Differentiating by patterns of interaction. *Merrill-Palmer Quarterly, 27,* 201–208.

Crittenden, P.M. (1988). Relationships at risk. In J. Belsky & T. Nezwarski (Eds.), *Clinical implications of attachment* (pp. 136–174). Hillsdale, NJ: Erlbaum.

Crittenden, P.M. (1989). Teaching maltreated children in the preschool. *Topics in Early Childhood Special Education, 9*(2), 16–32.

Culp, R.E., Watkins, R.V., Lawrence, H., Letts, D., Kelly, D.J., & Rice, M. (1991). Maltreated children's language & speech development: abused, neglected, and abused and neglected. *First Language, 11,* 337–389.

Donaldson, M. (1978). *Children's minds.* New York, NY: Norton.

Elmer, E. (1977). A follow-up study of traumatized children. *Pediatrics, 59,* 272–279.

Elmer, E., & Gregg, G. (1967). Developmental characteristics of abused children. *Pediatrics, 40,* 596–602.

Fox, L., Long, S.H., & Anglois, A. (1988). Patterns of language comprehension deficit in abused and neglected children. *Journal of Speech and Hearing Disorders, 53,* 239–244.

Gersten, M., Coster, W., Schneider-Rosen, K., Carlson, V., & Cicchetti, D. (1986). The socio-emotional bases of communicative functioning: quality of attachment, language development, and early maltreatment. In M. Lamb, A.L. Brown, & B. Rogoff (Eds.), *Advances in developmental psychology, Vol. 4* (pp. 105–151). Hillsdale, NJ: Erlbaum.

Greenspan, S.I. (1981). *Psychopathology and adaptation in infancy and early childhood: principles of clinical diagnosis and preventive intervention.* New York, NY: International Universities Press.

Hemphill, L., Picardi, N., & Tager-Flusberg, H. (1991). Narrative as an index of communicative competence in mildly mentally retarded children. *Applied Psycholinguistics, 12,* 263–279.

Hoff-Ginsberg, E. (1991). Mother–child conversation in different social classes and communicative settings. *Child Development, 62,* 782–796.

Kempe, C.H., Silverman, F.M., Steele, B.B., Droegemuller, W., & Silver, H.C. (1962). The battered child syndrome. *Journal of the American Medical Association, 181,* 17–24.

Lewis, D.O., Shanok, S.S., Pincus, J.H., & Glaser, G.H. (1979). Violent juvenile delinquents. *Journal of the American Academy of Child Psychiatry, 23,* 653–658.

Lynch, M., & Cicchetti, D. (1991). Patterns of relatedness in maltreated and nonmaltreated children: connections among multiple representational models. *Development and Psychopathology, 3,* 207–226.

Lynch, M.A., & Roberts, J. (1982). *The consequences of child abuse.* New York, NY: Academic.

Main, M., Kaplan, N., & Cassidy, J. (1985). Security in infancy, childhood, and adulthood: a move to the level of representation. Growing points in attachment theory. *Monographs of the Society for Research in Child Development, 50*(series no. 209), 66–104.

Martin, H.P., & Beezley, P. (1977). Behavioral observations of abused children. *Developmental Medicine and Child Neurology, 19,* 373–387.

Martin, H.P. Beezley, P., Conway, E., & Kempe, C.H. (1974). The development of abused children. *Advances in Pediatrics, 21,* 25–73.

Mash, E.J., Johnston, C., & Kovitz, K. (1983). A comparison of the mother–child interactions of physically abused and non-abused children during play and task situations. *Journal of Clinical Child Psychology, 12,* 337–346.

Masten, A.S., Best, K.M., & Garmezy, N. (1990). Resilience and development: contributions from the study of children who overcome adversity. *Development & Psychopathology, 2,* 425–444.

McCabe, A., & Peterson, C. (Eds.) (1991). *Developing narrative structure.* Hillsdale, NJ: Erlbaum.

McCauley, R.J., & Swisher, L. (1987). Are maltreated children at risk for speech and language impairment? An unanswered question. *Journal of Speech and Hearing Disorders, 52,* 299–303.

Morisset, C.E., Barnard, K.E., Greenberg, M.T., Booth, C.L., & Spieker, S.J. (1990). Environmental influences on early language development: the context of social risk. *Development and Psychopathology, 2,* 127–149.

Mueller, N., & Silverman, N. (1989). Peer relations in maltreated children. In D. Cicchetti & V. Carlson (Eds.), *Child maltreatment: theory and research on the causes and consequences of child abuse and neglect* (pp. 529–578). New York, NY: Cambridge University Press.

Oates, R.K., Peacock, A., & Forrest, D. (1984). The development of abused children. *Developmental Medicine and Child Neurology, 26,* 649–656.

Olson, S.L., Bates, J.E., & Bayles, K. (1984). Mother–infant interaction and the development of individual differences in children's cognitive competence. *Developmental Psychology, 20,* 166–179.

Pelton, L. (1978). Child abuse and neglect: the myth of classlessness. *American Journal of Orthopsychiatry, 48,* 608–617.

Rosenberg, M.S. (1987). Children of battered women: the effects of witnessing violence on their social problem-solving abilities. *Behavior Therapist, 4,* 85–89.

Salzinger, S., Feldman, R.S., Hammer, M., & Rosario, M. (1991). Risk for physical child abuse and the personal consequences for its victims. *Criminal Justice and Behavior, 18,* 64–81.

Santostefano, S. (1978). *A biodevelopmental approach to clinical child psychology.* New York, NY: John Wiley.

Schneider-Rosen, K., Braunwald, K.B., Carlson, V., & Cicchetti, D. (1985). Current perspectives in attachment theory: illustrations from the study of maltreated infants. Growing points in attachment theory. *Monographs of the Society for Research in Child Development, 50*(series no. 209), 194–210.

Sroufe, L.A. (1979). The coherence of individual development. *American Psychologist, 34,* 834–841.

Tarter, R.E., Hegedus, A.M., Wiastein, N.E., & Alterman, A.I. (1984). Neuropsychological, personality, and familial characteristics of physically abused delinquents. *Journal of the American Academy of Child Psychiatry, 23,* 668–674.

Toth, S.L., Manly, J.T., & Cicchetti, D. (1992). Child maltreatment and vulnerability to depression. *Development and Psychopathology, 4,* 97–112.

Trickett, P.K., Aber, J.L., Carlson, V., & Cicchetti, D. (1991). Relationship of socioeconomic status to the etiology and developmental sequelae of physical child abuse. *Developmental Psychology, 27,* 148–158.

Wasserman, G.A., Green, A., & Allen, R. (1983). Going beyond abuse: maladaptive patterns of interaction in abusing mother–infant pairs. *Journal of the American Academy of Child Psychiatry, 22,* 245–252.

Profiles of toddlers with slow expressive language development

Rhea Paul, PhD
Associate Professor
Speech and Hearing Sciences Program
Portland State University
Portland, Oregon

ONE OF THE MOST puzzling problems confronting clinicians is the toddler who appears normal in every way, but fails to begin talking. Although retrospective data suggest that children with learning disabilities frequently have histories of slow language growth (Catts & Kamhi, 1986; Maxwell & Wallach, 1984; Weiner, 1985), very little is known about the prognosis for 2-year-olds with delayed onset of language. Traditional wisdom counseled a "wait and see" attitude, and parents are still frequently told that their 2-year-old will grow out of the delay. Some researchers (see Whitehurst et al., this issue) continue to advocate this position. Although, no doubt, spontaneous improvement does occur for some children, there are other 2-year-olds for whom early expressive delays presage long-term difficulty in language and school achievement. The problem for clinicians is to decide which 2-year-old with slow speech development can confidently be left alone to outgrow the problem, and which should

Top Lang Disord, 1991,11(4),1–13
© 1991 Aspen Publishers, Inc.

be monitored closely or provided with some form of intervention.

NORMAL LANGUAGE DEVELOPMENT IN TODDLERS

Children exhibit communicative intentions by using gestures and nonconventional vocalizations to express requests and protests and to call attention to themselves and their actions before they say their first word at about 12 months (Chapman, 1981). Coggins (this issue) provides some details about the acquisition of communicative skills in this age group. By 15 months, average *expressive* vocabulary size is 10 words (Reich, 1986). Throughout this early period, receptive vocabulary size exceeds the number of words the child can produce. Comprehension of the first word is usually about 3 months earlier than production, and the first word understood is usually not the same one as the first produced. Comprehension of 50 words generally occurs at about 13 months of age (Benedict, 1979).

First words are acquired slowly in production, a word or two at a time from 12 to 18 months in normal children. At the point at which the child's expressive vocabulary reaches about 50 words, generally at about 18 months, two important things happen. First, there is a spurt of vocabulary growth. Spoken vocabulary increases to an average of over 150 words at 20 months (Dale, Bates, Reznick, & Morisset, 1989) and to over 200 words at age 2 (Reich, 1986). Second, children begin to combine words into simple two-word sentences, often called "telegraphic utterances" (Brown, 1973). These telegraphic utterances usually encode a small range of meanings,

known as semantic relations, that are related to the child's developing cognitive notions (see Thal, this issue), such as object permanence ("allgone milk") and possession ("my cookie").

Although these ages represent averages around which considerable variability exists, the data on the normal range of variation for expressive vocabulary size and use of telegraphic utterances suggests that 24 months is a point at which delays in these areas can be identified (see Rescorla, this issue). Miller (1981) reported that average mean length of utterance (MLU) in morphemes at 24 months is 1.5 to 2.4, indicating that 2-year-olds within the average range of language acquisition are using at least equal numbers of one- and two-word utterances. Several large-scale studies used to establish norms for standardized developmental scales (Bzoch & League, 1971; Capute et al., 1986; Coplan, Gleason, Ryan, Burke, & Williams, 1982; Frankenburg & Dodds, 1967; Rescorla, 1989; Resnick, Allen, & Rapin, 1984) support the notion that children who fail to produce 50 words and two-word combinations at 24 months can be considered delayed in expressive language development.

Stoel-Gammon (this issue) discusses the acquisition of phonology during this period. Briefly, children by the age of 2 produce about 70% of their target consonants correctly, produce 9 to 10 different consonant phones, and a variety of syllable types (Stoel-Gammon, 1987a), suggesting that they are at least moderately intelligible to those in their immediate environment.

Thus, by the age of 2, normal children produce frequent intentionally communicative acts, have an expressive vocabulary of at least 50 words and a substantially larger receptive vocabulary, have begun to put together multiword utterances, and are generally intelligible to those who know them well. It is possible to identify children who are delayed in language development by age 2, but there is little empirical evidence to resolve the issue of whether these early delays persist into the preschool and school-aged periods, or as many believe, simply resolve on their own. Many of the authors in this issue are engaged in trying to find the answer to this question.

TODDLERS WITH SLOW EXPRESSIVE LANGUAGE DEVELOPMENT

In the Portland Language Development Project (PLDP), a longitudinal study, Paul (1991) has been following children between 18 and 34 months of age whose parents reported small expressive vocabularies on the Language Development Survey (Rescorla, 1989), and comparing them with a group of normally speaking children.

Children in the PLDP study were considered slow in expressive language development if they produced fewer than 10 intelligible words at 18 to 23 months, or fewer than 50 words or no two-word combinations by 24 to 34 months.

A group of 30 children meeting the above criteria for slow expressive language development (SELD) was matched to a control group of 30 children on the basis of age, socioeconomic status (SES), race, birth order, and sex ratio. Average age was 25.4 months (SD 4.6) for the

SELD group and 25.2 months (SD 4.0) for the normal speakers. Sixty-nine percent of the normals and 76% of the SELDs were male. There was no difference in birth order between the two groups. The mean socioeconomic levels on the Hollingshead Scale (Myers & Bean, 1968) were similar, with the mean falling at the middle to lower-middle class level and a similar distribution of levels across the two groups. The proportion of homes in which English was the only language spoken (100% and 97%) was also similar. There were more children from nonwhite ethnic groups in the normal sample than in the SELD group (17% and 0%; respectively). All the subjects passed hearing screening at 25 dB. All had developmental quotients on the Bayley Scales of Infant Development (Bayley, 1969) of 85 or better, and all passed informal observational screening for neurological disorders and autism performed by author.

All the subjects were given an intensive assessment battery for receptive language, cognitive development, oral motor function, and adaptive behavior. Parents filled out questionnaires regarding demographic information, medical history, and child behavior. A videotaped free-play interaction between parent and child was analyzed for maternal linguistic input, child communicative behavior, and child phonological characteristics. Characteristics of this cohort at age 2 are presented here in order to draw a portrait of the toddler with SELD.

History of ear infections

Parents were asked to indicate the number of ear infections the child had experienced before the first evaluation. The number of ear infections reported in both diagnostic groups—SELD and normal—was high, 4 to 6 on the average, and not significantly different between the two. Although this is a very rough estimate of history of otitis media (OM), the fact that both groups report similar figures suggests that OM is very common in all children under 2. Paul, Lynn, and Lohr-Flanders (1990) noted that history of ear infections as reported by parents, a very rough estimate of otitis media, did not predict language outcome at either age 3 or 4 years, suggesting that OM is not the primary determining factor in either initial delay or persistence of delay in this population. Studies of OM report conflicting results on this issue (Friel-Patti, 1990). Clearly, more research is needed on this topic.

Pre- and perinatal history

Parents were asked to describe any pre- or perinatal problems experienced by the subjects, as well as any family history of language delay. Neither pre- nor perinatal problems reported by parents distinguished the groups. One factor that did differ between groups is the reported incidence of history of language, speech, or learning problems in other family members. This history was reported 3 to 4 times more frequently in the SELD group, indicating a possible genetic basis for at least some cases of the disorder. It may be that families with a late-talking child tend to think more of other family members who were slow to start talking, and this increased sensitivity to the issue could also be the source of the difference. Further research is needed to pursue this question.

Cognitive skills

On the Bayley Scale of Infant Mental Development, (Bayley, 1969), both groups scored within the normal range, but the normal group did score significantly higher, with a mean developmental quotient of 116, as opposed to 97 for the SELDs. Although it might appear that the normal group is performing at a superior, rather than average, level of intellectual development, recent data on the Bayley suggest that it may produce inflated scores in normal children (Campbell, Siegel, Parr, & Ramey, 1986). This factor may account for the apparent superior performance of the normal subjects. Nonetheless, the fact is that there is a significant difference in favor of the normals on this measure. Because many of the Bayley items require comprehension or expression of verbal material, it was possible that the difference between the two groups was attributable to low performance of the SELD group on the verbal items. To determine whether the verbal portion of the Bayley influenced SELD group performance, an item analysis was completed.

All the children tested passed all the items on the Bayley up to and including item 123. The last 40 items on the test (123–163) are equally distributed between verbal and nonverbal. There are 10 items that require expressive language, such as naming objects, naming pictures, and producing sentences; 10 that require responses based on understanding language, such as discriminating objects, pointing to pictures, and understanding prepositions; and 20 that require nonverbal responses, such as building a tower, imitating crayon strokes, and completing puzzles. A comparison was made between the proportion of the last 20 verbal items and the proportion of the last 20 nonverbal items passed by the subjects in the two diagnostic groups. First, the analysis revealed that the normal group passed a significantly higher proportion of both the receptive and expressive items, as well as the combination of both types of verbal items. There was no significant difference, though, in the average number of nonverbal items passed by subjects in the two groups. It would seem, then, that the SELD children are roughly comparable to their normally speaking counterparts in terms of nonverbal cognitive ability.

Adaptive skills

Parents of children in both groups were interviewed using the Vineland Adaptive Behavior Scales (Sparrow, et al, 1984; see Paul, Spangle-Looney, & Dahm, 1991, for a more detailed discussion). The groups did not differ on the Daily Living scale, consisting primarily of self-help items, or on the Motor scale, which assesses gross and fine motor development. There were, however, significant differences in expressive language, receptive language, and socialization on this measure.

The difference between the groups in terms of receptive level was examined further to look for subgroups based in receptive language skill within the SELD sample. Although the SELD group did not perform as well, on the average, as the normals, 71% of the SELD toddlers scored within 6 months of age level on this scale. Only 29% of the SELD sample identified solely on the basis of small expressive

vocabulary size, then, appear to show deficits on receptive skill concomitant with their expressive delays.

The significant difference between the groups in terms of socialization skill on the Vineland also was explored. Here, the results revealed that 62% of the SELD toddlers scored more than 6 months below age level, whereas none of the normal group did so. Because some of the items on the socialization scale required verbalization, such as saying "please" or addressing people by name, an item analysis to determine the influence of verbal performance on this scale was conducted. Results indicated that the normal subjects passed a significantly greater absolute number of nonverbal items, suggesting that the poor performance of the SELD children on the socialization scale went beyond an inability to engage in verbal social routines. These data imply that social skill deficits are associated with SELD. It could be that slowness in language growth and poor socialization are both related to an underlying decrement in motivation to interact. These children may experience somewhat less drive for interaction than other toddlers, which could result in less need to acquire language, even when the potential to do so exists. Although this suggestion is highly speculative, data on communicative intentions produced in this population can be interpreted in a similar light.

Communicative intentions

The box entitled "Scheme for Coding Communicative Intentions," provides the coding scheme used for analyzing expression of communicative intentions in the 10-minute, free-play, mother–child inter-

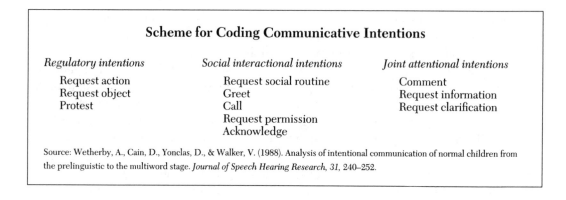

Scheme for Coding Communicative Intentions

Regulatory intentions	*Social interactional intentions*	*Joint attentional intentions*
Request action	Request social routine	Comment
Request object	Greet	Request information
Protest	Call	Request clarification
	Request permission	
	Acknowledge	

Source: Wetherby, A., Cain, D., Yonclas, D., & Walker, V. (1988). Analysis of intentional communication of normal children from the prelinguistic to the multiword stage. *Journal of Speech Hearing Research, 31,* 240–252.

actions that were videotaped. (See Paul & Shiffer, 1991, for a more detailed discussion.)

Paul and Shiffer (1991) showed that the SELD group produced significantly fewer communicative initiations, including nonverbal gestures and vocalizations, than did the normal children. Although SELD children expressed all the types of intentions that were expressed by the normal children, their overall frequency of communicative initiation was lower. However, the difference in frequency could primarily be accounted for by a difference in one particular type of communicative intention: the comment or joint attentional intention, used to focus the mother's attention on an object or activity. Commenting was the most frequent intention for both groups, but the normals commented significantly more often than the SELD group did. The difference between the groups in terms of expression of communicative intentions was a quantitative one, and limited to the intention primarily concerned with interaction for its own sake, rather than for the attainment of environmental ends. Again, the SELD group looked as if it was some-what less interested in interacting with others, even nonverbally.

Behavior

The two groups were compared on the Childhood Personality Scale (Cohen, 1975), a parent questionnaire. (See Paul & James, 1990, for a more detailed discussion.) The items on this scale were divided into four factors: (1) hyperactivity, (2) conduct, (3) relationships to others, and (4) affect/mood. Here, significant differences were found between the two groups on the hyperactivity and conduct factors only.

In addition, parents were asked to complete a questionnaire that listed a series of possible "problem behaviors" and to rate the presence of these problems in their child on a scale of "not at all," "some problem," or "serious problem." The SELD group was rated as showing significantly more problem behaviors on this instrument than was the normal group. The SELD toddlers, then, seemed to be perceived by their parents as overly active and more difficult to manage than normally speaking 2-year-olds.

Phonology

Paul and Jennings (in press) investigated syllable structure characteristics of the subjects' productions in both vocalizations and meaningful words, using an adaptation of Stoel-Gammon's (1987b) procedure for evaluating phonological structures in young children. The box entitled, "Scheme for Coding Syllable Structure Level" gives the coding criteria for this procedure, which scores syllable structures at three levels. Level 1 includes vowels, syllabic consonants, and consonant (C) vowel (V) syllables containing only glottal stops or glides; level 2 includes utterances with CV, VC, or CVC syllables with a single consonant type; level 3 includes syllables with more than one consonant type.

Paul and Jennings (in press) reported that the SELD toddlers were significantly less mature in terms of the complexity of their syllable structures. Whereas most normally speaking 2-year-olds produced a majority of syllables rated at level 3, with more than one different consonant, very few of these syllables were produced by the SELD group, whose syllables were primarily of the level 1 and level 2 variety. Similarly, the SELD group had significantly fewer consonants in their phonetic inventories—an average of 8, as opposed to 16 for the normal toddlers. The percentage of consonants produced correctly relative to adult target words was also significantly reduced in the speech of SELDs, with the normal toddlers producing about 70% correct consonants, and the SELDs producing only 56%. It seems clear, then, that SELD toddlers showed less maturity in phonological production than their peers with normal expressive vocabulary size.

This finding accords well with those of Whitehurst et al. (this issue). They report that, although expressive vocabulary size moves relatively quickly within the normal range after the slow start in these children, articulation skills continue to be poor throughout much of the preschool period. Our follow-up studies of these children (Paul, 1991) also suggest that a large proportion of 3- and 4-year-olds with a history of SELD have articulation deficits, both with and without concomitant expressive language delays. Whitehurst et al. (this issue) report that articulation deficits in their SELD subjects resolved more or less spontaneously by age 5. However, Shriberg and Kwiatkowski (1988) showed that 20% to 30% of children with apparently specific articulation difficulties in the preschool period required special education services once the child was in school,

---

Scheme for Coding Syllable Structure Level

Score 1: Utterances consisting of voiced vowel(s), syllabic consonants, or CV syllable(s) with only glottal stops or glides as consonants. Examples: /wawa/, /n̩/, /i/.

Score 2: Utterances consisting of CV, VC, or CVC syllable(s) in which only one consonant type appears (disregarding voicing differences). Examples: /gigi/, /dada/, /t di/.

Score 3: Utterances consisting of syllables with two or more different consonants. Examples: /c p/, /dali/.

Source: Stoel-Gammon, C. (1987b). Language production scale. In L. Olswang, C. Stoel-Gammon, T. Coggins, & R. Carpenter. (Eds.), *Assessing linguistic behaviors.* Seattle, WA: University of Washington.

even though the articulation disorder itself may have been resolved by this time. Thus, it would appear that the SELD toddlers' delays in phonological acquisition presage a substantial risk for articulation delay during the preschool period. This delay, in and of itself, and even if it appears to resolve by school age, seems to constitute a risk for special educational needs, possibly stemming from phonological processing problems (Catts, 1989).

Summary

These data indicate that children identified at age 2 on the basis of small expressive vocabulary alone resemble their normally speaking peers in terms of medical history of ear infections, and nonverbal cognitive skills. They differ from other toddlers, though, on a range of verbal and nonverbal parameters, including social skills, communicative behavior, maladaptive behavior, and phonological maturity. These differences suggest that late-talking toddlers may not be slow simply in the development of the ability to say words. These differences could be construed to suggest that the children would be at a substantial risk for long-term delay. What is the evidence for this position?

OUTCOMES OF SLOW EXPRESSIVE LANGUAGE DEVELOPMENT

Several researchers, including Paul (1991), Rescorla (1990), and Thal (1989) have reported follow-up studies on relatively large groups of toddlers identified at age 2 as slow in expressive vocabulary development. These researchers are consistent in reporting that 40% to 50% of their subjects do not "outgrow" their delays by age 3 years, when expressive language deficit is no longer measured by vocabulary size, but by maturity of sentence structures as indexed by MLU in morphemes (Miller, 1981), structural stage (Miller, 1981), Developmental Sentence Score (Lee, 1974), or productive syntactic level (Scarborough, 1990). Paul (1991), like Whitehurst et al. (this issue), reports that expressive vocabulary size quickly moves within the normal range in this population, without intervention. However, more complex expressive skills, such as sentence structures and use of complex sentences, remain delayed in a substantial proportion of the 3-year-olds studied.

Paul and Smith (1991) followed 28 SELD toddlers to age 4 and showed that 57% of the group continued to show expressive deficits, as indexed by MLU and Developmental Sentence Score. In addition, Paul and Smith found that SELD children with persistent expressive language delay also demonstrated significant deficits in their narrative skills, when assessed with a standardized story-retelling task (Renfrew, 1977). This finding is particularly significant because narrative skills in preschoolers have been shown to be one of the best predictors of school success. Thus, when fine-grained measures of expressive skills that tap more complex abilities than size of expressive vocabulary or general verbal fluency are employed, a substantial proportion of children with a history of SELD evidence chronic deficits, at least until age 4.

The children in the present study have not yet reached age 5, and, as such, cannot be compared directly with the subjects reported to have "caught up" to normals in the Whitehurst et al. work reported in this issue. Similarly, the children in this study were evaluated for receptive language skill on an instrument that is more sensitive to deficits in receptive language than is the Peabody Picture Vocabulary Test-Revised (PPVT-R) (Dunn & Dunn, 1981), which only evaluates receptive vocabulary under quite restrictive conditions. Even random pointing to one of four pictures provides a one-in-four change of being "correct." Thus, it is not clear whether the present sample is, in fact, more receptively impaired than Whitehurst et al.'s, or simply assessed in more depth in this area. In any case, studies that examine children with a variety of types of language delay in the preschool period and follow them into the school years consistently show very high risk for academic difficulty (Aram, Ekelman, & Nation, 1984; Aram & Nation, 1980; Garvey & Gordon, 1973; King, Jones, & Lasky, 1982).

Tallal (1988) suggests that many children who are diagnosed as language impaired in the preschool period frequently have their diagnoses changed to "learning disabled" when they reach school age, because it is the reading and writing deficits that become more obvious and salient. She argues that the two disorders are really manifestations of the same underlying deficit that is expressed in different ways at different points in development. Like Whitehurst et al. (this issue), Tallal observes that the oral language deficits that accompany the reading difficulties in

this population at school age are no longer obvious to the "naked ear," and may require more in-depth assessment in order to be tapped.

Scarborough and Dobrich (1990) present a model of the course of development of language skills in children with a history of SELD that includes a period of "illusory recovery" at about age 5, when SELD children appear to move within the normal range primarily because the rate of growth of their peers has slowed down considerably, only to speed up and again surpass the SELD children's rate at age 6 to 7. Thus, the issue of whether SELD children can be said to "catch up" by age 5, as Whitehurst et al. (this issue) claim, must be considered in light of

- whether the full range of language skills that are important at this age—and not detectable in measures of expressive vocabulary size, general verbal fluency, or unstructured conversation (such as complex sentence use and narrative skill)—is evaluated,
- whether any recovery that does appear to be completed by age 5 is stable, or will again be outpaced by development in normal children over the course of the next year or two, when their rate of language growth accelerates, in conjunction with the acquisition of literacy skills, and
- even if oral language skills do appear to eventually remain within the normal range by the end of the preschool period, whether the underlying processes that slowed them down at first continue to operate, now influencing primarily the learning of reading, writ-

ing, and spelling, as seems to be the case for so many youngsters with a history of language delay.

It would seem that the question of spontaneous recovery from early language delay must be phrased in terms of what we mean by "catch up." If we mean that children who start out with small expressive vocabularies and little speech achieve normal expressive vocabulary sizes and generally fluent production by age 5, the answer may be "yes" (Whitehurst et al., this issue). If we mean that children who start out with small expressive vocabularies do not have increased risk for long-term difficulties with complex, sophisticated language use or with the school curricula, then the answer is not yet clear. This author's view of the evidence available from a range of sources at this point in time suggests that 2-year-olds who are slow in their expressive development do experience considerable risk for chronic delays in advanced language skills and in school achievement, although many will recover spontaneously. The issue, therefore, is to find reliable predictors of good and poor outcomes that can be used to make decisions about which toddlers should be closely monitored or provided with early intervention, and which can be confidently left alone to undergo spontaneous recovery.

INTERVENTION ISSUES

Should toddlers or young preschoolers with SELD be provided with speech-language intervention? Although some might argue that intervention has only short-term effects and does not change the long-term course of SELD, this conclusion is based on the belief that SELD toddlers become normal by age 5, and thus, no intervention is required. For example, Whitehurst et al. (this issue) measured outcome only in terms of expressive vocabulary size and general verbal fluency, and not in terms of the areas intervention was most likely to have addressed, that is, sentence structure and complexity. If it is the case, as I have argued, the SELD changes its form with development and is manifested in deficits in complex language, advanced discourse skills, and academic achievement in the late preschool and school-aged period, then some attempt to lay the basis for these skills in an early intervention program may be effective, although further research will be needed to substantiate this view.

If the decision to provide intervention at age 2 is made, on what skills should intervention focus? One thing we do know about this population is that increasing expressive vocabulary may have little effect on outcome (Whitehurst, et al., this issue). Although it is tempting to say that because these children have small expressive vocabularies, what they need is to be taught larger ones, this approach does not seem to produce positive results. The deficits seen in these children in socialization and communication skills suggest that their slow language growth may be association with immature or underdeveloped interpersonal abilities. If this is the case, then intervention must focus first on the interpersonal, or pragmatic, aspect of language in order to be effective. Naming and labeling drills in and of themselves will not reach this goal.

These findings suggest a management program that should take place in a pragmatic context with a focus on interpersonal communication. Activities would include the production of multiword utterances encoding early semantic relations, at first using the words the child is already producing in holophrases. Later, new vocabulary items with controlled phonological shapes can be taught and eventually incorporated into the multiword utterances.

For example, a child who at 24 months produces only the words *mama, car, bye, shoe, hug,* and *doggy* might be engaged in a game in which photos of his mother, his dog, a shoe, and a toy car were lined up on the floor. The clinician might take one of the items and say to the child, "Hide mama. I'll close my eyes. You hide mama. I'll see if I can find mama. Hide mama." This could then be repeated with the other items. Then the clinician might say, "Now let's hug mama. I'll do it first. I'll hug mama. Now you do it. Hug mama." This would then be repeated for all items. Next the clinician could say, "Now you tell me what to do. I could hug mama or I could hide mama. I could hug the doggy or I could hide the doggy. What should I do? You tell me." If the child only produced one word, the clinician could feign confusion, and ask "Mama? Shall I hide mama? Or should I hug mama? You tell me what to do." The child could then be encouraged to take several turns. When two-word combinations of the agent–action form are produced consistently, new vo-

cabulary items, either nouns or verbs, can be added to the game.

It should be noticed that the words used contain only consonants already produced by the child, and only simple CVC syllable shapes. Also, the game is structured so that in order to accomplish the goal, to get the clinician to hide or hug one of the items, the child must produce both the target words. Neither alone will be sufficient to communicate the message. Finally, the game puts the child in an assertive position, where he tells the clinician what to do.

As the child gets older and improves in sentence length, intervention might focus on those skills known to be associated with school success, because this seems to be the area of deficit that is most likely to persist in this population. Given SELD children's poor phonological skills, and the known association between deficits in phonological awareness and in reading (Catts, 1989), a program during the late preschool period that focused on the development of phonological awareness through rhyming and segmentation activities may be useful (Bradley & Bryant, 1985). Even if phonological errors in production are the only obvious deficit these children are displaying in this period, phonological awareness activities, as an adjunct to articulation training, may have a preventative effect in helping to stave off early reading delay. Similarly, intervention that targeted the development of narrative skill and the comprehension and production of complex sentences may be of value. Of course, ongoing assessment is necessary both to ensure that the interventions are effective and to determine whether the child has moved within the normal range in the specific skills being addressed. Although these suggestions are speculative, their intent is to begin to connect the knowledge emerging about late-talking toddlers with more informed principles on which intervention may be based, and to stimulate research that will allow us to demonstrate whether such intervention is efficacious in either the short or long term.

REFERENCES

Aram, D., Ekelman, B., & Nation, J. (1984). Preschoolers with language disorders: 10 years later. *Journal of Speech and Hearing Research, 27,* 232–244.

Aram, D., & Nation, J. (1980). Preschool language disorders and subsequent language and academic difficulties. *Journal of Communication Disorders, 13,* 159–170.

Bayley, N. (1969). *Scales of infant mental development.* New York, NY: Psychological Corp.

Benedict, H. (1979). Early lexical development: Comprehension and production. *Journal of Child Language, 6,* 183–200.

Bradley, L., & Bryant, P. (1985). *Rhyme and reason in reading and spelling.* Ann Arbor, MI: University of Michigan Press.

Brown, R. (1973). *A first language.* Cambridge, MA: Harvard University Press.

Bzoch, K., & League, R. (1971). *Assessing language skills in infancy.* Baltimore, MD: University Park Press.

Campbell, S., Siegel, E., Parr, C., & Ramey, C. (1986). Evidence for the need to renorm the Bayley Scales of Infant Development based on performance of a population-based sample of 12 month old infants. *Topics in Early Childhood Special Education, 6,* 83–96.

Capute, A., Palmer, F., Shapiro, B., Wachtel, R., Schmidt, S., & Ross, A. (1986). Clinical linguistic and auditory milestone scale: Prediction of cognition in infancy. *Developmental Medicine and Child Neurology, 28,* 762–771.

Catts, H., & Kamhi, A. (1986). The linguistic basis of reading disorders: Implications for the speech-language pathologist. *Language, Speech and Hearing Services in Schools, 17,* 329–341.

Catts, H. (1989). Phonological processing deficits and reading disabilities. In A.G. Kamhi and H.W. Catts (Eds.), *Reading disabilities: A developmental language perspective.* Boston, MA: College-Hill Press.

Chapman, R. (1981). Exploring children's communicative intentions. In J. Miller (Ed.), *Assessing language production in children: Experimental procedures.* Baltimore, MD: University Park Press.

Cohen, D. (1975). *Childhood personality scale.* Washington, DC: National Institutes of Mental Health.

Coplan, J., Gleason, J., Ryan, R., Burke, M., & Williams, M. (1982). Validation of early language milestone scale in a high-risk population. *Pediatrics, 70,* 677–683.

Dale, P., Bates, E., Reznick, S., & Morisset, C. (1989). The validity of a parent report instrument of child language at twenty months. *Journal of Child Language, 16,* 239–250.

Dunn, L., & Dunn, L. (1981). *Peabody Picture Vocabulary Test* (Rev.). Circle Pines, MN: American Guidance.

Frankenburg, W., & Dodds, K. (1967). The Denver Developmental Screening Test. *Journal of Pediatrics, 71,* 181–191.

Friel-Patti, S. (1990). Otitis media: Implications for language learning. *Topics in Language Disorders, 11* (1).

Garvey, M., & Gordon, N. (1973). A follow-up study of children with disorders of speech development. *British Journal of Communication Disorders, 4,* 46–56.

King, R., Jones, D., & Lasky, E. (1982). In retrospect: A fifteen year follow-up of speech-language disordered children. *Language, Speech and Hearing Services in Schools, 13,* 24–32.

Lee, L. (1974). *Developmental sentence scoring.* Evanston, IL: Northwestern University Press.

Maxwell, S., & Wallach, G. (1984). The language-learning disabilities connection: Symptoms of early language disability change over time. In G. Wallach & K. Butler (Eds.), *Language and learning disabilities in school-aged children.* Baltimore, MD: Williams & Wilkins.

Miller, J. (1981). *Assessing language production in children: Experimental procedures.* Baltimore, MD: University Park Press.

Myers, J., & Bean, L. (1968). *A decade later: A follow-up of social class and mental illness.* New York, NY: Wiley.

Paul, R. (1991). Assessment of communication in toddlers: Why and how. *Clinics in Communication Disorders,* in press.

Paul, R., & James, D. (1990). Language delay and parental perceptions. *Journal of the American Academy of Child and Adolescent Psychiatry, 29,* 669–670.

Paul, R., & Jennings, P. (in press). Phonological behavior in normal and 'late-talking' toddlers. *Journal of Speech and Hearing Research.*

Paul, R., Lynn, T., & Lohr-Flanders, M. (1990). *Otitis media and speech/language development in late-talkers.* Paper presented at the American Speech-Language-Hearing Association National Convention, Seattle, WA.

Paul, R., & Shiffer, M. (1991). Expression of communicative intentions in normal and 'late-talking' young children. *Applied Psycholinguistics*, in press.

Paul, R., & Smith, R. (1991). *Narrative skills in four year olds with normal, impaired, and late-developing language.* Paper presented at the biennial meeting of the Society for Research in Child Development, Seattle, WA.

Paul, R., Spangle-Looney, S., & Dahm, P. (1991). Communication and socialization skills at ages two and three in 'late-talking' young children. *Journal of Speech and Hearing Disorders*, in press.

Reich, P. (1986). *Language development.* Englewood Cliffs, NJ: Prentice-Hall.

Renfrew, C. (1977). The Bus Story Language Test. Oxford: Author.

Rescorla, L. (1989). The language development survey: A screening tool for delayed language in toddlers. *Journal of Speech and Hearing Disorders, 54,* 587–599.

Rescorla, L. (1990). *Outcomes of expressive language delay.* Paper presented at the Symposium for Research in Child Language Disorders, Madison, WI.

Resnick, T., Allen, D., & Rapin, I. (1984). Disorders of language development: Diagnosis and intervention. *Pediatrics in Review, 6,* 85–92.

Scarborough, H. (1990). Index of productive syntax. *Applied Psycholinguistics, 11,* 1–22.

Scarborough, H., & Dobrich, W. (1990). Development of children with early language delay. *Journal of Speech and Hearing Research, 33,* 70–83.

Shriberg, L., & Kwiatkowski, J. (1988). A follow-up study of children with phonologic disorders of unknown origin. *Journal of Speech and Hearing Disorders, 53,* 144–155.

Sparrow, S., Balla, D., & Ciccetti, D. (1984). *Vineland Adaptive Behavior Scales.* Minneapolis, MN: American Guidance Service.

Stoel-Gammon, C. (1987a). Phonological skills of 2-year-olds. *Language, Speech and Hearing Services in the Schools, 18,* 323–329.

Stoel-Gammon, C. (1987b). Language production scale. In L. Olswang, C. Stoel-Gammon, T. Coggins, R. Carpenter (Eds.), *Assessing linguistic behaviors.* Seattle, WA: University of Washington.

Tallal, P. (1988). Developmental language disorders. In J. Kavanagh & T. Truss (Eds.), *Learning disabilities: Proceedings of the national conference.* Parkton, MD: York Press.

Thal, D. (1989). *Language and gesture in late talkers.* Paper presented at the biennial meeting of the Society for Research in Child Development, Kansas City, MO.

Weiner, P.S. (1985). The value of follow-up studies. *Topics in Language Disorders, 5,* (3), 78–92.

Wetherby, A., Cain, D., Yonclas, D., & Walker, V. (1988). Analysis of intentional communication of normal children from the prelinguistic to the multiword stage. *Journal of Speech and Hearing Research, 31,* 240–252.

Part II
Family/Caregiver/Peer Interactions with Very Young Communicatively Impaired Children

Mothers in dialogue with language-impaired children

Gina Conti-Ramsden, PhD
Lecturer, Education Department
University of Manchester
Manchester, England

ALL CHILDREN LEARNING to talk acquire their conversational skills within the context of dialogue and, most commonly, within the context of mother–child dialogues. Thus, it is not surprising that much research has concentrated on examining the nature of mothers' dialogues with normal language-learning children and with language-impaired children. Many of the studies comparing the characteristics of mothers' dialogues with language-impaired children to the characteristics of mothers' dialogues with normal language learners have been methodologically flawed. The claim that the linguistic input to language-impaired children is directive and controlling is no longer warranted. In fact the current state of knowledge on the general characteristics of mothers' dialogues with normal language-learning children across cultures and their correlation with the rate of language development forces a reformulation of thinking about language-impaired mother–child dyads. Such a reformulation

Top Lang Disord, 5(2), 58-68
© 1985 Aspen Publishers, Inc.

involves looking at how the language-impaired child acts on his or her linguistic environment within particular interaction situations instead of looking at the effect that linguistic input has on the language-impaired child.

TWO CATEGORIES OF CLINICAL THOUGHT

Clinician-researchers focusing in the area of child-directed speech fall mainly into two categories: those who argue that maternal speech to language-impaired children is *different* from that of normal language learning-children (Bondurant, Romeo, & Kretschmer, 1983; Buium, Rynders, & Turnure, 1973; Cardoso-Martins & Mervis, 1981; Ferracane & Dukes, 1981; Grossfeld & Heller, 1980; Marshall, Hegrenes & Goldstein, 1973; Schodorf & Edwards, 1981; Siegel, Cunningham, & van der Spuy, 1979; Wulbert, Inglis, Kriegsmann & Mills, 1975) and those who argue that maternal speech to language-impaired children is *similar* to that of normal language-learning children of the same language stage (Conti-Ramsden & Friel-Patti, 1983; Cramblit & Siegel, 1977; Lansky & Klopp, 1982; MacPherson & Weber-Olsen, 1980; Messick & Prelock, 1981; Rondal, 1977). Typically, investigators arguing that maternal speech to language-impaired children is *different* have found mothers of language-impaired children to be more directive and controlling (Bondurant et al., 1983; Buium et al., 1973; Marshall et al., 1973) than mothers of normal language-learning children. As a result, these investigators have entertained the possibility that the linguistic environment of language-impaired chil-

dren is less conducive for language learning than that of normal language-learning children. Furthermore, mothers of language-impaired children may actually maintain their children's language problem (Schodorf & Edwards, 1981), and linguistic input to language-impaired children may be somewhat deficient (Grossfeld & Heller, 1980). Conversely, investigators who argue for similarities have failed to replicate these findings (Conti-Ramsden & Friel-Patti, 1983; Lasky & Klopp, 1982). They found that mothers of the language impaired did not command, direct, or control their children more than mothers of normal language-learning children of the same language stage. What can account for such conflicting results?

METHODOLOGICAL ISSUES

Various methodological problems may account for the discrepant findings. First, the clinical populations examined are not comparable from study to study. Some clinician-researchers have included in their population of language-impaired subjects children with known genetic abnormalities and cognitive deficits (Buium et al., 1973; Cardoso-Martins & Mervis, 1981; Marshall et al., 1973; Rondal, 1977); others have deliberately excluded such subjects from their studies (Conti-Ramsden & Friel-Patti, 1983; Lasky & Klopp, 1982; MacPherson & Weber-Olsen, 1980). The earlier studies tended to have loosely defined subjects such as "mongoloids" or "retardates" without an attempt to control for the range of linguistic and cognitive difficulties of such children. The later studies, some influenced by the work of Stark and

Tallal (1981), used stricter subject criteria in an attempt to study more homogeneous groups of children. Thus the problem is a double-edged sword. Studies with either loosely specified or different criteria of language impairment often produce conflicting results; studies with strictly defined criteria may yield results that are not easily generalized to the population of language-impaired children. Given the heterogeneity of the population, using an all-encompassing term such as "language impairment" may be misleading. Instead, subgroups of language-impaired children should be recognized with an attempt to explicitly specify and describe their characteristics. All conclusions and recommendations should be restricted to only those children who are comparable.

Second, some clinician-researchers have compared language-impaired children to their chronological age-mates (Bondurant et al., 1983; Marshall et al., 1973; Wulbert et al., 1975) and others have attempted to match language-impaired children to normal language-learning children of the same language stage (Conti-Ramsden & Friel-Patti, 1983; MacPherson & Weber-Olsen, 1980; Rondal, 1977) and to children of the same mental age (Cardoso-Martins & Mervis, 1981). This difference reflects another historical trend. In the mid-1960s Menyuk's (1964) suggestion that language-impaired children were *qualitatively* different from their chronological age-mates was widely accepted. However, following Brown's (1973) stage concept, researchers and clinicians began to compare language-impaired children with normal language-learning children of the same language stage as measured by mean length of utterance (MLU). The findings

of such studies not only failed to replicate the findings of the earlier studies but they revealed that language-impaired children performed similarly to younger, normally developing children of the same MLU level on a variety of language measures. (Folger & Leonard, 1976; Leonard, Bolders & Miller, 1976; Leonard, Steckol & Schwartz, 1978). The only differences noted were *quantitative:* Language-impaired children tended to use their language skills less frequently than their normal language learning counterparts.

The effect of mothers' speech modifications change as their children's communicative abilities develop. For example, Gleitman, Newport, and Gleitman (1984) found that the effect of maternal yes/no questions on their normal language-learning children's auxiliary growth was insignificant for children between 18 and 21 months but reliably significant in children from 24 to 25 months. Therefore, in order to compare maternal speech to children, whether language-impaired or not, the children *must* be at a similar stage of language development. It has been obvious for a long time that matching children for chronological age does not necessarily ensure similarity in the children's language development. It has been more recently discovered that similarity in language-impaired and normal language-learning children's MLUs does not guarantee equivalent mastery of linguistic structures by both groups of children (Johnston & Kamhi, 1980).

The social interaction abilities of language-impaired children also appear to be different from MLU matches. Friel-Patti and Harris (1984) compared language-impaired children with both their chronological age-mates and their MLU matches. They found that the social interaction of the language-impaired children was better than that of their MLU matches but not as advanced as that of their chronological age-mates. Moreover, some language-impaired children appear to have difficulties with specific aspects of conversational competence. Conti-Ramsden and Friel-Patti (1983, 1984) found that language-impaired children initiate and dialogue significantly less often than their MLU counterparts.

The same problem arises when considering cognitive variables. Johnston (1982) demonstrated that similar mental ages for language-impaired and normal language-learning children (derived from the Leiter International Performance Scale) do not guarantee similar abilities for both groups of children. Similarly, Kamhi (1981) found that the nonlinguistic symbolic and conceptual abilities of language-impaired children were better than those of their MLU-matched controls but poorer than those of their mental age peers. As Newhoff and Browning (1983) contend when studying interaction, cognitive/linguistic comparability between language-impaired children and normal language learning children may be impossible because of the reciprocal nature of interaction: Mothers affect their children and children, in turn, affect their mothers. Thus, as soon as the child fails to develop language appropriately, the interaction of the mother and child may be different.

Consequently, within the interactive framework, the clinician-researcher has two main choices, which are not mutually exclusive: a) to acknowledge that comparability between dyads involving language-impaired children and normal language-learning children is not viable and then concentrate on controlling as many relevant variables as possible, and b) to remain within the population of language-impaired children, identifying and comparing different interactional styles in language-impaired dyads, deriving histories of interaction after following a variety of language-impaired dyads over time, and so on. The latter approach needs to be explored before clinician-researchers can identify the development of different kinds of language impairment.

Third, some clinician-researchers interested in mothers' speech to language-impaired children have focused on one half of the dyad (the mother) more than on the child (Bondurant et al., 1983; Buium et al., 1973; Cramblit & Siegel, 1977; Petersen & Sherrod, 1982; Wulbert et al., 1975). Others have attempted to capture the dyadic nature of the conversational interaction between mothers and their language-impaired children (Conti-Ramsden & Friel-Patti, 1983; Lansky & Klopp, 1982; MacPherson & Weber-Olsen, 1980; Messick & Prelock, 1981; Newhoff, Silverman, & Millet, 1980).

A large body of literature now supports the view that the characteristics of mother–child discourse result from the mutual regulation of behaviors of both interactants (Conti, 1981; Conti-Ramsden & Friel-Patti, 1983; DeVilliers, 1983; Snow & Ferguson, 1977). From birth, the child is seen as an interactant with the external world. Piaget described this interaction between the child and the environment as basically need oriented: The child interacts with the environment in order to maintain equilibrium. Piaget (1960) suggested that the child is biologically determined to achieve equilibrium and to adapt to the environment. Schaffer (1977, 1979) has also suggested that infants are preadapted to behave in certain ways that elicit responses from caregivers, which in turn contribute to their learning. Newhoff and Launer (1984) have discussed at length this mutual involvement suggesting that the child is a social interactor from birth and that learning is essentially social. Thus, although clinician-researchers interested in maternal speech to language-impaired children have acknowledged the bidirectionality of the influences within the interaction, not all have used methodologies involving dyadic measures. Indeed, investigators who have focused on the linguistic behaviors of only one conversational partner (usually the mother) have removed the context in which discourse occurs, attempting later the almost impossible task of reintegrating their findings into an interactive, discourse frame. Similarly, remediation of language impairment has tended to focus only on one member of the dyad (first the child and then the mother), thus missing the important contribution that each partner makes to the dyad. Many clinicians seem to put into practice the view that each participant in the interaction is an equally contributing member of the interchange. Even Newhoff and Browning (1983), who discuss and defend this position, continue to talk about "caregiver training" and suggest that training *before* motherhood may be successful. How could it succeed if the partner with whom the mother will interact is not born yet? An interactive approach demands interactive therapy or a therapy of interaction. Even the moth-er–child dyad appears to be too narrow a unit of intervention.

These methodological problems have challenged the findings of studies that described mothers of language-impaired children as more directive and controlling than mothers of normal language-learning children. This suggestion is no longer warranted. As a result of the methodological change, it now appears that mothers of language-impaired children do not command, direct, or control their children any more than mothers of normal language-learning children of the same language stage (Conti-Ramsden & Friel-Patti, 1983; Lasky & Klopp, 1982; Messick & Prelock, 1981).

EFFECTS OF MOTHER–CHILD DIALOGUE CHARACTERISTICS

Once the characteristics of mothers' dialogues with their language-impaired children are accurately described, the question arises as to what their effect may or may not be on how these children themselves learn to talk. To answer this question it is important to know how the mother–child relationship contributes to normal language acquisition and how much variation exists from culture to culture.

Studies with normal language-learning children

Features of the speech used by adults in addressing young, normal language learning children are so well known and well documented in the literature that the term *motherese* has been coined to refer to them as a cluster of co-occurring behaviors. The speech addressed to normal language-learning children is reported to be much simpler in both syntax and semantics, as well as more redundant than the speech addressed to adults (Snow, 1972); it is slower, clearer, and more fluent (Broen, 1972); and has an exaggerated intonation pattern (Garnica, 1977). What effect do these characteristics have on the child learning language?

During the 1970s a variety of studies attempted to correlate mothers' speech characteristics with their children's rate of language learning. Cross (1977, 1978) in her study of mothers of linguistically advanced and unadvanced children, found that mothers who used more semantically related utterances and less directive ones had children who were linguistically more advanced. Similarly, Newport, Gleitman, and Gleitman (1975, 1977) found that mothers' use of imperatives correlated negatively with children's language growth. These investigators, along with Furrow, Nelson, and Benedict (1979), also found that mothers' use of yes/no questions accelerated the child's acquisition of verbal auxiliaries.

While the findings correlating semantic relatedness with speed of language acquisition and directiveness with delay in the acquisition process are rather intuitive, other significant correlations found in these studies are counterintuitive. For example, Furrow et al. (1979) found that mothers' use of verbs correlated *negatively* with the acquisition of MLU and verbs. As a result, much debate has arisen concerning the robustness of the results and the appropriateness of the methodologies used. Subsequently, Gleitman et al. (1984) reanalyzed their earlier data and

their previous findings discussed in detail as well as those of Furrow et al. (1979), and made a serious effort to explain all three analyses. They concluded that their correlational findings were stage dependent; that is, the characteristics of maternal speech varied with the language stage of the child. Most of the correlations they found were limited to the younger group of children (children between 18 and 21 months) with the single exception of maternal yes/no questions, which had an effect on auxiliary growth for the older group (children between 24 to 27 months) but were not significant for the younger group. Thus, their reanalysis confirmed their previous finding that selected features of mothers' speech influence the children's rate of language acquisition, with the proviso that this phenomenon is stage dependent. They then probed further to try to ascertain what or who was responsible for the changes over time. Was it the mothers' speech? Or was it the child's use of the speech provided by the mother? Gleitman et al. (1984) found that there were no major changes in mothers' language over the period observed (from 1 to 3 years of age). What *was* changing was the child's focus and use he or she made of the linguistic material provided by the mother. In this sense, it was the child who changed rather than the mother.

Thus, the fact seems to be that the language-learning child exploits linguistic material at one stage but not another. Furthermore, the linguistic material presented by the mother (at least for the ages of 1 to 3 and for the linguistic features studied by Gleitman et al., 1984) appears to remain constant over time. Consequently, the results have thrown the research ball back into the child's court. The question is no longer what the characteristics of mothers' speech do for the child learning language but how and to what extent the child himself or herself filters and organizes the information provided by the mother. The current state of knowledge on the relationship between maternal speech and normal language learning emphasizes the need to look at the characteristics of the child as a language learner, without neglecting the ways in which these characteristics interact with specific properties of the environment.

Cross-cultural studies

Knowledge about the features of motherese and their relative effect on normal language development has largely been based on studies of middle-class families in the United States and Western Europe. A broader look at other cultures reveals that the characteristics of mothers' dialogues with their children vary greatly from culture to culture and that children learn to talk under a very wide range of interactive situations. Cross-cultural studies of interaction between children and their caregivers have been reviewed by Newhoff and Launer (1984) and Lieven (1984) at length. The latter reviewed the work of Schieffelin (1979), Ochs (1982), and Brice Heath (1983).

Schieffelin's (1979) cross-cultural work has been based on the Kaluli community of Papua New Guinea. She found that the Kaluli mothers are the primary caregivers until the child is about 3 years old. In this community, mothers are thought to be responsible for "teaching" children how to talk. This "teaching" is mainly achieved

Knowledge about the features of motherese and their effects on normal language development has largely been based on studies of middle-class families in the United States and Western Europe.

by the use of the *elema* strategy, which commands the child to imitate. *Elema* means "say what I say," and the child is constantly directed to repeat what is said to him or her. In some ways, the Kaluli mother is like a theater producer, supplying the correct lines for the child to imitate.

Ochs (1982) studied the caregiver–child verbal interaction in a rural community of Western Samoa. Unlike the Kaluli people, Samoan communities distribute their caregiving responsibilities over several family members and over several generations. Caregiver's talk to Samoan children is highly directive; they instruct the child what to say through elicited imitation. Ochs also points to the almost complete absence of expansions in caregivers' speech to Samoan children.

In America, Brice Heath (1983) has observed the Trackton community from the Piedmont Carolinas. In this community, children are verbally ignored until they can talk. Adults rarely address children when they are beginning to talk, nor do they pay attention to what the children are saying until they can put together multiword utterances. In this sense, young Trackton children receive no feedback for their verbal efforts, nor semantically related expansions.

It is evident that children from other cultures learn to talk under conditions of very little or no semantically related, child-directed talk and in highly directive and controlling environments. Given this evidence, researchers such as Ochs (1982) surmise that the characteristics of mother-ese that have been thought to aid language learning cannot be considered to be universally natural. Lieven (1984) has argued that children who are not provided by adults with externalized supports for language (like semantically related utterances) find ways of providing that support for themselves. She hypothesizes that a sort of "self-scaffolding" occurs. Lieven also argues that although the Kaluli, Samoan, and Trackton children's linguistic environment is directive and unresponsive, it is also child-centered in the sense that adult–child interactions are initiated once children show interest in what is going on around them. It is rather difficult, however, to reconcile the cross-cultural data available with Lieven's latter arguments.

The language-impaired mother–child dyad

The current state of knowledge affords little guidance for the language-impaired mother–child dyad. It has been shown that (a) normal language-learning children are exposed to a variety of interactive environments; (b) mother's dialogues with their normal language-learning children are vastly different in character from culture to culture; and (c) whatever the characteristics of mothers' dialogues with their children, motherese does not change over time; instead, children's selective use of these characteristics changes. These suggestions have shifted importance away from to the input to language-learning children and onto the child's responses to the input he or she receives during mother–child interaction.

Thus, the question of the effect of mothers' speech on language-impaired children's language development is no longer crucial. The new question is how the language-impaired child acts on his or her linguistic environment and within which interaction situations.

Insufficient evidence is available at present to delineate language-impaired children's predispositions for organizing and filtering linguistic information or to compare these with the predispositions of normal language-learning children. Nonetheless, Lieven (1984) suggests that normal language-learning children have a variety of pathways into learning language that may not be available to language-impaired children. In other words, language-impaired children may well be restricted in their abilities to organize and filter linguistic information, and these restrictions may vary among different subgroups of language-impaired children. Thus, children with phonological problems are likely to differ from children who have receptive and expressive language problems. Once again, it may be misleading to use the all-encompassing term "language impairment"; instead, subgroups of language-impaired children should be identified and described in detail.

For the normal language-learning child, a variety of interactive styles appears to offer enough for the child to learn language. But is it the same for the language-impaired child? Can the language-impaired child develop under a variety of interactive conditions as do normal language-learning children? These questions have not yet been answered and research, together with intervention, is greatly needed. One task facing the clinician-researcher is to determine *how* particular features of the interactive environment do or do not match the language-impaired children's predisposition to organize linguistic information. Different subgroups of language-impaired children may match

---

> *One task facing the clinician-researcher is to determine* how *particular features of the interactive environment do or do not match the language-impaired child's predisposition to organize linguistic information.*

---

with different types of interactive env on-ments. Thus, there may be no one "optimal" match; instead, a variety of interactive styles and ranges within these styles exists from which language-impaired children derive their linguistic information.

Given the reciprocity of interaction, the effect that each partner has on the other is difficult to determine when viewing only the mother–child dyad in research or in intervention. Stylistic matches and mismatches are difficult to identify. The influences of mother on child and of child on mother are so intimately related that the mother's style is difficult to isolate from the child's style. It is important to observe both mothers and children interacting with other partners. In this way, the specific aspects of the interaction that are heavily influenced by the participant's interactive style can be disentangled from those that are not. In addition to identifying interaction matches and mismatches, it will be important to identify those aspects of mothers' and children's interaction that change little across partners, that is, each individual's style. Knowledge of the individual's style of interaction may be very important for intervention. Consider, for example, the following spontaneous comments about interaction from two mothers and their children. The first mother talks about her interaction with her normal language learning, 2-year-old daughter:

She is just wonderful. We love to chat together. We do it for hours. She comes out with these enormous sentences! She is so aware of everything. She is great company. T. Hague (personal communication, March, 1984).

Contrast these comments with those of the second mother who is talking about her interaction with her language-impaired, 5-year-old daughter:

I am a naturally quiet person and we are a na .rally quiet family. We [herself and her husband] can just sit with each other all evening without saying anything and we are happy. Since I was told I should try to talk more to our daughter and draw her into conversation more, I don't talk to her naturally anymore. My voice pitch changes about an octave higher when I talk to her. It makes me so aware, I could kick myself. A. Neville (personal communication, April, 1984).

These two mothers' individual styles are clearly different. Knowledge of such individual styles allows the clinician to plan therapy that will be best suited to the natural style of the mother and the family. The aim should be to shape the interaction, if necessary, not to destroy it. In the future, clinician-researchers involved in the therapeutic process may be able to identify interactive styles that match the predispositions of different subgroups of language-impaired children, and design therapies of interaction that build on the natural inclinations of these children's families.

REFERENCES

Bondurant, J.L., Romeo, D.J., & Kretschmer, R. (1983). Language behaviors of mothers of children with normal and delayed language. *Language, Speech and Hearing Services in Schools, 14,* 233–242.

Broen, P.A. (1972). The verbal environment of the language-learning child. *American Speech and Hearing Association Monographs, 17.*

Brown, R. (1973). *A first language.* Cambridge, MA: Harvard University Press.

Brice Heath, S. (1983). *Ways with words.* Cambridge: Cambridge University Press.

Buium, N., Rynders, J., & Turnure, J. (1973). Early maternal linguistic environment of normal and nonnormal language-learning children. *Proceedings of the 81st Annual Convention of the American Psychological Association,* 79–80.

Cardoso-Martins, C., & Mervis, C.B. (1981, March). *Maternal Speech to prelinguistic Down syndrome children.* Paper presented at the Gatlinburg Conference for Research on Mental Retardation/Developmental Disabilities, Gatlinburg, Tennessee.

Conti, G. (1982). *Mothers in dialogue: Some discourse features of motherese with normal and language impaired children.* Unpublished doctoral dissertation, University of Texas at Dallas.

Conti-Ramsden, G., & Friel-Patti, S. (1983). Mothers' discourse adjustments to language-impaired and non-language-impaired children. *Journal of Speech and Hearing Disorders, 48,* 360–367.

Conti-Ramsden, G., & Friel-Patti, S. (1984). Mother–child dialogues: A comparison of normal and language impaired children. *Journal of Communication Disorders, 17,* 19–35.

Cramblit, N.S., & Siegel, G.M. (1977). The verbal environment of a language-impaired child. *Journal of Speech and Hearing Disorders, 42,* 474–482.

Cross, T.G. (1977). Mothers' speech adjustments: The contribution of selected child listener variables. In C.E. Snow & C.A. Ferguson (Eds.), *Talking to children: Language input and acquisition.* Cambridge, England: Cambridge University Press.

Cross, T.G. (1978). Mothers' speech and its association with rate of linguistic development in young children. In N. Waterson and C. Snow (Eds.), *The Development of Communication.* New York: Wiley.

deVilliers, J. (1983). Patterns of verb use in mother and child. *Papers and Reports on Child Language Development, 22,* 43–48.

Ferracane, B.J., & Dukes, P.J. (1981, November). *Mother–child dyad: What are you doing?* Paper presented at the American Speech-Language-Hearing Association Convention, Los Angeles.

Folger, M., & Leonard, L. (1976). Language and sensorimotor development during the early period of referential speech. *Journal of Speech and Hearing Research, 21,* 519–427.

Friel-Patti, S., & Harris, M. (1984). *Language impaired children's use of play and socially directed behaviors.* Manuscript submitted for publication.

Furrow, D., Nelson, K., & Benedict, H. (1979). Mothers' speech to children and syntactic development: Some simple relationships. *Journal of Child Language, 6,* 423–442.

Garnica, O.K. (1977). Some prosodic and paralinguistic features of speech to young children. In C.E. Snow & C.A. Ferguson (Eds.), *Talking to children: Language input and acquisition.* Cambridge, England: Cambridge University Press.

Gleitman, L.R., Newport, E.L., & Gleitman, H. (1984). The current status of the motherese hypothesis. *Journal of Child Language, 11,* 43–79.

Grossfeld, C. & Heller, E. (1980). *Follow the leader: Why a language impaired child can't be "it."* (*Working Papers in Experimental Speech-Language Pathology and Audiology.* Vol. 9) New York: Department of Communication, Arts and Sciences, Queens College of the City University of New York.

Johnston, J.R. (1982). Interpreting the Leiter IQ: Performance profiles of young normal and language-disordered children. *Journal of Speech and Hearing Research, 25,* 291–296.

Johnston, J., & Kamhi, A. (1980, June). *The same can be less: Syntactic and semantic aspects of utterances of language-impaired children.* Paper presented at the meeting of the Symposium on Research on Child Language Disorders, Madison, Wisconsin.

Kamhi, A.G. (1981). Nonlinguistic symbolic and conceptual abilities of language-impaired and normally developing children. *Journal of Speech and Hearing Research, 24*, 446–453.

Lasky, E.Z., & Klopp, K. (1982). Parent-child interactions in normal and language-disordered children. *Journal of Speech and Hearing Disorders, 47*, 7–18.

Leonard, L., Bolders, J., & Miller, J. (1976). An examination of the semantic relations reflected in the language usage of normal and language disordered children. *Journal of Speech and Hearing Research, 19*, 371–392.

Leonard, L., Steckol, K., & Schwartz, R. (1978). Semantic relations and utterance length in child language. In F. Peng & W. Von Raffler-Engle (Eds.), *Language acquisition and developmental kinesis*. Tokyo: Bunka Hyoron.

Lieven, E.V.M. (1984). Interaction style and children's language learning. *Topics in Language Disorders, 4*(4), 15–23.

MacPherson, C.A., & Weber-Olsen, M. (1980). Mother speech input to deficient and language normal children. *Proceedings from the First Wisconsin Symposium on Research in Child Language Disorders, 1*, 59–79.

Marshall, N., Hegrenes, J., & Goldstein, S. (1973). Verbal interactions: Mothers and their retarded children versus mothers and their nonretarded children. *American Journal of Mental Deficiency, 77*, 415–419.

Menyuk, P. (1964). Comparison of grammar of children with functionally deviant and normal speech. *Journal of Speech and Hearing Research, 7*, 109–21.

Messick, C.K., & Prelock, P.A. (1981, November). *Successful communication: Mothers of language-impaired children vs. mothers of language-normal children.* Paper presented at the American Speech-Language-Hearing Association Convention, Los Angeles.

Newhoff, M., & Browning, J. (1983). Interactional variation: A view from the language-disordered child's world. *Topics in Language Disorders, 4*, 49–60.

Newhoff, M., & Lanner, P.B. (1984). Input as interaction: Shall we dance? In R.C. Naremore (Ed.), *Language science: Recent advances*. San Diego, CA: College-Hill Press.

Newhoff, M., Silverman, L., & Millet, A. (1980). Linguistic differences in parents' speech to normal and language disordered children. *Proceedings from the First Wisconsin Symposium on Research in Child Language Disorders, 1*, 44–57.

Newport, E.L., Gleitman, L.R., & Gleitman, H. (1975). A study of mothers' speech and child language acquisition. *Papers and Reports on Child Language Development, 10*, 111–116.

Newport, E.L., Gleitman, L.R., & Gleitman, H. (1977). Mother, I'd rather do it myself: Some effects and non-effects of maternal speech style. In C.E. Snow & C.A. Ferguson (Eds.), *Talking to children: Language input and acquisition*.

Ochs, E. (1982). Talking to children in Western Samoa. *Language in Society, 11*, 77–104.

Petersen, G.A., & Sherrod, K.B. (1982). Relationship of maternal language to language development and language delay in children. *American Journal of Mental Deficiency, 86*, 391–398.

Piaget, J. (1960). *Psychology of Intelligence*. New Jersey: Littelfield, Adams and Co.

Rondal, J.A. (1977). Maternal speech to normal and Down's syndrome children matched for mean length of utterance. In E. Meyers (Ed.), *Quality of life in severely and profoundly mentally retarded people: Research foundations for improvement*. Washington, DC: American Association of Mental Deficiency.

Schaffer, H. (1979). *Studies in mother–infant interaction*. London: Academic Press.

Schaffer, H.R. (1979). Acquiring the concept of dialogue. In M. Bornstein & W. Kessen (Eds.), *Psychological Development from Infancy: Image to Intention*. Hillsdale, NJ: Erlbaum.

Schieffelin, B.B. (1979). Getting it together: An ethnographic approach to the study of the development of communicative competence. In E. Ochs & B.B. Schieffelin (Eds.), *Developmental Pragmatics*. New York: Academic Press.

Schodorf, J.K., & Edwards, H.T. (1981, November). *Analysis of parental discourse to linguistically disordered and normal children.* Paper presented at the American Speech-Language-Hearing Association Convention, Los Angeles.

Siegel, L.S., Cunningham, C.E., & van der Spuy, H.I.J. (1979, April). *Interaction in delayed and normal preschool children with their mothers.* Paper presented at the Society for Research in Child Development, San Francisco, California.

Snow, C. (1972). Mothers' speech to children learning language. *Child Development, 43*, 1–22.

Snow, C.E., & Ferguson, C.A. (1977). (Eds.), *Talking to children: Language input and acquisition*. Cambridge, England: Cambridge University Press.

Stark, R.E., & Tallal, P. (1981). Selection of children with specific language deficits. *Journal of Speech and Hearing Disorders, 46*, 114–122.

Wulbert, M., Inglis, S., Kriegsmann, E., & Mills, B. (1975). Language delay and associated mother-child interactions. *Developmental Psychology, 11*, 61–70.

A family involvement model for hearing-impaired infants

Mary Trabue Fitzgerald, PhD
Consultant

Rebecca M. Fischer, MSc
Coordinator, Hearing Impaired Services
Mama Lere Parent Infant Training
  Program
Bill Wilkerson Hearing and Speech
  Center
Nashville, Tennessee

OVER THE PAST two decades the development of early intervention programs for parents of hearing-impaired children has received increased attention. The relatively brief history of early intervention programs for hearing-impaired infants and toddlers has progressed through three distinct phases. During the 1960s, the focus of pioneering parent-involvement projects was essentially individualized and child-oriented. That is, parents were trained to implement specific curriculum objectives prescribed by professionals. Pediatric audiologists developed identification and intervention projects that incorporated comprehensive neonatal screening programs, early introduction of wearable amplification, assessment of auditory and language abilities, and intensive training of residual hearing to enhance the development of communication skills (Knox & McConnell, 1968; Pollack, 1970). Recognizing the critical importance of parents to children's early

Top Lang Disord, 1987, 7(3), 1–18
© 1987 Aspen Publishers, Inc.

habilitation, these original models used mothers to teach specific auditory and linguistic skills in home therapy sessions during the period between the detection of a significant hearing loss in infancy and school-based educational services for hearing-impaired children, typically available by age 3.

From the intensive emphasis on parental implementation of auditory–oral training curricula, practitioners gradually expanded their pioneering projects. Parental education regarding the nature of hearing impairment and its impact on the family (Luterman, 1979; Murphy, 1979), as well as specific guidance for parents in teaching functional language skills in routine daily activities (McConnell, 1974; Simmons-Martin, 1981), was incorporated. This second phase of parent involvement programs for hearing-impaired infants was characterized by an active role for parents as full participants in more global habilitation efforts including statewide service delivery models such as the SKI-HI program (Clark & Watkins, 1978) and the UNISTAPS network (Northcott, 1972).

Two separate developments in the field during the decade of the 1970s resulted in this gradual shift toward more emphasis on parental guidance. First, research in the area of normal language acquisition documented the crucial role of maternal–child interactions in the development of communication during the prelinguistic and early linguistic period (see Snow & Ferguson, 1977, and Weiss, 1986, for more recent review). This research provided a strong impetus for recognizing parents as the primary communicative interactants and language models for young hearing-impaired children (Kretschmer &

Kretschmer, 1979). Secondly, the implementation of P.L. 94-142, mandating the participation of parents in educational placement and planning decisions, stimulated more active parent–professional partnerships in all phases of the habilitation process.

The decade of the 1980s has witnessed a continued expansion of the scope of services to families of young hearing-handicapped children. For example, several recent curricula have delineated specific target behaviors for both parents and infants with respect to auditory development, presymbolic communication, initial speech objectives, and receptive and expressive language (Hasenstab & Horner, 1982; Schuyler, Rushmer, Arpan, Melum, Sowers, & Kennedy, 1985). During this third phase of parent-involvement programs, the extended family network as well as extrafamilial caregivers are often included as direct targets of intervention. This expanded scope reflects societal pressures and demographic changes in family patterns, including dual-career and single-parent households. Many programs emphasize the needs of parents and significant others such as siblings, grandparents, and other caregivers for supportive counseling to cope with stress associated with detecting and dealing with a hearing handicap (Moses, 1985; Murphy, 1979).

Pragmatically based research on the quality of caregiver–child interactions among hearing-impaired infants (Blennerhassett, 1984; Matey & Kretschmer, 1985; Weiss, 1986) has focused attention on the variety of sociocommunicative contexts in which young deaf children develop functional communication skills. This gradual evolution toward an integrated, ecological perspective for family involvement projects results from the recognition that the hearing-impaired infant is a member of a family system and a communication network. Such an assumption dictates that intervention efforts must be directed at the systems level rather than exclusively at the child or parent level. This entire range of relationships within the infant's environment must be targeted to develop social networks within which families and alternative caregivers can achieve confidence in their roles, facilitate the interaction patterns that form the basis for language acquisition, and thus ameliorate communication disorders that are secondary to significant hearing impairments.

As an example of this evolutionary process in serving families with hearing-impaired infants and toddlers, the basic assumptions and major components of the Mama Lere Parent–Infant Training Program of the Bill Wilkerson Hearing and Speech Center at Vanderbilt University in Nashville, Tenn., are presented as a model for assessing family needs and developing integrated habilitation program. Finally, critical issues in future intervention efforts with families of hearing-impaired children are discussed.

PREMISES OF THE MAMA LERE PARENT–INFANT TRAINING PROGRAM

The evolution of the Mama Lere Training Program over the past two decades, from a child-oriented model (Knox & McConnell, 1968) to a family-focused project (Fitzgerald & Bess, 1982; Bill Wilkerson Hearing and Speech Center, 1984), is

based on two premises:

1. Families are the social context in which all children, including those with significant hearing losses, grow and develop. Because professionals responsible for habilitation change frequently during the educational process, only families can provide continuous support and ongoing commitment to hearing-impaired children's optimum development. Thus, families in keeping with their own values and choices have a right and a responsibility for maximum involvement in the planning and implementation of early intervention programs.

2. In order to facilitate this meaningful involvement for parents and significant others, the unique needs of each family for emotional support, accurate, understandable information, and specific guidance to optimize their child's communicative development must be recognized and incorporated into individual habilitation plans. In addition, ongoing assessment of both child progress and family status must provide for frequent monitoring and for necessary modifications of specific interventions.

Based on these premises, the Mama Lere Program addresses the multiplicity of child and family concerns and builds on individual strengths within each system of significant others to create an effective intervention plan.

Service delivery components

Within this ecological framework, the Mama Lere Project has evolved four service delivery components, shown in Figure 1.

Supportive counseling

The family support component represents a process in which parents and others who are significant in infants' lives are offered a variety of opportunities to meet their expressed needs for sharing individual concerns with staff members and developing mutual support systems with other families who face similar problems. A number of professionals in early intervention (Luterman, 1979; Moses, 1985; Turnbull & Turnbull, 1986) have concluded that supportive counseling is the first service that should be provided to families following the initial diagnosis of a handicap and that assistance should be extended beyond the early periods of grief and adjustment to include establishing a

Significant Others

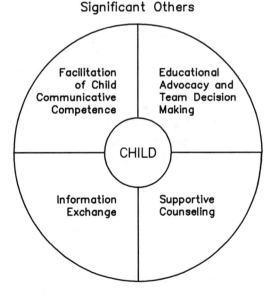

Figure 1. Service delivery components in an ecological framework.

permanent mutual support network for families of handicapped children to meet the varying and changing needs of significant others as children grow and mature.

Many families choose to share their concerns in individual sessions with staff members; some participate in group discussions with other parents and invited counselors.

In the Mama Lere program, these needs are addressed through a number of options from which families can select the types of services that they prefer. Many families choose to share their concerns in individual sessions with staff members; some participate in group discussions with other parents and invited counselors. A number of significant others prefer informal group sharing experiences or one-to-one conversations with families whose situations closely match their own. The development of a "parent-to-parent" system, in which families with older hearing-impaired children who have been in the program over an extended period of time are paired with families of newly diagnosed children, has been particularly successful. Feedback from significant others participating in this program suggests that the intimacy and the intensity of support offered by peers who have confronted similar circumstances may be more effective than professional counseling for many families.

Information exchange

In the information-sharing component of the Mama Lere Program, adult family members, older siblings, and other important caregivers begin to acquire the knowledge base and form attitudes necessary to become effective change agents through discussing observations of their children's current level of functioning, the communication environment available in the social network, and management of hearing impairments and amplification systems. The emphasis is on sharing perceptions, exchanging observations, and a commitment by the professional staff that significant others are indeed experts concerning their own children and that a variety of family structures and attitudes regarding child development can provide appropriate contexts for hearing-impaired infants.

Strategies that have proven particularly effective in facilitating open exchanges of information and opinions include family discussion groups planned and implemented by parents to address high-priority topics such as child management, coping with stress, hearing impairment and adolescence, and new technological advances. Weekend and evening parent meetings offer opportunities to explore basic information concerning audition, hearing aid management, speech development, and language facilitation with newly enrolled families in a context of mutual support. These concepts are then examined in greater detail in individual family sessions through interviews, discussion, and demonstration, as well as selected videotape and print media. Through these types of activities, significant others explore their own attitudes and learn to understand their children's developmental needs as an essential step in the family-based habilitation effort.

Educational advocacy

The major premise of the Mama Lere advocacy component is the position that advocacy is a positive process involving both rights and responsibilities and that families of hearing-impaired infants can learn advocacy skills as well as other important parenting skills (Fitzgerald, 1984). Advocacy training for individual families involves the following process:

1. Development of a thorough understanding of the educational needs and local placement options available to hearing-impaired children (Nix, 1977; Testut & Baldwin, 1977).
2. Information about families' rights to appropriate educational services and parental involvement in the planning process (Turnbull & Turnbull, 1986).
3. Training in skills necessary to actively collaborate and negotiate in decision-making conferences as full participants (Muir, Milan, Branston-McLean, & Berger, 1982).
4. Training in critical evaluation and independent monitoring of services offered (Ross & Calvert, 1977).
5. Development of an awareness of continuing political responsibilities for insuring appropriate services (Northcott, 1980).

Frequently used activities for achieving these objectives, such as on-site observations, negotiation training through role playing, group parent meetings, community advocacy workshops, and panel discussions are matched to individual family styles and needs. Families with school-age hearing-impaired children and outside child advocates often assist the staff in implementing various aspects of the training model, and significant others routinely are introduced to local organizations specializing in advocacy for all handicapped individuals while still in the infant program. The choice of specific activities depends on the age of the children and the number of families involved as well as the educational options available within a local school system and the amount of time available for individual family advocacy training.

Survey data (Fitzgerald, 1984) collected from parents who have participated in the Mama Lere Program indicate that knowledge of their child's educational needs was clearly ranked as the highest priority objective by families, closely followed by knowledge of educational options and potential placements. Following participation in advocacy training, parents rated themselves as knowledgeable in these areas and indicated a high degree of satisfaction with individual advocacy training sessions and small-group discussions offered by preschool and parent–infant specialists. In contrast to other reported surveys of parental participation in educational decision making (Lusthaus, Lusthaus, & Gibbs, 1981), these families reported high levels of active participation in their children's Individualized Education Program conferences and standard multidisciplinary team staffings.

Facilitation of communicative competence

The fourth and most familiar component of the Mama Lere family involvement project is facilitation of adult–child interactions during which the staff and significant others explore techniques and strategies to enhance the development of functional communication skills for individual children (Bill Wilkerson Hearing and Speech Center, 1984; Fitzgerald & Bess, 1982). This process involves analyses of communicative interactions between hearing-impaired infants and significant others in daily caregiving routines and play sessions using clinical observations (Cole & St. Clair-Stokes, 1984; Russo & Owens, 1982) and modeling by the habilitation specialists of specific types of interactions that are associated with language acquisition in normally developing infants. Family members are encouraged to incorporate basic principles of reciprocity, contingency, and semantic relatedness into daily routines in their homes and caregiving settings. The use of communication sampling enables staff members and parents to examine which particular adult facilitation strategies appear to be most reinforcing for individual infants in specific contexts and to monitor both adult and child progress on a regular basis. Individualized objectives in speech, language, audition, and other developmental domains are defined by the staff and family through the instructional decision-making model described later (Fischer & Kenworthy, in press). Then specific instructional strategies, including a combination of incidental techniques and directed teaching activities, are developed for achieving those objectives within an integrated approach to communication training.

By incorporating multiple objectives into familiar contexts with a variety of significant others in natural communicative environments, the principles of pragmatic language theories (Bruner, 1983; Prutting, 1982) are implemented in a habilitative process that maintains the specificity of individualized objectives, which are periodically evaluated. This integrated approach to curriculum management is particularly effective in preserving and supporting the natural facilitative interactions between infants and their families while targetting a developmentally appropriate sequence of communication skills for hearing-impaired infants. In addition, specific training in the management of amplification devices (Bill Wilkerson Hearing and Speech Center, 1984), in establishing listening skills through a program of sequenced auditory experiences (Bill Wilkerson Hearing and Speech Center, 1984), and in enhancing infant vocalizations that are the precursors of later speech development (Ling, 1976; Ling & Ling, 1978) are offered to those family members or significant others who have the major responsibility for daily care.

These four service-delivery components of supportive counseling, information exchange, advocacy training, and facilitation of communicative competence are woven into a wide variety of intervention plans individually tailored to the unique requirements of each child and family as determined during the assessment–intervention decision-making process.

Assessment–intervention decision-making model

Assessment approach

One of the distinguishing characteristics of the Mama Lere Parent–Infant Program is the individuality of each assess-

ment and intervention plan. The model (adapted from Kenworthy & Fischer, in press) shown in Figure 2 involves the evaluation of both child and family status, including the child's capabilities as an interlocutor and the significant other's concerns and attitudes.

Evaluating the skills of hearing-impaired infants entails assessing level of functioning in a number of different areas directly and indirectly related to communication development. Following the areas of identification and referral, the sensory/perceptual and communicative level of function is determined using a variety of assessment procedures selected to accurately evaluate the status of both child and family. After interpretation of test results, appropriate amplification or alternative devices are selected, and the infant's performance with the recommended instrument provides a baseline for intervention in the auditory domain.

A similar procedure is followed in assessing the child's communication skills. By carefully selecting evaluation instruments appropriate for the infant and family, the outcome of the assessment process provides answers to five important questions, which in turn enable the clinician to intervene effectively.

First, at what level of ability is the infant currently functioning? Information on language production (i.e., syntax, semantics, pragmatics, phonology, voice) and comprehension (i.e., semantics, syntax, situational), cognition, gross and fine motor skills, oral–motor skills, self-help, and personal–social skills assists the assessment team in delineating communication abilities as well as other behaviors. In selecting evaluation instruments, the ob-

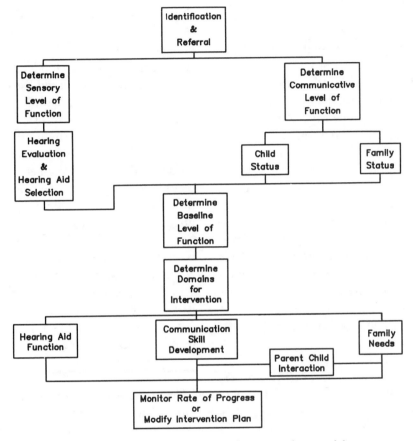

Figure 2. Assessment–intervention decision-making model.

jectivity of formal tests is combined with parental interviews and observation sampling procedures to assess language comprehension and production (see Hasenstab & Horner, 1982, for a review of assessment procedures). In addition, cognitive skills are evaluated as they relate to the infant's linguistic level. The result of such an assessment is a broad perspective of the child's abilities and a delineation of developmental areas that require intervention. Especially important to note is large discrepancies in the child's performance across skill areas. Such differences may dictate the need for modification in the intervention approach or therapeutic emphasis (Miller, 1981).

Second, what is the next stage or level in developing the infant's communication skills? Because few assessment tools provide comprehensive therapeutic outlines, the linkage between assessment and intervention is weak in many currently available programs for hearing-impaired children. Testing provides information on the child's current level, but few suggestions are offered on the next appropriate objectives. Thus it is important that the evaluation team choose assessment tools that provide information that can be used in conjunction with a selected outline for language intervention.

At the Mama Lere Parent–Infant Training Program, an outline for the development of communicative competence serves as a guide for language intervention. This comprehensive but flexible guide ensures that important communication milestones are addressed in an individualized approach adapted to the needs of each child and family. Following initial interviews with the parents and observation of parent and child, the clinician determines the child's approximate level of linguistic competence and then selects appropriate test procedures to facilitate examination of the child's current communication abilities and designation of future goals and objectives as defined in the outline.

Third, at what rate is the infant developing communication skills? Little normative data is available to compare the performance of an individual child with other hearing-impaired infants. Yet it is crucial that such information on rate of progress be included where possible in order to ensure that the therapy strategies employed are effective. The Grammatical Analysis of Elicited Language Tests (Moog & Geers, 1979; Moog, Kozak, & Geers, 1983) are syntactically based assessments that provide normative data on hearing-impaired children, while a number of comprehensive language outlines (Bloom & Lahey, 1978; Miller, 1981) also provide a means of comparing the performance of hearing-impaired children with that of their normal-hearing peers.

Fourth, what is the most effective intervention approach to achieve immediate goals and objectives? Another outcome of

the assessment procedure is the formulation of strategies for developing more advanced communication skills. Rarely is this areas included in standard evaluation protocols, yet it is essential for the success of any intervention program. The habilitation specialist gains information on the appropriateness of structured versus unstructured activities, communication mode, and specific language facilitation techniques in eliciting the desired communication from the infant. Through language-sampling procedures, the significant others and the child are observed with respect to the "matching" of their communication behaviors. From this analysis, the clinicians can determine the family's strengths and weaknesses in facilitating the child's language learning and decide on the focus for therapy.

Through language-sampling procedures, the significant others and the child are observed with respect to the "matching" of their communication behaviors.

Finally, what are the strengths and needs of the family and significant others in the child's life? Through open-ended interviews addressing such areas as family resources, interactions, functions, and the family life cycle, the dynamics of the family system are described. Only by first meeting the needs of the family and viewing the child as a part of a communication and family system can individualized therapeutic goals for the child be achieved. In many ways, the information gained about the family system provides the clinician with important clues concerning the most effective intervention approaches for the infant.

As a result of this assessment process, which is ongoing rather than time-bound, the intervention specialists develop individualized therapy plans that incorporate the strengths of the family–child system and have as a primary goal the continued development of the infant as a communicator and the strengthening of the parent–child interaction.

Intervention

Once baseline functioning levels are established through initial assessment, intervention focuses on three domains that are continually monitored: family status, hearing aid functioning, and communication skill development (Fischer & Kenworthy, in press).

Acknowledging the impact of a hearing-impaired child on the family, parents and siblings participate in a variety of experiences and activities with professionals and other families through the four service-delivery components depicted in Figure 1. The intervention plan is determined by the individual family's needs and concerns, capitalizes on the strengths of the significant others, and addresses any vulnerabilities (Luterman, 1979; Moses, 1985). Thus the uniqueness of each family system provides the framework for managing all other aspects of the habilitation program.

The importance of audition as a modality for processing linguistic input is underscored through systematic 3-month re-evaluations and the prominent role of the daily hearing aid monitor program (Han-

ners & Sitton, 1974). Over the past 15 years, a comprehensive system has evolved that includes the use of the Five Sound Test (Ling & Ling, 1978), a live-voice presentation of several vowels and consonants spanning the speech spectrum, to note changes in hearing aid function or the child's detection of the speech signal. Careful instruction and demonstration of the effects of noise and distance on the ability of the infant to interpret verbal messages and achieve meaningful auditory experience is provided for adult family members.

Building communication skills of the hearing-impaired child involves elaborating on the existing skills of the child and significant others. For the most part, available parent–infant curricula provide guidance for the development of speech, language, and audition as distinct areas, defining goals and objectives within each constituent domain (Hasenstab & Horner, 1982; Schuyler et el., 1985). While this approach helps to clarify goals and emphasizes the hierarchical nature of communication skills, it fails to address the parallel development of language, speech, and auditory abilities and the interaction among skill areas. As a result, the teaching of communicative competence is often fragmented such that language, speech, and auditory objectives are "taught" as "activities" rather than developed within an integrated communication setting. It is therefore necessary to provide some means of reintegrating separate skill sequences derived from available curricula in a manner that helps clinicians design therapy plans that incorporate each of the three skill areas into functional communication exchanges.

Recognizing that parent–child dialogues are the underlying motivation and the natural context for the acquisition of communicative competence, the Mama Lere Program has developed a framework (shown in Figure 3) that highlights the interaction between emerging child behaviors and adult facilitative behaviors as well as the integration of communication skills in the language, speech, and auditory domains. Language, speech, and auditory skills are delineated for each developmental stage (prelinguistic, single word, and word combination levels). Then both adult and child behaviors are defined for the integrated communication skills at each successive level. Using the framework as a guide, clinicians plan intervention activities and strategies that capitalize on and use the naturally occurring, normal interactions between caregivers and infants to develop and integrate communication skills. One of the early therapeutic goals is to match adult and child behaviors to facilitate the emergence of communicative competence. For example, at the prelinguistic level, a pragmatic goal for both parent and child is to develop strong turn-taking skills, so that the adult reinforces infant vocalizations and the infant increases vocal efforts. Although these might be defined as language goals, the reciprocity established between the adult and the child also provides a context for practicing speech sounds. The Ling Speech Program (Ling, 1976) is easily adapted to the emerging and facilitating behaviors of the hearing-impaired infant and parent by incorporating babbling practice (repetition and alternation of syllables) into short games and songs shared by the dyad. Similarly, a simple calling

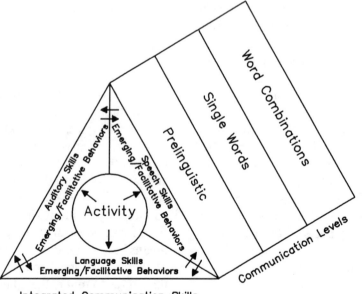

Figure 3. Framework depicting the interaction between emerging child behaviors and adult facilitative behaviors.

game used to develop auditory attention also incorporates the pragmatic goal of establishing reciprocity in early communicative exchanges.

For example, at the level of word combinations, one language goal might be the answering of *wh*-questions when reading a simple story. Specific objectives might include: (a) answering routine questions; (b) using two-word utterances to express location and possession; (c) discriminating between two-word linguistic units; and (d) practicing phonemic-level speech. Using "The Three Bears," questions such as *Where is Mama Bear's chair?* or *Where is Papa Bear's bed?* facilitate the accomplishment of receptive language objectives while helping the child retell the story encourages the use of phrases such as *Baby Bear's bowl*, incorporating expressive language and speech objectives. In this approach, particular importance is placed on integrating semantic, syntactic, and pragmatic language functions with other communication skills to expedite the natural learning of objectives.

An essential component of effective intervention programs is the continual monitoring of rate of progress within the framework of staffing procedures involving family members. The results of both formal tests and observational measures are useful in determining whether the child's communication skills continue to improve with respect to chronological age. Intervention approaches, intensity of programming, educational placement, mode of communication, and parental commitment all affect performance. Lack of progress may dictate a reevaluation of program targets and methods, and modifications in one or more areas to better match the individual needs of the family and child. Discussion of recommendations and new procedures with significant others ensures that changes in programming are clearly understood and supported by all team members.

Like other family-oriented approaches (Moses, 1985; Turnbull & Turnbull, 1986), the intervention model used by the Mama Lere Program recognizes the individuality of each family and emphasizes the relationship between professionals and the parents as they work together to develop a program tailored to the needs of the child and family. It seeks to maximize the flexibility of the habilitation program, allowing the team to modify a number of intervention components and to provide support for the family's efforts. As such, this model can be used with many different service delivery systems or curricula and focuses on providing the best options for each individual family, taking into account the differences in approaches and families. The developmentally based communication framework integrates

> *The developmentally based communication framework integrates component skills and incorporates each with naturally occurring dialogues between the adult and infant, again emphasizing the uniqueness of the parent–child relationship.*

component skills and incorporates each within naturally occurring dialogues between the adult and infant, again emphasizing the uniqueness of the parent–child relationship. Thus, rather than fitting every family into a specified curriculum, the model allows the early intervention specialists to create a variety of individualized programs using each family system as the foundation on which to develop infant communication abilities.

The following case studies demonstrate how the intervention strategies and focus are designed with respect to the child's rehabilitative needs and to family dynamics.

CASE STUDY 1

Larry (not his real name) was identified at 2;5 years of age as demonstrating a moderately severe bilateral sensorineural hearing loss with recurrent middle ear infections. He was the only child of a single mother who had no immediate family in Nashville, Tennessee and was living with a friend until she could afford an apartment of her own. Shortly after enrollment, Larry was dismissed from the day care program because of biting and other aggressive behaviors.

Formal testing was attempted but could not be conducted because of Larry's noncompliant behavior and a short attention span. Observation and parents' reports indicated that Larry was functioning at approximately the 6–12 month level with respect to speech and language skills, while gross and fine motor skills were within normal limits for a 2-year-old. Results of a cognitive screening and play assessment revealed cognitive skills clustered at the 9–12-month level and immature play behaviors. Observation of parent and child indicated that Larry's lack of

attention and inappropriate behavior made it difficult to sustain meaningful interaction, although for short periods of time reciprocal play was established and maintained. He refused to wear amplification for extended periods of time. Larry was referred for a comprehensive psychological and medical evaluation, and the mother was encouraged to obtain professional counseling to deal more effectively with the challenges facing her.

Larry's mother declined to pursue the referrals, but wanted to continue weekly therapy. An initial intervention program was designed to provide emotional support for the parent and to share information on normal child development with the expectation that, in the future, Larry's mother would feel more comfortable pursuing the program's recommendations for further testing and counseling. Therapy emphasized the use of all modalities to develop basic prelinguistic communication skills such as joint referencing, focused attention, and reciprocity. Activities were designed to enhance parent–child interaction in unstructured daily routines and informal play. Behavior management techniques that ignored undesirable behaviors and reinforced appropriate interactive behaviors were introduced. In addition, middle-ear function was monitored, and a schedule for daily hearing-aid use was developed to gradually increase Larry's tolerance for hearing aids.

Following 4 months of therapy and increased problems in the second day-care placement, Larry's mother agreed to place her child in a behavior-disordered class at a local mental health facility in addition to continuing therapy. Two months later, professionals at both institutions again encouraged the mother to arrange for additional testing, and she agreed.

Following the evaluation, Larry was enrolled in a private school for emotionally disturbed children with supplemental services from the public-school hearing-impaired itinerant teaching program. Through observation and case conferences, professionals remain in close contact and reinforce goals developed jointly. Larry's mother has become an effective advocate for her son and knowledgeable about his educational needs.

Larry is now 4 years old and uses sign language and speech to respond to limited requests and to label objects and actions during highly structured activities.

CASE STUDY 2

Dana (not her real name) was identified at 12 months of age as demonstrating a profound bilateral sensorineural hearing loss. She was the only child of a young rural couple who live 1.5 hours from Nashville, Tennessee. Strong family support for this couple was provided by both maternal and paternal grandparents. Results of informal testing, observation, and an interview with the parents suggested that Dana's language skills clustered at the 3–9 month level, while other developmental areas were age-appropriate.

Therapy sessions were scheduled late in the afternoons and on Saturday to accommodate the father's work schedule and enable him to participate. Other family members were encouraged to attend the bimonthly sessions as well as workshops and parent meetings. The parents were "paired" with another rural family who had a hearing-impaired child 1 year older than Dana. Through long-distance telephone conversations, the two families shared experiences and similar educational concerns. Intervention focused on the development of communication skills through the auditory mode, emphasizing interaction between parents and child during play and daily activities. Advocacy issues were discussed to prepare Dana's parents for their role in securing rehabilitation services for their child in a small rural community where alternatives within the local school system were limited.

At 4 years of age, Dana's language skills were assessed to be at the 24–30-month level. Following reevaluation, it was decided to integrate Dana in a preschool class with other normal-hearing children. A staff member accompanied Dana's mother in investigating the few preschool programs available in a nearby town. In this manner, the parent was trained to observe features such as class size, acoustic treatment, qualities of the teacher, curriculum, and schedule, which were all important in selecting an educational setting for Dana.

At 6 years of age, Dana and her family moved into town where the public school program was considered to be superior to that in the surrounding county. At this time, Dana's communication skills were evaluated by the school district and determined to be commensurate with those of entering normal-hearing kindergartners. Yet school personnel, who had no previous experience in mainstreaming hearing-impaired children, were hesitant to integrate Dana and suggested a self-contained classroom for hearing-impaired children using total communication. Using their advocacy training, Dana's parents persuaded the district to place their child in the mainstreamed kindergarten classroom on a trial basis, contingent on her ability to perform at grade level. They also secured audiological services and an auditory trainer for classroom use.

Dana, now 7, is mainstreamed in a first-grade classroom and is performing at grade level.

These two case studies demonstrate some of the child and family variables that are important considerations in developing dynamic intervention approaches. Although many differences existed between the two families, both were given information that enabled them to become effective advocates for their child and to pursue and select appropriate education options.

FUTURE CHALLENGES

The gradual evolution of programs for hearing-impaired infants and toddlers over the past 20 years represents a significant shift toward integrated, ecological models based firmly in research on normal language acquisition and the primacy of significant others in the development of communicative competence. This shifting perspective presents numerous challenges to early interventionists who will attempt to implement service delivery systems in the future.

Despite recently initiated research projects to develop new procedures for cost-effective screening for hearing losses and other communicative disorders in com-

munity primary health care settings, the median age of entrance into the diagnostic and intervention services at the Bill Wilkerson Center and the Mama Lere Program is close to 2 years. Thus, early detection of hearing loss remains an elusive goal after more than 20 years of experience in providing readily available assessment and habilitation services for infants and toddlers regardless of the family's economic status. Perhaps those concerned with health care needs and services for young children have yet to make a major commitment to the concept of valid and reliable screening and identification programs to detect hearing impairment within the first year of life (Bess & McConnell, 1981).

An even greater challenge is to provide intervention specialists with the perspectives, knowledge, and skills needed to establish ecologically based family involvement models (Northcott, 1973). The traditional coursework and clinical practicum experiences of personnel preparation programs in audiology, speech–language pathology, and education of the hearing-impaired rarely train students to work effectively with family-related problems, to integrate communication objectives, or to participate in interdisciplinary teams addressing the multiplicity of family and infant needs. Without axiological frameworks and theoretical models that support the value of family-oriented, pragmatically based interventions, and lacking preservice or inservice experience in exemplary service-delivery systems, practitioners remained tied to child-oriented, segmented curricula. Similarly, effective implementation of ecological habilitation programs requires recognition and consideration of varying family values, structures, and sociocultural backgrounds as well as differences in the degree of participation families choose (Turnbull & Turnbull, 1986). Families at different stages in their development (Turnbull & Turnbull, 1986) and adjustments to living with a hearing-handicapped child (Murphy, 1979) require different balances of support, information, and specific training.

The development of liaisons with service-delivery systems at the preschool level and beyond presents another challenge for ecological family involvement models. While providing assistance to individual families in selecting appropriate educational placements through strong advocacy components, habilitation specialists must also work diligently with other professionals to ensure that intervention techniques and integrated curricula that enhance the communicative competence achieved in infant projects are available to all children as they graduate to formal education institutions. Likewise, early interventionists must assist families in identifying additional community resources to meet their unique financial, medical, and social needs as well as providing linkages with local, state, and national advocacy organizations for hearing-impaired individuals.

• • •

The need for additional longitudinal research that documents the efficacy of early intervention and addresses the issue of the "fit" between family characteristics and specific intervention options remains a major challenge. New assessment approaches are urgently needed (Wolery & Bailey, 1984) that measure variables not only concerning the child but also concerning characteristics of families such as stress, support systems, attitudes toward child-rearing, and sense of control both as outcome and as mediating variables. Such assessment will evaluate the long-term as well as short-term effects of early intervention with hearing-impaired children. The significant methodological difficulties in producing sound efficacy data, including threats to internal validity, extensive reliance on pretest/posttest designs, a narrow range of outcome measures, and weak linkages between programmatic goals and dependent measures (Strain, 1984; White, Mastropieri & Castro, 1984), must not deter continued early intervention research. Although caution should be exercised in generalizing from specific small samples to the general population of hearing-impaired children, the limited evidence available from several established family-involvement models for hearing-impaired infants including the Mama Lere Project (Fitzgerald & Bess, 1982; Hanners, 1977; McConnell, 1974; McConnell & Liff, 1975; Simmons-Martin, 1981; Weiss, Goodwin & Moores, 1975) suggests that many hearing-impaired children who participate in family-focused infant programs have the capability to develop functional oral and written language to learn in regular academic settings with supportive help, and to achieve academically and linguistically at substantially higher levels than national samples of hearing-impaired children at the elementary and secondary school levels.

REFERENCES

Bess, F.H., & McConnell, F.E. (1981). *Audition, education, and the hearing-impaired child.* St.Louis, MO: C.V. Mosby.

Bill Wilkerson Hearing and Speech Center. (1984, July). *Programming for preschool hearing-impaired children.* Symposium presented at the Bill Wilkerson Hearing and Speech Center, Nashville, TN.

Blennerhassett, L. (1984). Communicative styles of a 13-month-old hearing impaired child and her parents. *Volta Review, 86,* 217–228.

Bloom, L., & Lahey, M. (1978). *Language development and language disorders.* New York: Wiley.

Brunner, J.S. (1983). *Child's talk: Learning to use language.* New York: Norton.

Clark, T.C., & Watkins, S. (1978). *The SKI-HI model: A comprehensive model for identification, language facilitation, and family support for hearing handicapped children through home management, ages birth to six* (3rd ed.). Logan, UT: Utah State University.

Cole, E., & St. Clair-Stokes, J. (1984). Caregiver-child interactive behavior: A videotape analysis procedure. *Volta Review, 86,* 200–217.

Fischer, R.M., & Kenworthy, O.T. (in press). Intervention with preschool hearing-impaired children, In D.E. Yoder & R.D. Kent (Eds.), *Decision making in speech-language pathology.* Toronto: B.C. Decker.

Fitzgerald, M.T. (1984, June). *Advocacy training for parents of hearing-impaired children: A five stage model.* Paper presented at the meeting of the Alexander Graham Bell Assn. for the Deaf, Portland, OR.

Fitzgerald, M.T., & Bess, F.H. (1982). Parent/infant training for hearing-impaired children. *Monographs in Contemporary Audiology, 3*(3).

Hanners, B.A. (1977). *A study of language skills in thirty-four hearing impaired children for whom remediation began before age three.* Unpublished doctoral dissertation, Vanderbilt University, Nashville, TN.

Hanners, B.A., & Sitton, A.B. (1974). Ears to hear: A daily hearing aid monitoring program. *Volta Review, 76,* 530–536.

Hasenstab, M.S., & Horner, J. (1982). *Comprehensive intervention with hearing-impaired infants and preschool children.* Rockville, MD: Aspen Systems Corporation.

Kenworthy, O.T., & Fischer, R.M. (in press). Assessment and the hearing-impaired child. In D.E. Yoder & R.D. Kent (Eds.), *Decision making in speech-language pathology.* Toronto: B.C. Decker.

Knox, L.L., & McConnell, F. (1968). Helping parents to help deaf infants. *Children, 15,* 183–187.

Kretschmer, R., & Kretschmer, L. (1979). The acquisition of linguistic and communicative competence. Parent-child interactions. *Volta Review, 81,* 306–322.

Ling, D. (1976). *Speech and the hearing-impaired child: Theory and practice.* Washington, DC: Alexander Graham Bell Assn. for the Deaf.

Ling, D., & Ling, A.H. (1978). *Aural habilitation: Foundations of verbal learning in hearing-impaired children.* Washington, DC: Alexander Graham Bell Assn. for the Deaf.

Lusthaus, C.S., Lusthaus, E.W., & Gibbs, H. (1981). Parents' roles in the decision process. *Exceptional Children, 48,* 256–267.

Luterman, D. (1979). *Counseling parents of hearing-impaired children.* Boston: Little, Brown.

Matey, C., & Kretschmer, R. (1985). A comparison of mother's speech to Down's Syndrome, hearing-impaired children. *Volta Review, 87,* 205–215.

McConnell, F.E. (1974). The parent teaching home: An early intervention program for hearing-impaired children. *Peabody Journal of Education, 51,* 162–170.

McConnell, F.E., & Liff, S. (1975). The rationale for early identification and intervention. *Otolaryngology Clinics of North America, 8,* 77–87.

Miller, J.F. (1981). *Assessing language production in children.* Baltimore: University Park Press.

Moog, J.S., & Geers, A.E. (1979). *Grammatical analysis of elicited language—simple sentence level.* St. Louis, MO: Central Institute for the Deaf.

Moog, J.S., Kozak, V.J., & Geers, A.E. (1983). *Grammatical analysis of elicited language—presentence level.* St. Louis, MO: Central Institute for the Deaf.

Moses, K.L. (1985). Dynamic intervention with families. In *Hearing-impaired children and youth with developmental disabilities: An interdisciplinary foundation for service.* Washington, DC: Gallaudet College Press.

Muir, K.A., Milan, M.A., Branston-McLean, M.E., & Berger, M. (1982). Advocacy training for parents of handicapped children: A staff responsibility. *Young Children, 37,* 41–46.

Murphy, A.T. (Ed.). (1979). The families of hearing-impaired children. *Volta Review, 81*(5).

Nix, G. (Ed.). (1977). *The rights of hearing-impaired children.* Washington, DC: Alexander Graham Bell Assn. for the Deaf.

Northcott, W.H. (1972). *Curriculum guide: Hearing-impaired children—birth to three years, and their parents.* Washington, DC: Alexander Graham Bell Assn. for the Deaf.

Northcott, W.H. (1973). Competencies needed by teachers of hearing-impaired infants, birth to three years, and their parents. *Volta Review, 75,* 532–544.

Northcott, W.H. (1980). On behalf of parents in the IEP process. *Volta Review, 82,* 7–13.

Pollack, D. (1970). *Educational audiology for the limited hearing infant.* Springfield, IL: Charles C Thomas.

Prutting, C.A. (1982). Pragmatics as social competence. *Journal of Speech and Hearing Disorders, 47,* 123–134.

Ross, M., & Calvert, D.R. (1977). Guidelines for audiology programs in education settings for hearing-impaired children. *Volta Review, 79*(3), 153–161.

Russo, J.B., & Owens, R.E. (1982). The development of an objective observation tool for parent-child interaction. *Journal of Speech and Hearing Disorders, 47,* 165–173.

Schuyler, V.S., Rushmer, N., Arpan, R.K., Melum, A., Sowers, J., & Kennedy, N. (1985). *Parent-infant communication* (3rd ed.). Portland, OR: Infant Hearing Resource.

Simmons-Martin, A. (1981). Efficacy report: Early education project. *Journal of the Division for Early Childhood, 4,* 5–10.

Snow, C.E., & Ferguson, C.A. (Eds.), (1977). *Talking to children: Language input and acquisition.* Cambridge: Cambridge University Press.

Strain, P.S. (1984). Efficacy research with young handicapped children: A critique of the status quo. *Journal of the Division for Early Childhood, 9*(1), 4–10.

Testut, E.W., & Baldwin, R.L. (1977). Educational options. *Volta Review, 79,* 281–286.

Turnbull, A.P., & Turnbull, H.R. (1986). *Families, professionals and exceptionality: A special partnership.* Columbus, OH: Charles E. Merrill.

Weiss, A. (Ed.), (1986). Language disorders and hearing impairment: Implications from normal child language. *Topics in Language Disorders, 6*(3).

Weiss, K.C., Goodwin, M.W., & Moores, D.F. (1975). *Characteristics of young deaf children and early intervention programs* (Research Report 91 Proj. No. 332189). (DHEW Grant No. OE–09–33219–4533(032)). Minneapolis: University of Minnesota.

White, K.R., Mastropiere, M., & Casto, G. (1984). An analysis of special education early childhood projects approved by the joint dissemination review panel. *Journal of the Division for Early Childhood, 9*(1), 11–26.

Wolery, M., & Bailey, D.E. (1984). Alternative to impact evaluations. Suggestions for program evaluation in early intervention. *Journal of the Division for Early Childhood, 9*(1), 27–37.

Peers as communication intervention agents: Some new strategies and research findings

Howard Goldstein, PhD
Associate Professor of Communication and Psychiatry
Department of Communication

Phillip S. Strain, PhD
Associate Professor of Child Psychiatry & Special Education
School of Medicine
University of Pittsburgh
Pittsburgh, Pennsylvania

AMONG THE social deficits of handicapped children, a lack of communicative interaction skills is of utmost concern. Communicative interaction skills provide the primary means of control over the social environment. Furthermore, when interaction is infrequent, the handicapped child is not only conceding control over the environment, but opportunities for learning language and other skills are greatly diminished. Consequently, interventions that focus on the early use of language skills to engage others in conversational interchanges are needed.

As handicapped children have been mainstreamed into regular education, their lack of social and communication

Support for this article was provided by Contract No. 300-82-0368 (Early Childhood Research Institute) from the U.S. Department of Education and Grant No. MH37110-5 from the National Institutes of Mental Health to the University of Pittsburgh. The opinions expressed herein do not necessarily reflect the position or policy of either agency and no official endorsement should be inferred.

Top Lang Disord, 1988, 9(1), 44–57
© 1988 Aspen Publishers, Inc.

skills have become increasingly apparent. Many handicapped children are socially withdrawn and rarely interact with peers. Frequently, peers will attempt to interact initially, but lack of response from the handicapped children may extinguish these attempts. One approach has been to teach communicative skills to the handicapped children directly. Another, less direct approach has been to teach peers to initiate and sustain communicative interaction with these children.

Two peer intervention strategies developed from studies of social and play skills of handicapped and nonhandicapped children in developmentally integrated settings follow. In the first intervention, normally developing peers are taught to use strategies that promote interaction on the part of initially socially withdrawn classmates. In the second intervention both handicapped and nonhandicapped children are taught sociodramatic play scripts that provide a basis for improved interaction during free play. These interventions represent effective ways to expand communication training in integrated settings.

ENHANCING SOCIAL INTERACTION AMONG CHILDREN

The literature on social interaction provides a conceptual and procedural basis for developing peer-mediated communicative interventions. Several researchers have shown that peers may help to increase the positive social behavior of handicapped children (e.g., Guralnick, 1986; Hendrickson, Strain, Tremblay, & Shores, 1982; Strain, 1977; Strain, Shores, & Timm, 1977). It has been suggested that

observation of peer models and interaction with peers may aid linguistic–communicative development of handicapped children (Guralnick, 1976, 1981a, 1981b; Guralnick & Paul-Brown, 1977, 1980, 1984). Although peers have served as models and reinforcement agents in structured language intervention sessions (e.g., Guralnick, 1976) they have rarely been used as change agents to promote communicative interaction in less structured situations.

Several methods have been used to investigate the social interaction of children. These include

- descriptive studies of normal, handicapped, and integrated groups of children (e.g., Fenrick, Pearson, & Pepelnjak, 1984; Guralnick & Paul-Brown, 1977, 1980, 1984; Tremblay, Strain, Hendrickson, & Shores, 1981);
- empirical research on training specific skills to handicapped children (e.g., Kohl, Beckman, & Swenson-Pierce, 1984); and
- empirical research on training peers to be intervention agents (e.g., Goldstein & Ferrell, 1987; Goldstein & Wickstrom, 1986; Odom, Hoyson, Jamieson, & Strain, 1985; Strain, Hoyson, & Jamieson, 1985).

Descriptive studies

A number of variables have been shown to significantly alter the rate of social interaction between children. These variables include the number and kinds of materials available, the sex of the children available for interaction, physical arrangement of space, and teacher involvement in directing activities (see Tremblay,

Strain, Hendrickson, & Shores, 1981). Other descriptive studies have evaluated the attending behavior (Fenrick, Pearson, & Pepelnjak, 1984), language skills (Guralnick & Paul-Brown, 1977, 1980, 1984, 1986), and play skills (Faught, Balleweg, Crow, & Van Den Pol, 1983; Peterson & Haralick, 1977) of handicapped as well as normally developing children in integrated and segregated settings, primarily during free play. Tremblay et al. (1981) examined the social behavior of normal preschool children to provide a normative basis for subject and target behavior selection. Peterson and Haralick (1977) found that nonhandicapped children in developmentally integrated preschools tended to interact more frequently with other nonhandicapped children. Nevertheless, handicapped and nonhandicapped children did interact in almost 30% of the observed play intervals. Isolated play was dominant when only handicapped children were in the play setting. When both nonhandicapped and handicapped children were available, parallel and cooperative play accounted for 65% of the intervals. These authors conclude that while little exclusion or rejection of handicapped children was evident, the types of play in the integrated groups were less complex than the play between nonhandicapped children. Other researchers have obtained similar results (Beckman & Kohl, 1984; Faught, Balleweg, Crow, & Van Den Pol, 1983; Kohl & Beckman, 1984).

Training handicapped children

Rarely have researchers directly taught severely handicapped children to interact socially with their nonhandicapped peers. Absence of research in this area may be due to the difficulty of the task, inconsistencies of results, or the amount of time required to teach these specific skills.

Kohl, Beckman, and Swenson-Pierce (1984) used an indirect approach by teaching functional toy use to three handicapped children. Increases in functional toy use were not consistently associated with increases in social interaction, however. Kohler and Fowler (1985) had more success using a more direct approach. Teaching handicapped children and their peers to invite others to play and to use amenities (e.g., Thank you, Please) increased appropriate social interaction for both the handicapped children and their peers. These behaviors were maintained after teacher reinforcement was withdrawn, leading the authors to conclude that the reciprocity of these behaviors functions as a natural reinforcer to maintain these skills. Further research is needed to identify behaviors, which can be easily taught to handicapped children, that initiate and sustain interaction with nonhandicapped peers most effectively.

TRAINING PEERS AS INTERVENTION AGENTS

As an alternative approach, training normally developing peers to interact and use strategies to encourage severely handicapped children to communicate has proven rather successful. For example, Odom, Hoyson, Jamieson, and Strain (1985) trained normally developing children in an integrated preschool to act as peer confederates. During intervention, a significant increase in social interaction was observed; however, a high level of teacher prompting was necessary to sustain this increase.

Teaching peers to facilitate communicative interaction during play times

Appropriate social skills include both verbal and nonverbal behavior. More recent work has focused on the verbal component of communicative–social interaction between handicapped and nonhandicapped children (Goldstein & Ferrell, 1987; Goldstein & Wickstrom, 1986). These studies demonstrate that normally developing children can be taught to use specific strategies to increase communicative interaction.

The purpose of the first study (Goldstein & Wickstrom, 1986) was to determine whether normally developing children could be prompted to use strategies that promoted communicative interaction on the part of their autistic classmates who had limited language production skills, but rarely interacted with peers. Posters depicting the use of the strategies were used to help teach the strategies, to prompt strategy use nonintrusively, and to keep track of reinforcement.

The selection of strategies was based upon peer-mediated interventions focusing on social interaction, developmental literature, and the practices speech–language pathologists and special educators typically use to evoke conversations in unstructured situations. The strategies taught to peers were:

- establishing functional eye contact;
- describing one's own or other children's play;
- initiating joint play;

- repeating, expanding, or requesting clarification of utterances made by the handicapped child;
- establishing joint focus of attention; and
- prompting requests.

A preliminary cost–benefit analysis provided a basis for eliminating less useful strategies from the training package. *Establishing joint focus of attention* and *promoting requests* were relatively ineffective strategies and in addition, *prompting requests* took an inordinate amount of time to teach. Goldstein and Ferrell (1987)

The specific steps to implement peer intervention include teaching peers to use facilitative strategies and then prompting and reinforcing the use of the strategies during play with a handicapped classmate.

---

determined that peer intervention remained effective when the number of strategies taught to peers was reduced from six to four.

The specific steps to implement this peer intervention include (1) teaching peers to use facilitative strategies and then (2) prompting and reinforcing the use of the strategies during play with a handicapped classmate.

Teaching strategies to peers

A teacher and an adult "actor" conduct the training of nonhandicapped peers. A parent can serve as the actor. Training can be accomplished with as few as one child and as many as six children at a time. During training, the peers are told that they are learning how to get their friends to talk with them. A training script is available (Goldstein, 1987) for introducing the behavioral strategies to the children.

The script provides directions to the adults (teacher and actor) for: (1) modeling the use of the strategies for getting others to talk and (2) encouraging the children to practice verbalizing the intent of these strategies.

During training, the strategies are introduced one at a time using a direct instruction approach. After the required responses are modeled by the adults and verbally rehearsed according to the prepared script, each child practices using the strategies with the adult actor. The actor pretends to be a handicapped child and makes it progressively more difficult for the peers to evoke appropriate responses. The actor waits for longer time periods before responding to the peers' initiations. Thus, the peers experience more realistic, difficult situations and learn to be persistent and to modify their use of the strategies.

A set of posters illustrating each of the four strategies is employed in training and is used to prompt the use of the strategies. These posters can later be available during daily free play periods and can be used to prompt the use of the strategies by the peers. The peers practice employing the strategies with the adult actor serving as the handicapped child until each child demonstrates independent use of the strategies. Mastery can be set at four uses of the strategies in the role-play situation without prompting. The children have to be persistent to use the strategies successfully. Thus, the adult actor becomes a more reticent responder over the course of training to give the peers practice with more challenging situations.

Observing and prompting structured free play

During structured free play, two or three nonhandicapped peers are paired with a handicapped child for 5 to 10 minutes. During a longer free play period the nonhandicapped peers can be paired with two or more handicapped children in succession. Before each play period it is helpful to remind the peers that they are to try to get the handicapped child to talk with them. The teacher lists the strategies that the peers have been taught. For example the teacher might say, "Remember, you can get your friend to look at you, you can suggest some things to do together, you can talk about what you are doing, and you need to listen to your friend and make sure you understand what he or she said, so you can repeat it."

During the session the teacher tries not to be an active interacter. When the teacher becomes involved, interaction among the children tends to be inhibited. In addition to prompting the peers to use the four strategies, the teacher is responsible for overall monitoring of the activity (e.g., the teacher may redirect the activity to facilitate cooperative play, may have to resolve conflicts, and may have to confiscate disputed materials).

The teacher prompts strategy usage in a nonintrusive manner. The best way to prompt is by pointing to the poster depicting the strategy that the teacher believes will promote communicative interaction. It is sometimes necessary to say the name of the peer to draw attention to the poster. An alternative way to prompt, when necessary, is to whisper a suggestion into the ear of a peer.

During free play sessions the teacher monitors the number of times the peers use the facilitative strategies effectively. One can put little tokens on the posters or checks on a blackboard above the posters. Different areas of the posters can be set aside for different peers. At the end of the free play period the teacher can count the number of successful strategy uses. This can be used as a basis for a reinforcement system whereby the children can earn stickers, small toys, privileges, or treats when they meet a criterion (e.g., five successful uses of a strategy per child).

Experimental results

When this training regimen was introduced in the Goldstein and Wickstrom (1986) study, it resulted in higher rates of interaction for each of the handicapped children that persisted above baseline levels after teacher prompting was withdrawn. Immediate increases in the number of responses per session were shown to be under experimental control for all three subjects. The increased rate of responding was attributable primarily to on-topic responses for all three subjects, as well as imitative responses for one subject. Initiations, on the other hand, showed more gradual improvements in two subjects and inconsistent change in one subject.

Additional questions raised by this first study required investigation. For example, the efficacy of using peers as mediators of a classroomwide intervention had

not been evaluated. In addition, it was important to examine generalization to other free play periods and determine whether interaction might be augmented further by providing tangible reinforcement to target children. Thus, Goldstein and Ferrell (1987) systematically replicated the earlier research, extending it by

- determining the efficacy of teaching all six normally developing classmates to serve as peer confederates,
- examining the relationship between target children's rates of initiations and responses and the behavior displayed by peers and the teacher,
- determining whether teacher reinforcement of the target child would augment the effects of the peer-mediated intervention, and
- assessing the extent of generalization of interaction skills with previously trained peers at other play times.

Significant increases in communicative interaction occurred when the peers were prompted to use the strategies with the three autistic classmates. In particular, increases in the handicapped children's response rates were demonstrated during free play observations. In addition, fewer initiations by two of the handicapped children during the peer intervention were shown to be attributable to reductions in teacher prompting. Although most strategy use by peers was prompted during the initial intervention phases, prompting dropped gradually while peer strategy use was maintained. Generalization to other settings was demonstrated by only one subject.

Results of these studies have been quite encouraging. The teaching and prompting of specific strategies to facilitate interaction among autistic children and their normally developing peers appears to be an effective method for increasing interaction among children in integrated settings. These studies on communicative interaction among handicapped and normally developing children have resulted in a number of findings that are summarized below.

- Peers' use of several facilitative strategies has resulted in higher rates of communicative interaction in handicapped preschoolers, especially in the most relevant, on-topic verbal response category.
- Effects of peer intervention on the initiations of autistic preschoolers have been inconsistent. One possible confounding variable was the tendency of teachers to prompt the handicapped preschoolers prior to the peer intervention. Subsequent experimental analyses have indicated that sharp reductions in teacher prompting of the handicapped children were responsible for reductions in initiation rates.
- Maintenance and generalization of effects although not consistently impressive, are encouraging. Peer-mediated interventions to promote social interaction that have not focused on communication have rarely resulted in as much maintenance and generalization (e.g., Day, Powell, Dy-Lin, & Stowitschek, 1982; Odom, Hoyson, Jamieson, & Strain, 1985). This may indicate that communicative behaviors that have been targeted have greater potential for naturally reinforcing, reciprocal in-

teraction. Nevertheless, further research is needed to discover the best methods for increasing and generalizing interactions.
- Reinforcement of handicapped children (in addition to reinforcement for peers' strategy use) resulted in maintenance of improved initiation rates that were initially associated with increased teacher prompting. Teaching more specific facilitative strategies to handicapped children is likely to enhance the success of a peer-mediated treatment approach further.
- Peer strategy use was maintained even though a natural (i.e., unprogrammed) decline in teacher prompting was demonstrated as the study progressed. Furthermore, handicapped preschoolers were equally responsive to teacher-prompted and unprompted strategy use by their peers. This finding is suggestive of the potential for peers to take on more responsibility for instituting the intervention independently, perhaps from the initial stages of intervention.

Teaching handicapped children and peers to interact during sociodramatic play

Children engaged in sociodramatic play take on roles and interact with other children to act out themes or episodes. Such play is typical of 3- to 7-year old children. Although a number of investigators have sought to measure, describe, and compare sociodramatic play skills across ages, sexes, cultures, and socioeconomic groups (Eifermann, 1971; Iwanaga, 1973; Rosen, 1974; Smilansky, 1968), relatively little research has explored ways to promote the development of sociodramatic play.

Researchers have attempted to determine whether training children in sociodramatic play enhances their subsequent performance on cognitive, social, and language measures. In one of the earliest interventions of this kind, Smilansky (1968) compared the effects of three treatments on the development of sociodramatic play and related skills. Smilansky found no significant gains from an experiential enrichment treatment, significant improvement using play skills treatment, and the greatest improvement using a combination of the two treatments. Smilansky also analyzed the verbal behavior of the children in her study. She found increases in play-related conversation, range of vocabulary, and sentence length accompanying improvement in sociodramatic play skills. She contended that the improvement in verbal behaviors resulted from play situations that forced children to draw on and better utilize their language skills.

In other studies using play skill interventions, a number of secondary effects have been found. Sociodramatic play training has resulted in more complex play and an increase in vocabulary and

---

Teaching children to play in a sociodramatic manner appears to enhance their performance on cognitive, social, and language measures.

---

verbal expression scores (Lovinger, 1974); improved group problem-solving and role-taking skills (Rosen, 1974); increases in intelligence test scores; improved interpretation of sequential events; and enhanced ability to distinguish between fantasy and reality, to empathize, and to delay impulse (Saltz, Dixon, & Johnson, 1977). In summary, teaching children to play in a sociodramatic manner appears to enhance their performance on cognitive, social, and language measures.

Many educators as well as special educators have incorporated sociodramatic play training into curricula for preschool children. The usual approach to such training involves setting the stage for sociodramatic play by making specific materials available and by providing informal teacher intervention during the play, in the form of participation and/or direction of activity. The effectiveness of such informal training has not been demonstrated with language-handicapped children nor with normally-developing children who may have limited knowledge of sociodramatic themes or scripts. For instance, a child may be familiar with the customer role in a grocery store, but may have more difficulty enacting the check-out clerk or stockperson roles.

Once children are taught all the roles and routines of a sociodramatic theme, they may need little additional intervention. Nelson and Gruendel (1979) have discussed how such shared knowledge enhances children's social or communicative speech. They contend that egocentric or noncommunicative speech, which reportedly accounts for 30% to 60% of the language occurring when young peers are together, is due to children's lack of shared knowledge or context. Children are much more likely to engage in interactive communication when they share a social script, a script for the routine events to be expected in a particular situation. Research on social scripts (Bower, Black, & Turner, 1979; Nelson & Gruendel, 1979) provides a conceptual framework for teaching sociodramatic play skills. Furthermore, peer intervention approaches can be augmented by teaching sociodramatic scripts to children with varying developmental levels.

Recently, a research team (Goldstein, Wickstrom, Hoyson, Jamieson, & Odom, 1988) completed two studies in which handicapped and normally developing peers were taught all relevant roles and behaviors associated with common play scenarios. The handicapped children used one-to-three word utterances but seldom used their language during social play. In the first experiment, triads that included one autistic child and two nonhandicapped preschoolers were taught to enact a hamburger stand script that incorporated motor–gestural and verbal responses for each of three roles. After the children learned to enact the hamburger stand script during training, prompting them to stay in their roles resulted in improved social and communicative interaction during free play. In the second experiment, these effects were replicated with triads consisting of heterogeneous groupings of language-delayed children who were taught a barbershop script. Thus, script training was similarly beneficial for a variety of handicapped and nonhandicapped preschoolers.

The specific steps to implement this script training intervention include (1) teaching scripts to children and then (2) encouraging role-related behavior during free play.

Sociodramatic script training

Training is conducted for approximately 15 minutes per day for at least one week. One teacher is needed to conduct script training sessions with each group of three children. Scripts have been devised to include three roles. An example of a script for a shoe store activity is included in the Appendix (additional scripts are available in Goldstein, 1987). Each child is provided opportunities to perform each role. When the script is first introduced it may be possible to go through the script just once in 15 minutes. It becomes easier to get through the script after a couple of days of training, however. The script specifies motor–gestural as well as verbal behaviors. These responses are adapted to the skill level of individual children.

When the script is first introduced, the teacher models responses and tells children whose turn it is, what to do, and what to say. Thereafter, the teacher attempts to employ fewer prompts and less explicit prompts. The hierarchies that follow provide examples of increasingly less intrusive prompts. For motor–gestural responses:

- Tell child what to do and provide full physical assistance (e.g., "Put these french fries in the container" while using manual guidance to help the child with the task).

- Tell child what to do and provide partial physical assistance.
- Tell child what to do and provide minimal physical assistance.
- Tell child what to do and point or gesture to indicate desired response or pertinent context.
- Tell child what to do.
- Tell child it is his or her turn and point or gesture.
- Point or gesture.
- Ask child "what do you do next?".

For verbal responses:

- Ask child to imitate and model the response, e.g., "You say, I want a hamburger and french fries."
- Ask child to imitate and model the beginning of the response, e.g., "You say, I want a . . .".
- Tell child it is his or her turn and point or gesture to indicate the relevant contextual information.
- Point or gesture to indicate the relevant context.
- Reiterate the prior child's behavior and ask the child, "What do you say?".
- Ask child "What do you say to the *cook*?".
- Remind child it is his or her turn.

After progressing through the script once, reassign children to different roles. Each time the children practice the activity, fewer and less intrusive prompts are provided. Two teaching strategies should be emphasized: (1) Be patient. Allow a child 5 seconds to respond. Within this time span, other children sometimes help the child by repeating the child's "cue" or by offering a suggestion of what the child needs to do. This should be encouraged.

(2) Be sensitive to the children's adaptations of the script. Slight modifications are not only permissible, but are helpful in providing novelty so the children do not get bored. One should intervene only when it appears that opportunities for one of the children to get involved is diminished.

Training continues until each of the children is able to perform the roles independently. The criterion for independent performance entails receiving prompts that specify responses on less than 20% of the role-specific behaviors on at least two consecutive days. Then the sociodramatic play interaction is encouraged during free play.

Observing and prompting structured free play

Up to 10 minutes can be devoted to a sociodramatic play activity during free play. At the beginning of the activity, the teacher reminds the children what the three roles they learned were and helps assign each of the three children to a role. When children have finished a play episode one should help them switch roles so that each child has an opportunity to be each character.

Again, an effort is made to not become actively involved. Active teacher involvement tends to inhibit interaction among the children. Although prompting may be necessary, it should be kept to a minimum. The most frequent prompting should be reminders about the activity and the role that a child is portraying (e.g., "Remember, you are the salesperson at the hamburger stand"). It may be necessary to redirect the activity on occasion and/or take away disputed materials. Once the children have learned the roles during script training, it is rarely necessary to specify desired responses. But, sometimes it is helpful to ask a child "What do you do now?".

Sociodramatic play following script training reflected more sophisticated social interaction among handicapped and nonhandicapped preschoolers (Goldstein, Wickstrom, Hoyson, Jamieson, & Odom, 1988). Advancements were seen in the ability of preschoolers to interact in groups of three and to exchange sociodramatic roles. It is worth noting that improvements in interaction were evident in theme-related behavior not specifically targeted in the script. Script training seems to impose an expectation of interaction and communication among children. This is especially important in mainstreamed classrooms, where structure often must be imposed to ensure that handicapped children are engaged in social interaction (see Strain & Odom, 1986). In addition, there may be long-term benefits to the heterogeneous grouping of children. For example, the more linguistically sophisticated children may model more advanced language skills for less sophisticated peers.

•   •   •

Both of the peer-based interventions described in this article can be thought of as adjuncts to ongoing teacher-mediated interventions in the language domain. These strategies in no way take the place of or supersede other intervention modalities. On the contrary, they provide the opportunity and take full advantage of the influence that peers naturally exert on one another.

Handicapped children talking in as little as single-word utterances benefit from these interventions. Peer-mediated intervention most often has been implemented with autistic children who evidence an inappropriate amount of isolate or parallel play as well as a low rate of communicative interaction with peers (Goldstein & Ferrell, 1987; Goldstein & Wickstrom, 1986). Other children with developmental disabilities who do not demonstrate such severe social deficits have also benefited from these interventions. The sociodramatic script training intervention has been implemented with children who were responsive to peers in conversational contexts, even though they initiated to peers only occasionally. They also were demonstrating some pretending or theme-related play, although their expressive language repertoires were sometimes quite limited. It is notable that the normally developing children involved in script training also made significant improvements in the quality of their playtime interactions with peers (Goldstein, Wickstrom, Hoyson, Jamieson, & Odom, 1988).

As data mount to indicate the developmental advantages that accrue to handicapped children who have regular exposure to normally developing peers (Strain, Hoyson, & Jamieson, 1985; Strain & Odom, 1986), it is likely that many more young children with serious communication problems will be educated along with normally developing peers. The script training and the peer-strategy-use interventions represent potent and cost-effective ways to expand communication training in integrated settings.

REFERENCES

Beckman, P.J., & Kohl, F.L. (1984). The effects of social and isolate toys on the interactions and play of integrated and nonintegrated groups of preschoolers. *Education and Training of the Mentally Retarded, 19,* 169–175.

Bower, G.H., Black, J.B., & Turner, T.J. (1979). Scripts in memory for text. *Cognitive Psychology, 11,* 177–250.

Day, R.M., Powell, T.H., Dy-Lin, E.B., & Stowitschek, J.J. (1982). An evaluation of the effects of a social interaction training package on mentally handicapped preschool children. *Education and Training of the Mentally Retarded, 17,* 125–130.

Eifermann, R.R. (1971). Social play in childhood. In R.E. Herron & B. Sutton-Smith (Eds.), *Child's play* (pp. 270–297). New York: Wiley & Sons.

Faught, K.K., Balleweg, B.J., Crow, R.E., & Van Den Pol, R.A. (1983). An analysis of social behaviors among handicapped and nonhandicapped preschool children. *Education and Training of the Mentally Retarded, 18,* 210–214.

Fenrick, N.J., Pearson, M.E., & Pepelnjak, J.M. (1984). The play, attending, and language of young handicapped children in integrated and segregated settings. *Journal of the Division for Early Childhood, 8,* 57–67.

Goldstein, H. (1987). *Teaching strategies for promoting communication skills.* Unpublished manuscript, University of Pittsburgh, Early Intervention Research Program.

Goldstein, H., & Ferrell, D.R. (1987). Augmenting communicative interaction between handicapped and nonhandicapped preschool children. *Journal of Speech and Hearing Disorders, 52,* 200–211.

Goldstein, H., & Wickstrom, S. (1986). Peer intervention effects on communicative interaction among handicapped and nonhandicapped preschoolers. *Journal of Applied Behavior Analysis, 19,* 209–214.

Goldstein, H., Wickstrom, S., Hoyson, M., Jamieson, B., & Odom, S. (1988). Effects of sociodramatic play training on social and communicative interaction. *Education and Treatment of Children, 11,* 97–117.

Guralnick, M.J. (1976). The value of integrating handicapped and nonhandicapped preschool children. *American Journal of Orthopsychiatry, 46,* 236–245.

Guralnick, M.J. (1981a). The efficacy of integrating handicapped children in early education settings: Research implications. *Topics in Early Childhood Special Education, 1,* 57–71.

Guralnick, M.J. (1981b). Programmatic factors affecting child social interactions in mainstream preschool programs. *Exceptional Education Quarterly, 1,* 71–91.

Guralnick, M.J. (1986). The peer relations of young handicapped and nonhandicapped children. In P.S. Strain,

M.J. Guralnick, & H.M. Walker (Eds.), *Children's social behavior: Development, assessment, and modification* (pp. 93–140). New York: Academic Press.

Guralnick, M.J., & Paul-Brown, D. (1977). The nature of verbal interactions among handicapped and nonhandicapped preschool children. *Child Development, 48,* 254–260.

Guralnick, M.J., & Paul-Brown, D. (1980). Functional and discourse analyses of nonhandicapped preschool childrens' speech to handicapped children. *American Journal of Mental Deficiency, 84,* 444–454.

Guralnick, M.J., & Paul-Brown, D. (1984). Communicative adjustments during behavior request episodes among children at different developmental levels. *Child Development, 55,* 911–919.

Guralnick, M.J., & Paul-Brown, D. (1986). Communicative interactions of mildly delayed and normally developing preschool children: Effects of listener's developmental level. *Journal of Speech and Hearing Research, 29,* 2–10.

Hendrickson, J.M., Strain, P.S., Tremblay, A., & Shores, R.E. (1982). Relationship between toy and material use and the occurrence of social interactive behavior by normally developing preschool children. *Psychology in the Schools, 18,* 500–504.

Iwanaga, M. (1973). Development of interpersonal play in three-, four-, and five-year old children. *Journal of Research and Development in Education, 6,* 71–82.

Kohl, F.L., & Beckman, P.J. (1984). A comparison of handicapped and nonhandicapped preschoolers' interactions across classroom activities. *Journal of the Division for Early Childhood, 8,* 49–56.

Kohl, F.L., Beckman, P.J., & Swenson-Pierce, A. (1984). The effects of directed play on functional toy use and interaction of handicapped preschoolers. *Journal of the Division for Early Childhood, 8,* 114–118.

Kohler, F.W., & Fowler, S.A. (1985). Training prosocial behaviors to young children: An analysis of reciprocity with untrained peers. *Journal of Applied Behavior Analysis, 18,* 187–200.

Lovinger, S. (1974). Socio-dramatic play and language development in preschool disadvantaged children. *Psychology in the Schools, 11,* 313–320.

Nelson, K., & Gruendel, J.M. (1979). At morning it's lunchtime: A scriptal view of children's dialogues. *Discourse Processes, 2,* 73–94.

Odom, S.L., Hoyson, M., Jamieson, B., & Strain, P.S. (1985). Increasing handicapped preschoolers' peer social interactions: Cross-setting and component analysis. *Journal of Applied Behavior Analysis, 18,* 3–16.

Peterson, N.L., & Haralick, J.G. (1977). Integration of handicapped and nonhandicapped preschoolers: An analysis of play behavior and social interaction. *Education and Training of the Mentally Retarded, 12,* 234–245.

Rosen, L. (1974). The effects of sociodramatic play on problem-solving behavior among culturally disadvantaged preschool children. *Child Development, 45,* 920–927.

Saltz, E., Dixon, D., & Johnson, J. (1977). Training disadvantaged preschoolers on various fantasy activities: Effects on cognitive functioning and impulse control. *Child Development, 48,* 367–380.

Smilansky, S. (1968). *The effects of sociodramatic play on disadvantaged preschool children.* New York: Wiley.

Strain, P.S. (1977). An experimental analysis of peer social initiations on the behavior of withdrawn preschool children: Some training and generalization effects. *Journal of Abnormal Child Psychology, 5,* 445–455.

Strain, P.S., Hoyson, M., & Jamieson, B. (1985). Normally developing preschoolers as intervention agents for autistic-like children: Effects on class deportment and social interaction. *Journal of the Division for Early Childhood, 9,* 105–115.

Strain, P.S., & Odom, S.L. (1986). Preventive discipline in early childhood special education. Invited article, *Teaching Exceptional Children, 19,* 26–31.

Strain, P.S., Shores, R.E., & Timm, M.A. (1977). Effects of peer social initiations on the behavior of withdrawn preschool children. *Journal of Applied Behavior Analysis, 10,* 289–296.

Tremblay, A., Strain, P.S., Hendrickson, J.M., & Shores, R.E. (1981). Social interactions of normal preschool children. *Behavior Modification, 5,* 237–253.

Caregiver–child interaction and language acquisition of hearing-impaired children

O.T. Kenworthy, PhD
Division of Hearing and Speech Sciences
School of Medicine
Vanderbilt University
Nashville, Tennessee

IMPROVEMENTS in auditory and speech-sound development have long been used to measure the success of aural rehabilitation (e.g., Ling, 1976; Pollack, 1970). Ross and Tomassetti (1978) note that one of the primary assumptions underlying this approach is that "whatever serves to improve the speech discrimination will serve the needs of the hearing impaired child" (p. 420). Consequently,

The interaction data for the normal-hearing/hearing-impaired dyads were extracted from videotapes collected as part of two grants funded by the Spencer Foundation, Sub-Grants #133–A270 and #133–A908, granted to Dr. Robin Chapman through the School of Education, University of Wisconsin Graduate School, Madison, Wisconsin. Special recognition is due to Mrs. Dorothy Hayes and Dr. Kristine Retherford for their filming of the original tapes. Data analysis was also supported by funds granted through the College of Letters and Sciences of the University of Wisconsin Graduate School. Dr. Jim Verhoeve, Dr. Mary Roach, Mr. Bruce Orchard, and Dr. Cliff Gilman also assisted in the data analysis. The write-up of these results was also supported in part by a grant from the Robert Wood Johnson Foundation to the Division of Hearing and Speech Sciences of the Vanderbilt University School of Medicine.

TLD, 1986, 6(3), 1–11
© 1986 Aspen Publishers, Inc.

aural rehabilitation professionals have placed a good deal of emphasis on listening skills and speech-sound production. While some attention has been devoted to speech and language development as an outcome of natural interactions (e.g., Simmons-Martin & Calvert, 1979), the clinical implementation of the traditional (speech-based) philosophy has generally focused on speech production, often at the expense of conversational interaction.

While auditory and speech-sound development clearly play an important role in aural rehabilitation, some researchers and clinicians have recently questioned the scope and sequence of intervention that adopts such a perspective for preschool children (R. Kretschmer, personal communication, April, 1984). The question has arisen as to whether difficulties in language use noted in school-aged hearing-impaired children may be an unintended residual effect of intervention strategies that focus on teaching speech rather than facilitating language and interaction (Wilbur, 1977).

In contrast to speech-based methods, some researchers and clinicians have adopted a language-based approach that emphasizes the importance of conversational interaction during the preschool period. With this approach, the assumption is that approximations to adult speech models are an outgrowth of the children's developing desire to make their specific communicative intent clear. The language-based approach assumes that, in addition to overcoming the lack of normal-hearing sensitivity and speech discrimination, hearing-impaired children also face the formidable task of acquiring their native language. Indeed, a good deal

of evidence suggests that normal-hearing sensitivity and speech discrimination are not sufficient conditions to ensure normal language development (see Rees, 1978 for a review of pragmatics).

In short, the intervention plan for the hearing-impaired preschooler should be directed toward developing an adequate language base. Hence, the focus of early intervention should be on facilitating communicative interaction and linguistic growth, not auditory and speech-sound development *per se*. In this way, whatever auditory skills the child may present, or subsequently acquire, may be integrated into a solid linguistic framework. This framework makes it clear to the child that language is a tool for both initiating and responding to requests.

Under this concept of intervention, speech and hearing remediation for the hearing-impaired preschooler parallels the language and speech development of normal-hearing children. The content and sequence of the intervention plan is based on knowledge about normal language and speech development. In addition, the combined communication strategies of the caregiver and the child are the focus of treatment.

For the sake of brevity and clarity, further discussion will presume that appropriate selection, fitting, and monitoring of amplification are an integral part of ongoing management (see Ross & Tomassetti, 1978, for further discussion). The language-based approach is also predicated on at least four other basic assumptions about language and speech development:

1. Language development is predictably associated with the context, or

interaction, within which the child learns language.

2. Hearing-impaired children have the potential to learn language in a sequence and manner similar to normal-hearing children.

3. The presence of hearing impairment in the child changes the language-learning context, particularly the language input to the child, in significant but alterable ways.

4. Realigning language input to the hearing-impaired child to conform with the interactions observed in normal-hearing dyads will facilitate language and speech learning in the hearing-impaired child.

INTERACTION AND LANGUAGE ACQUISITION

Since the late 1960s, knowledge of language acquisition has undergone a steady metamorphosis. The unit of analysis has extended gradually to the conversation, and the process has increasingly been considered a synergistic or interactional one. This evolution began with a reconsideration of the child's abilities and motivations. Landmark work by Brown (1973) and Bloom (1970), among others, focused attention on how children's language productions differ qualitatively from those of adults. The focus of research and clinical inquiry expanded to incorporate meaning (semantics) as well as structure (syntax). At the same time, Bloom's "rich interpretation" of children's one- and two-word utterances signaled the importance of context in language learning. The effects of context were initially analyzed in terms of how the setting influences the child's

meaning. Less attention was directed to how modifications or models provided by the caregiver affect the child's language development.

More recently the focus of research on caregiver-child interaction has expanded from the description of child-directed talk to investigation of the specific relationships between such talk and subsequent language learning. While a causal relationship has not been conclusively established, sufficient evidence exists to support a clear association between the quality or content of the dyadic interaction and the rate of the child's language learning. What seems critical is that the adult's utterances or actions should be linked to the topic, meaning, or surface structure of the immediately preceding utterances or actions of the child (e.g., Bloom, Rocissano, & Hood, 1976).

At the interactional and conversational level, Bruner (1975) observes early on that the caregiver seeks to routinize the interaction and to ensure joint attention by referring primarily to objects being acted on or actions being participated in by the child. In this way, the caregiver provides the child with a simplified and focused context, thereby reducing the child's processing load and highlighting certain components, relationships, and sequences

---

The caregiver provides the child with a simplified and focused context, thereby reducing the child's processing load and highlighting certain components, relationships, and sequences within each interaction.

within each interaction. Establishing mutual regard in this way also provides the child with repeated and consistent models for the lexicogrammatical markers and relationships required to express various communicative intents. As Bruner (1975) notes, the transition from prelinguistic to linguistic mappings of experience is "made possible by the presence of an interpreting adult who operates not so much as a corrector or reinforcer but as a provider, an expander, and an idealizer of utterances (p. 17)."

These same general processes of simplification (or highlighting, modeling, and expansion) are also apparent in the form and content of the caregiver's utterances. Despite methodological differences, studies by Cross (1977), Furrow, Nelson, and Benedict (1979), Folger and Chapman (1978), Newport, Gleitman, and Gleitman (1977), and Barnes, Gutfreund, Satterly, and Wells (1983) all demonstrate that the use of certain sentence types and semantically related utterances by the caregiver correlate with later language learning by the child.

Specifically, the use of yes/no questions has been correlated with the child's acquisition of auxiliary verbs in English. This apparently occurs because yes/no questions place the auxiliary in the sentence-initial position where the verb form is more perceptually salient. Similarly, the use of expansions and repetitions with expansions has been correlated with increases in children's responsiveness and increases in mean length of utterance (MLU). These utterances repeat the child's meaning, allowing the child to focus on the syntactic elaboration modeled by the adult. While the caregiver

probably does not consciously intend to teach specific aspects of language to the child, it is likely that the linguistic modifications the caregiver uses to engage the child in dialogue facilitate language learning. The effectiveness of such conversational and linguistic adjustments, however, depends on how well the caregiver focuses and elaborates on the child's communicative attempts.

HEARING IMPAIRMENT, INTERACTION, AND ACQUISITION

Does such child-focused, linguistically contingent interaction take place between normal-hearing caregivers and hearing-impaired children? Certainly, the intelligibility of the hearing-impaired child's speech presents a problem. Moreover, hearing-impaired children tend to rely heavily on systematic but idiosyncratic nonverbal cues that depart from the communication-mode expectations of most normal-hearing interactants (Goldin-Meadow & Feldman, 1977; Alegria, 1981). The combination of these two factors may place an unmanageable conversational burden on the caregiver and disrupt the early patterns of dyadic interaction that are considered critical to language acquisition. Consequently, the language-learning difficulties of the hearing-impaired child may be linked, in part, to breakdowns in early communicative interaction (Brasel & Quigley, 1977; Wilbur, 1977).

Sequence and manner of acquisition

Several recent studies have provided data suggesting that hearing-impaired children can learn language in the same sequence and manner as normal-hearing children. In particular, Weiss, Carney, and Leonard (1985) noted recently that hearing-impaired children are perceived to produce contrastive stress patterns similar to those noted for a younger sample of normal-hearing children matched for mean length of utterance (MLU). Since the topic-comment structure of conversation is marked by contrastive stress (Campbell & Shriberg, 1982), the findings of Weiss, Carney, and Leonard (1985) suggest that hearing-impaired children may possess the ability to monitor conversational interchanges, at least at a prosodic level. However, since these authors found no relationship between degree of hearing loss and the production of contrastive stress, it leaves open the question of whether previous conversational experience influenced the acquisition of this skill.

A similar concern might be raised about certain syntactic deficits commonly noted in hearing-impaired children. Wilbur (1977) noted that hearing-impaired students correctly produce such forms and structures as pronouns and complex sentences but failed to apply them at appropriate times. Wilbur concluded that "as long as the modifications that arise from pragmatic context are ignored in language programs, deaf students' facility with English will continue to be stilted and stereotyped (p. 91)."

Several other studies have found that hearing-impaired children apply the same semantic and pragmatic functions as normal-hearing children, but at a later age (e.g., Skarakis & Prutting, 1977; Curtiss, Prutting, & Lowell, 1979). Moreover, McKirdy and Blank (1982) note that hear-

ing-impaired preschoolers are less adept at applying these functions to the dialogue roles of speaker-initiator and speaker-responder. In general, hearing-impaired preschoolers are less able to sustain dialogue and often respond inappropriately to the overtures of their conversational partners. In summary, these results suggest that hearing-impaired children learn the same content and structures of language that normal-hearing children do but may fail to integrate or apply them adequately within a conversational setting. The question remains whether their conversational shortcomings result from inappropriate input during the early language-learning period.

Caregivers' input

Several studies have questioned whether normal-hearing/hearing-impaired dyads interact less effectively than dyads composed of two normal-hearing people. Like McKirdy and Blank (1982), Greenberg (1980a, 1980b) and Meadow, Greenberg, Erting, and Carmichael (1981) have observed that the communicative attempts expressed by both dyad types are similar. Yet these studies have also observed that the quantity and quality of interaction in normal-hearing/hearing-impaired dyads may be constrained by the communication methods and communicative competence of the dyad. In particular, Meadow, Greenberg, Erting, and Carmichael (1981) note that dyads using the same communication mode, in which either both interactants are normal-hearing or both are hearing-impaired, did not differ significantly from one another in terms of the quality and duration of conversational episodes. In addition, both of these dyad types participate in significantly longer and more complex interactions than normal-hearing/hearing-impaired dyads and dyads using either a simultaneous (sign plus speech) or an aural/oral mode of communication.

However, Greenberg (1980a, 1980b) also found that hearing-impaired dyads with a high rating for communicative competence sustain significantly longer and more complex interactions than dyads that were rated low in communicative competence, regardless of the communication mode used. The cumulative results of these studies suggest that the method of communication is secondary in importance to the competent sharing of information and sustained interaction. Moreover, these findings imply that the nature of the child's handicap may affect the manner in which normal-hearing/hearing-impaired dyads interact.

Other studies of conversational interaction between normal-hearing caregivers and hearing-impaired children have supported this implication, particularly along the social-emotional dimension (Brinich, 1980; Cross, Johnson-Morris, & Nienhuys, 1980; Hyde, Elias, & Power, 1980). It has been consistently noted that normal-hearing caregivers of hearing-impaired children tend to be more physically manipulative, more dominant, and more verbally controlling than their counterparts in normal-hearing dyads. These differences have also been observed regardless of whether these two dyad types have been matched for chronological age or language level (Cross, Johnson-Morris, & Nienhuys, 1980). Discrepancies exist in the literature, however, concerning differences in interaction within the two kinds of dyad.

Recently, Kenworthy (1984) examined whether the presence of hearing impairment in the child influenced the caregiver's use of linguistic adjustments in seven normal-hearing/hearing-impaired dyads in which the children were learning language through the aural/oral mode. Examples of the various coding categories investigated are presented in Table 1. Comparable data for normal-hearing dyads were obtained from several studies, including Gallagher (1981), Retherford, Schwartz, and Chapman (1981), van Kleeck and Carpenter (1980), Cross (1977), Folger and Chapman (1978), and Ninio and Bruner (1978).

The vast majority of the utterances used by mothers in the normal-hearing/hearing-impaired dyads were either noncontingent in form or otherwise unrelated to the discourse features in question. Compared with results obtained for normal-hearing dyads, these findings revealed a considerably lower prevalence of the contingent categories than would be expected. Furthermore, no clear relationship was evident between the intelligibility of the child's qualifying utterances and the mother's use of contingent queries.

The vast majority of the utterances used by mothers in the normal-hearing/hearing-impaired dyads were either noncontingent in form or otherwise unrelated to the discourse features in question.

Table 1. Examples of coding categories for utterances of normal-hearing mothers while interacting with hearing-impaired children (after Kenworthy, 1984)

Mother's utterance[a]	Category	Contingency
The car is going.	Expansion	Y
The truck is running.	Alternative	Y
The car is going fast.	Modification	Y
Which car is going? What is going?	Request for specification	Y
The *car* is going?	Request for confirmation	Y
What?	Neutral query	Y
The car what?	Specific constituent repetition	Y
Say car?	Request for imitation	Y
Car go.	Other repetition	Y
The car is blue. The car is blue.	Self-repetition	N
Hmm. Okay. Uhuh.	Conversational device	N
This is a ball. That's right.	Labeling statement	N
Oh wait (*grabs toy*).	Not applicable	N
That might . . . or (*unintelligible*)	Uncodable	N

[a]Each example is considered as a response to the child saying "car go," except self-repetitions and labeling statements, which are monologic and do not share the same referent as the child's utterance or action. Also, the contingent query categories assume a return to a turn at speaking, as discussed by Garvey (1977) and Gallagher (1981).

Thus, not only was the rate of contingent queries well below expectations, but the distribution of these queries relative to the child's speech intelligibility was unexpected. Specifically, unintelligible utterances by the child were not queried by the mother.

These findings suggest that the presence of hearing impairment in the child may substantially alter the linguistic input the caregiver provides. At an interactional level, several studies have found that normal-hearing caregivers of hearing-impaired children are more verbally (and physically) dominant and controlling. At the conversational level, normal-hearing caregivers of hearing-impaired children have been observed to offer substantially fewer semantically-related utterances than have been offered to normal-hearing children by their mothers.

INTERACTION AND INTERVENTION

Insight into the management implications of the findings described here is afforded by two examples of how conversations in normal-hearing/hearing-impaired dyads may vary. The two examples given in Table 2 are adapted from Kenworthy's (1984) transcripts and represent two children who evidenced similar hearing sensitivity but showed disparate gains in mean length of utterance (MLU). The better-ear, unaided pure-tone averages (500, 1,000, and 2,000 Hz) for these two children were 100 and 110 dB HL, respectively, yet the first child achieved the lower residual gain score for MLU while the second child obtained the higher residual gain score.

The two conversational episodes in

Table 2. Examples of typical mother–child interaction sequences in two NH/HI dyads

Example 1	Example 2
C: bah (*points to window*)	C: abah
M: This is a nice truck (*holds up toy*).	M: What?
C: bah (*repeats without pointing*)	C: abah (*points to window*)
C: (*walks to window*)	M: You want it open?
M: Jerry. (*pause*) Jerry. Come here.	C: ah (*nods head yes*)
(*pause*) Look at this nice farm	M: What do you want?
C: (*points to toy*).	C: obeh
	M: Okay. Here. You do it (*lifts child up to window*).

Table 2 contrast distinctly in the nature of the linguistic interaction provided by the two normal-hearing mothers. Nevertheless, the turn-taking structures of the two interactions are similar. The degree of reciprocity evident in each case is nearly identical. Although the limited number of child utterances per turn might prompt some concern, neither mother seems to dominate the available floor time.

Actual measures of reciprocity, such as utterances per turn or unconditional and transitional probabilities based on percentage of talk by each interactant, might also support the view that these dyads behave similarly and in a reciprocal fashion. Such measurements might further lead to the conclusion that it is the *child's* conversational deficit that requires direct intervention. That is, such an analysis could suggest that communication breakdown would not occur if each child more clearly specified the referent by speaking more descriptively and intelligibly. Such a perspective could easily lead to an intervention plan aimed at vocabulary building and several concomitant speech-production targets. Such strategies might also be implemented by labeling a limited array of objects and actions and requiring the child to imitate the clinician's productions. If the child spontaneously labels one of the actions or objects provided, the clinician can seize the opportunity to correct the child's production in a natural language sequence. In this way, the child may learn more words, speak more clearly, and participate better in the conversation.

When analyzed according to the adult's role in maintaining linguistic contingency and how well such contingency facilitates language growth, the outcome is different. In each case, the interaction begins with an utterance whose referent is unclear given the speech signal alone. To understand the child's communicative intent, the mother must divert her gaze toward the child and scan for nonverbal, or back-channel cues. If these cross-modal cues fail to clarify the child's message, the mother may choose to query further or abandon the child's topic and introduce a new topic.

In the second example, the mother lacks the necessary back-channel cues to ascertain the child's intent. Therefore, she chooses to offer the neutral query,

"What?" The first mother, on the other hand, overlooks the available nonverbal cue of pointing and chooses to redirect the conversation to a referent that was clear to her. This tendency toward redirecting the topic and action sequence of the interaction was maintained throughout the conversation. Unlike the second mother, who focused on the *child's* intent, the first mother chose to impose her intent (topic) on the child. The result is a parallel, didactic interchange, from which the child ultimately withdraws, instead of an interactive and engaging learning opportunity that accommodates the child's egocentricity.

In contrast to the first mother, the second mother remains committed to estab-

---

In contrast to the first mother, the second mother remains committed to establishing the topic initiated by the child by continuing to query when the back-channel cues remain ambiguous.

---

lishing the topic initiated by the child by continuing to query when the back-channel cues remain ambiguous. As a result, she not only keeps the child's interest, she also supplies a seemingly inadvertent model for the child's speech target, "open." Consequently, the child approximates the modeled target and realizes the desired intent. The second mother requires reassurance and guidance from a clinician while the first mother might benefit from more direct instruction.

Thus, when analyzed with respect to linguistic contingency, these two interactions suggest several important clinical principles. First, casual or informal observation, as well as measures of reciprocity, are inadequate for assessing conversational interaction. Second, measures of linguistic contingency should be part of the assessment battery and should be used to help determine the scope and sequence of intervention. Third, cross-modal cues such as gestures play an important role in establishing and maintaining interaction and should not be discouraged as long as they are consistent with the intended message. Fourth, assessment and intervention during the preschool period should focus on both the child and the child's primary interactant.

Finally, clinicians whose remediation is structured like that of the second mother should be encouraged by the numerous findings suggesting that such structures are successful. In addition to the anecdotal evidence presented here, several recent studies have found that such interactions facilitate acquisition of syntax (Goldstein, 1984), word combinations (Schwartz, Chapman, Terrell, Prelock, & Rowan, 1985), and spontaneous imitations (Scherer & Olswang, 1984). Such sequences may also afford opportunities to alter the child's speech productions successfully without using direct corrective feedback. Example 1, however, points to the need to remain equally mindful of what is meant by seizing teaching opportunities within natural language sequences. Those who would choose to *teach* speech or language to the child by constraining and directing the interaction, may wish to reconsider their approach given the findings presented here about how children *learn* to speak.

REFERENCES

Alegria, J. (1981). The development of referential communication in deaf and hearing children: Competence and style. *International Journal of Behavioral Development, 4,* 295–312.

Barnes, S., Gutfreund, M., Satterly, D., & Wells, G. (1983). Characteristics of adult speech which predict children's language development. *Journal of Child Language, 10,* 65–84.

Bloom, L. (1970). *Language development: Form and function in emerging grammars.* Cambridge, MA: MIT Press.

Bloom, L., Rocissano, L., & Hood, L. (1976). Adult-child discourse: Developmental interaction between information processing and linguistic knowledge. *Cognitive Psychology, 8,* 521–552.

Brasel, K., & Quigley, S. (1977). Influence of certain language and communication environments in early childhood on the development of language in deaf individuals. *Journal of Speech and Hearing Research, 20,* 81–84.

Brinich, P. (1980). Childhood deafness and maternal control. *Journal of Communication Disorders, 12,* 75–81.

Brown, R. (1973). *A first language.* Cambridge, MA: Harvard University Press.

Bruner, J. (1975). Ontogenesis of speech acts. *Journal of Child Language, 2,* 1–19.

Campbell, T.C., & Shriberg, L. (1982). Associations among pragmatic function, linguistic stress and natural phonological processes in speech-delayed children. *Journal of Speech and Hearing Research, 25,* 547–553.

Cross, T. (1977). Mother's speech adjustments: The contributions of selected child listener variables. In C.E. Snow & C.A. Ferguson (Eds.), *Talking to children: Language input and acquisition.* Cambridge, England: Cambridge University Press.

Cross, T., Johnson-Morris, J., & Nienhuys, T. (1980). Linguistic feedback and maternal speech: Comparison of mothers addressing hearing and hearing-impaired children. *First Language, 1,* 163–189.

Curtiss, S., Prutting, C., & Lowell, E. (1979). Pragmatic and semantic development in young children with impaired hearing. *Journal of Speech and Hearing Research, 22,* 534–552.

Folger, J., & Chapman, R. (1978). A pragmatic analysis of spontaneous imitations. *Journal of Child Language, 5,* 25–38.

Furrow, D., Nelson, K., & Benedict, H. (1979). Mother's speech to children and syntactic development: Some simple relationships. *Journal of Child Language, 6,* 423–442.

Gallagher, T. (1981). Contingent query sequences within adult-child discourse. *Journal of Child Language, 8,* 51–62.

Garvey, C. (1977). The contingent query: A dependent act in conversation. In M. Lewis & L. Rosenblum (Eds.), *Interaction, conversation and the development of language.* New York: Wiley & Sons.

Goldin-Meadow, S., & Feldman, H. (1977). The development of language-like communication without a language model. *Science, 197,* 401–403.

Goldstein, H. (1984). Effects of modeling and corrected practice on generative language learning of preschool children. *Journal of Speech and Hearing Disorders, 49,* 389–398.

Greenberg, M. (1980a). Mode use in deaf children: The effects of communication method and communication competence. *Applied Psycholinguistics, 1,* 65–80.

Greenberg, M. (1980b). Social interactions between deaf preschoolers and their mothers: The effects of communication method and communication competence. *Developmental Psychology, 16,* 465–474.

Hyde, M., Elias, G., & Power, D. (1980). *The use of verbal and nonverbal control techniques by mothers of hearing-impaired infants.* Mt. Gavatt, Australia: Mt. Gavatt College of Advanced Education, Center for Human Development.

Kenworthy, O.T. (1984). *The influence of selected discourse and auditory factors upon the language acquisition of hearing-impaired children.* Unpublished doctoral dissertation, University of Wisconsin–Madison.

Kretschmer, R.R. (1984, April). *Language of the hearing-impaired child.* Workshop presented at Tennessee State University, Nashville.

Ling, D. (1976). *Speech of the hearing-impaired child: Theory and practice.* Washington, DC.: Alexander Graham Bell Assn. for the Deaf.

McKirdy, L., & Blank, M. (1982). Dialogue in deaf and hearing preschoolers. *Journal of Speech and Hearing Research, 25,* 487–499.

Meadow, K., Greenberg, M., Erting, C., & Carmichael, H. (1981). Interactions of deaf mothers and deaf preschool children: Comparisons with three other groups of deaf and hearing dyads. *American Annals of the Deaf, 126,* 455–469.

Newport, E., Gleitman, H., & Gleitman, L. (1977). Mother, I'd rather do it myself: Some effects and non-effects of maternal speech style. In C.E. Snow & C.A. Ferguson (Eds.), *Talking to children: Language input and acquisition.* Cambridge, England: Cambridge University Press.

Ninio, A., & Bruner, J. (1978). The achievements and

antecedents of labelling. *Journal of Child Language, 5,* 1–15.

Pollack, D. (1970). *Educational audiology for the limited hearing infant.* Springfield, IL: Charles C Thomas.

Rees, N. (1978). Pragmatics of language: Applications to normal and disordered language development. In R. Schiefelbusch (Ed.), *Bases of language intervention.* Baltimore, MD: University Park Press.

Retherford, K., Schwartz, B., & Chapman, R. (1981). Semantic roles and residual grammatical categories in mother and child speech: Who tunes into whom? *Journal of Child Language, 8,* 583–608.

Ross, M., & Tomassetti, C. (1978). Hearing aid selection for preverbal hearing impaired children. In D. Pollack (Ed.), *Amplification for the hearing-impaired* (2nd ed.). New York: Grune and Stratton.

Scherer, N., & Olswang, L. (1984). Role of mothers' expansions in stimulating children's language production. *Journal of Speech and Hearing Research, 27,* 387–396.

Schwartz, R., Chapman, K., Terrell, B., Prelock, P., &

Rowan, L. (1985). Facilitating word combination in language-impaired children through discourse structure. *Journal of Speech and Hearing Disorders, 50,* 31–39.

Simmons-Martin, A., & Calvert, D. (Eds.). (1979). *Parent-infant intervention.* New York: Grune and Stratton.

Skarakis, E., & Prutting, C. (1977). Early communication: Semantic functions and communicative intentions in the communication of the preschool child with impaired hearing. *American Annals of the Deaf, 122,* 382–391.

van Kleeck, A., & Carpenter, R. (1980). The effects of children's language comprehension level on adults' child-directed talk. *Journal of Speech and Hearing Research, 23,* 546–569.

Weiss, A., Carney, A., & Leonard, L. (1985). Contrastive stress production in hearing-impaired and normal-hearing children. *Journal of Speech and Hearing Research, 28,* 26–35.

Wilbur, R. (1977). An explanation of deaf children's difficulty with certain syntactic structures of English. *The Volta Review, 79,* 85–92.

Part III
Caregivers and Clinicians: Language Assessment and Intervention

Preschool language intervention: some key concerns

Sandy Friel-Patti, PhD
Associate Professor

Janice Lougeay-Mottinger, MA
Coordinator of Clinical Practicum
The University of Texas at Dallas
Callier Center for Communication
  Disorders
Dallas, Texas

THE IDEA THAT SYNTAX is central to a theory of language learning has given way to the more recent assertion that learning how to use language to encode cognitive knowledge in a social context is the focal issue of language development. Rees (1978) stated that "the uses of language become the motivating force for learning language as well as the major determiners of which language forms are to be learned" (p. 261). For the better part of a decade, clinicians have tried to extend the pragmatic model of language learning to the assessment and treatment of language-impaired children. Their efforts to integrate a broad interpretation of pragmatic theory into clinical procedures have led to a fundamental change in the approach to intervention planning (Craig, 1983; Prutting & Kirchner, 1983).

The broad interpretation of pragmatic

The authors have chosen to use the pronoun she for clinicians and he for clients because it reflects the customary clinical composition.

theory suggests that communicative functions are the principal motivation for language growth (Bates, 1976; Halliday, 1975; MacNamara, 1972; Muma, 1978; Rees, 1978), and that conversation and structural development are functionally inseparable. Pragmatics is not simply a taxonomy of language uses; syntax and semantics are thought to develop in order to clarify pragmatic functions.

The clinician who interprets current theory in this way must alter customary intervention procedures to incorporate these views. An integrative approach to intervention must preserve communicative exchanges that occur naturally as conversational interactions (Bloom & Lahey, 1978; Lucas, 1980; Muma, 1978; Seibert & Oller, 1981). The inherently reinforcing quality of effective communication must become the motivating factor in children's learning. Language growth should be facilitated via experiences with functional communication. Operant procedures are no longer necessary since the natural consequences of the communicative exchanges serve to reinforce and shape appropriate communication. Structural and conversational rules are learned as interdependent aspects of communication.

To achieve these goals, the clinician must shift her role from teacher to facilitator. Rather than serving as an active provider of information to the child (Muma, 1978), she must provide interactive sequences of events that encourage the child to communicate, and she must afford natural consequences for his participation. She must structure these interactions to increase the frequency of opportunities for the child to use targeted components and to increase the contingency of natural consequences (Bloom & Lahey, 1978). In this way, the clinician structures an environment that preserves the inherent motivation of natural communicative exchange.

The child's role also shifts from that of a passive recipient of information to an active participant inducing critical information. In such a context, both the clinician and the child work harder at the communicative interaction than either would work within a more traditional approach.

The clinician who accepts this broader interpretation of pragmatic theory cannot simply add goals for language use to existing programs. She faces the difficult task of providing interactions and experiences that will maximize the child's communicative potential. The available literature to help apply these ideas in the clinical setting is sparse, and there are few empirical studies to help evaluate past efforts (Craig, 1983).

The present article addresses the clinical issues that must be considered in planning preschool language intervention programs aimed at integrating pragmatic theory into the treatment plan. Solutions are offered for two common problems clinicians encounter in implementing a pragmatically based intervention plan.

CLINICAL ISSUES

Clinician as facilitator

The clinician's role in the intervention procedure is to facilitate the child's inductions regarding language use (Bloom & Lahey, 1978). By manipulating the environment, the clinician can encourage the learning of effective communicative strategies. Constable (1983) proposed that the clinician is responsible for creating systematized, linguistically enhancing experiences. The clinician should take into account the competencies the child is attempting to acquire. In this way, the clinician–child interaction can be defined as a speaker–listener paradigm that provides a basis for successful communication.

When translated into behavior, the clinician's role becomes one of structuring intervention activities to provide opportunities for the child to use communication meaningfully, while increasing the frequency of experiences with particular language events. Learning environments must be provided that are inherently interesting to the child and that stimulate his curiosity about language use. The clinician creates linguistically stimulating circumstances that are systematically arranged to meet the child's specific communicative goals through conversation.

Using Nelson and Gruendel's (1979) idea that the development of topic-relevant dialogue results from the child's ability to build shared social scripts, Constable (1983) proposes intervention strategies using social routines or scripts. Familiar routines such as birthday parties, food preparation, washing dishes, and so on are viewed as appropriate tasks for facilitating progressive language use. In routine events such as this, Constable suggests, language clinicians can provide conversational support to facilitate cognitive and communicative growth. They can structure these routines to demand increasing specificity in order to achieve communicative success.

Intervention strategies designed to improve language learning through participation in conventionalized routines and the development of scripts for these situations presumes that each script, as a conceptual unit, has psychological reality for the child. Conti-Ramsden and Friel-Patti (1984a) have recently reported difficulties in delineating scripts within dialogue. The concept of a script as representing any number of routine, sequential events can be loosely interpreted to include all events, including sets of events that are not scripted. Thus it is difficult to differentiate scripted from nonscripted conversations. Such problems undoubtedly also arise when planning an intervention program using scripts as a facilitative context. The suggestion that scripted contexts facilitate language learning is certainly appealing, underlining the need for an operational definition of the script. Without such a definition and in the absence of any evidence that scripts have psychological reality for the child, the claim that scripts facilitate language in dialogue is circular.

The clinician must be both an active, careful speaker and an active, creative listener. She provides the experiences and

---

An intervention strategy that stresses the importance of preserving an interactive environment and natural consequences for facilitating language learning must consider the role of play in children's learning.

---

assumes responsibility for making them effective in meeting the child's needs. The resulting interaction is a true discourse in which the clinician meets constraints established by the child's message and subsequently establishes new constraints to which the child must relate (Prutting, 1982). Because the interaction is dynamic, the clinician must be prepared to adapt her behavior in accordance with the child's behavior.

The role of play in children's learning

An intervention strategy that stresses the importance of preserving an interactive environment and natural consequences for facilitating language learning must consider the role of play in children's learning. It is commonly held that children learn about conversational demands and rules of discourse while interacting with their peers in play experiences. While peers may certainly contribute to a child's pragmatic learning and rule induction, of greatest importance is his verbal interaction with the clinician. The evidence suggests that verbal interaction with adults rather than peers is a major factor affecting children's development of communicative competence (McCartney, 1984). Interaction and play with peers is an inherently motivating forum for stabilization of language learning. Thus clinicians should capitalize on the appeal of play while at the same time preserving a low clinician-to-child ratio.

During play activity, the clinician can provide the children with a linguistic representation of their experience. Information is presented that can be used later by the child in communicative interactions

relating to the topic. Once the child has had sufficient experience with an activity to possess a base of knowledge about it, the clinician can probe for specific responses. She asks questions designed to encourage particular communicative functions or forms, or semantic relations. The clinician then remarks on what the child has said, often presenting new information. She provides a situationally appropriate model of mature speech. This factor enhances the child's understanding of how language functions in the environment and how it can be used to meet needs and manipulate interactions (Strong, 1983).

Input provided by the clinician

During the language-learning period, children proceed along a continuum of communicative partners: Beginning with primarily parent–child interactions, they move to parentally mediated interactions with adults and peers, and finally to peer interactions (Corsaro, 1981). Children frequently experience greater communicative success when interacting with adults because the adults exercise control of the interaction and adapt their style to the child's communicative limitations. Such modification of linguistic output by adults interacting with children is well documented (Conti-Ramsden & Friel-Patti, 1983, 1984b; Cross, 1977; Gleason and Weintraub, 1978; Snow, 1972). While there has been considerable speculation concerning the purpose for these speech style modifications, adult motivations probably change as the child changes (Brown, 1977; Gleason & Weintraub, 1978; Snow, 1977). Thus, when interacting with infants, the adults are primarily establishing an affectional bond. With preschoolers, however, the adult input could be seen as facilitating the abstraction of linguistic meaning and providing information about the world.

The view of language acquisition that emphasizes the child's linguistic experiences must assume that language learning occurs because of linguistic input rather than in spite of it. The speech that is directed to the child has the greatest effect on language development. What is important is the child's use of the input, the interpretation he places on it, and how he organizes the information gained for later learning (Kuczaj, 1982).

De Villiers and deVilliers (1978) distinguish *input,* the linguistic information to which the child is exposed, from *intake,* the child's selective use of the input. Thus, the same linguistic input and experiences may lead to different acquisition patterns for different children. Nelson (1973) examined the effects of adult input on language learning in normal children. She found that, when semantically related expansions of children's utterances were provided by the examiner, children were observed to subsequently use the modeled forms. Cross (1977, 1978) also looked at adult expansions as input and found a positive effect on language acquisition. Moerk (1983) reexamined transcripts described by Brown (1973) and found considerable consistency of specific teaching techniques and types of linguistic input between mothers and young language-learning children.

Wilcox (1984) states that adults can achieve cognitive and verbal synchrony with the child more easily than other children can, thereby enhancing both comprehension and participation in the communicative interaction. The clinician needs to provide input language that will enable the child to become a communicative partner in conversation. The clinician must use communicatively useful language in order to provide the child with environmental phrases related to home or school life (Snow, Midkiff-Borunda, Small, & Proctor, 1984).

Parents as clinical partners

In much of the cited literature, the communicating pairs have been mothers and their children. Mothers of language-impaired children also have the ability to modify their verbal behavior to match the level of their language-impaired children (Friel-Patti, 1980; Conti-Ramsden & Friel-Patti, 1983, 1984a). Involving parents in the intervention process has been common practice for years. Clinicians feel that mothers do well at reinforcing goals, aiding in generalization, and modeling appropriate language. Home programs are often devised to provide added practice in specific skills (Muma, 1978), and parents routinely serve as agents of carryover (Craig, 1983). However, Muma (1983) suggests that parents need assistance in identifying target behaviors before they can take an active role in intervention. They must first learn to identify the skills that are being stressed by the clinician and produced by the child before they can learn to use facilitation techniques.

Although parents naturally modify their input, they do not change it as effectively nor as consistently as clinicians do to meet children's needs. Often parents try to teach correct words, and they consistently correct inaccurate productions. This practice has been found to slow children's language learning (Cardoso-Martins & Mervis, 1981; Grossfeld & Heller, 1980). Bowerman (1976), also reporting on the role of negative feedback on inadequate performance, concluded that such feedback is not required for language learning and, furthermore, it does not seem to accelerate it. Wilcox (1984) notes that the research on negative feedback has been done with normal populations and it is possible that with language-impaired populations both negative and positive feedback are warranted.

Recently, Newhoff and Browning (1983) have suggested that language-impaired children affect the language that is addressed to them by their feedback or lack of it. Because of the bidirectional influence of one partner on the other in an interaction, the variation in linguistic abilities of the language-impaired children should be considered in any explanation of differences in the speech addressed to them. A clinician who is skilled at monitoring progress must make the decision about the most effective type of feedback to use with a particular child. Parents lack knowledge about normal language development and the ability to break tasks down into smaller steps needed to plan and carry through intervention. With clinician direction, however, parents can and do play a critical role in the intervention program. What parents of language-impaired children are trained to do has been demonstrated to affect what their children learn (Tiegerman & Siperstein, 1984).

The clinician's role in pragmatic intervention is complex and requires consider-

able planning as well as skill. It would be far easier to target a goal and set up an operant program to train it. Steckol (1983), however, warns that the stimulus–response format may increase the likelihood that the child will be language-learning disabled when he reaches school age. She suggests that we may be contributing to pragmatic deficits that become apparent in older language-impaired children during our early intervention. The inability to use language appropriately may reflect both a persistent language disorder and be a function of the remediation techniques used. By training a child to seek unnatural reinforcers for language, giving reinforcement only for linguistically complete utterances when eliptical responses are appropriate, clinicians may indeed be facilitating the development of inappropriate conversational rules.

Although the task of applying a broad interpretation of pragmatics to intervention procedures is difficult, the advantages of structuring remediation in this fashion far outweigh any disadvantages. Among the fundamental parameters of an intervention program identified by Bloom and Lahey (1978), Muma (1978), and others are two dimensions clinicians find particularly difficult to incorporate within an interactive pragmatic setting: (a) allowing for individual differences among children; and (b) providing a mechanism for being accountable for children's progress.

CLINICAL IMPLICATIONS

Meeting pragmatic needs of individual children in a group

The preference for group rather than individual language intervention with a preschool population is well documented in the literature (Blank, Rose, & Berlin, 1978; Bloom & Lahey, 1978). In a group setting, the natural consequences for communicative interactions seldom need to be contrived by the clinician, therefore, the group is well suited for pragmatically based therapy. Given the inherent differences among language-impaired children, however, to meet the individual needs of a group of children who are all involved in

---

Given the inherent differences among language-impaired children, however, to meet the individual needs of a group of children who are all involved in the same activity is a difficult task.

---

the same activity is a difficult task. Children in preschool language intervention programs are seldom a homogeneous group. It is quite possible that in a group of 10 preschoolers as many as 30 goals are targeted. Although each goal is not necessarily stressed in each activity, it is desirable that all activities meet some targeted need for each child. What occurs too often, for example, is that while the group is involved in an activity stressing expression of prepositional concepts, the four children in the group who are already competent in that area are encouraged not to respond so that the children who need the practice get it.

When using the more traditional, operant intervention techniques, clinicians list goals and then plan an activity to work on each one. It is obvious to the child what he is expected to do. It is easy for the clinician to determine whether the child has performed successfully.

In contrast, in an interactive situation neither the expectations of the clinician nor the performance of the child is as easily discernible. The clinician must set up a communicative situation that provides a natural conversational interaction that is specific to the goals of the children involved. Pragmatic intervention programs described in the literature (Constable, 1983; Kunze, Lockhart, Didow, & Caterson, 1983; Strong, 1983) encourage the clinician to use an activity that will be interesting for the children as well as providing opportunities for each child to respond relative to his goals. The clinician must structure what she says and does to facilitate appropriate performance from each member of the group. This goal is not easy, but it can be done. Careful planning and organization will make it work. A chart to help in organization is presented in Table 1. The goals for each child in the group are listed in abbreviated form.

The grid makes it obvious which goals, if any, several children have in common. The clinician selects an interactive activity such as making popcorn. Then, considering the children's goals, she plans the process, her questioning strategies and stimulation techniques, and the involvement of each student. In this way she is able to provide opportunities for all the children in the group to use language consistent with their goals during the activity. In addition, as a result of peer interactions, many of the goals will be reinforced in ways that cannot be anticipated fully by the clinician. Once the

Table 1. Chart to facilitate efficient planning for group intervention

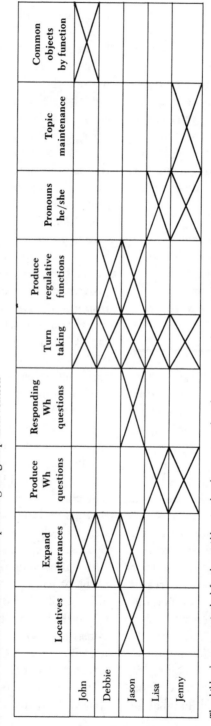

	Locatives	Expand utterances	Produce Wh questions	Responding Wh questions	Turn taking	Produce regulative functions	Pronouns he/she	Topic maintenance	Common objects by function
John		X			X				X
Debbie		X			X	X			
Jason	X	X		X	X	X			
Lisa			X		X		X		
Jenny			X				X	X	

The children's names are in the left column. Abbreviated goals are written along the top. An X in the square indicates the child listed is working on that goal.

planning is done for one interactive activity, the same strategies can be used again in other activities.

The clinician as facilitator is responsible for making the communication happen. By carefully preparing so that her role is specifically defined and the children's responses are anticipated, she can meet the needs of even a heterogeneous group of language-impaired preschoolers.

Accountability

Another major problem faced by clinicians relates to measuring students' progress. It is considerably easier to record data relative to children's individual goals if a traditional operant approach is used than in the interactive situation described. Of course, charting can be done efficiently in a group situation. With careful preparation and planning the clinician can accomplish efficient data collection.

Strong (1983) presents a recording system designed to tally linguistic forms and communicative functions in a variety of imitative and spontaneous situations. Several suggestions are given to help organize charting procedures. For example, she suggests that a clinician could choose to focus on only one linguistic form or function per activity for recording purposes. Although the activity afforded opportunities to elicit several linguistic forms and functions, it may not be possible to keep track of all the responses during the session. Thus, on one occasion in the cooking activity, the use of requestives for each child was charted. During a subsequent activity, requests for information would be charted. An alternative would be selecting one child to chart in each activi-

ty. All the goals for that child would be charted, but data might be collected only once every three weeks. Strong also recommends use of videotape if the clinician wishes to chart all goals for each child during a single activity.

If recordkeeping interferes with the natural interaction of the activity, a baseline measuring procedure can be used. Specific elicitation techniques can be structured to evaluate the child's performance relative to his goals. At predetermined intervals each child is evaluated (one to one) to monitor his progress in each area. In this more structured situation,

---

Obviously the interaction is less natural and some of the pragmatic skills present within a group of peers may not be evident in the structured situation.

---

charting responses is considerably less complicated than in a group interaction. In this way a probe testing situation is designed to evaluate the progress being made by the child. Obviously the interaction is less natural and some of the pragmatic skills present within a group of peers may not be evident in the structured situation. Some goals, however, can be effectively monitored in this way.

When it was necessary to track children's productions during the group interaction, a color-coded card system was used. Each color represented a goal; that is, red indicated *wh*-question production, and so on. A jar was used for each child. When the child gave an appropriate response the colored card responding to that response was placed in his jar. This was done unobtrusively by the clinician for the purpose of recording responses at a later time.

Table 2 presents a chart designed to be used during an activity with three children. The goals targeted during the activity include prepositional concepts, transportation vocabulary, formulation and response to wh-questions and use of subject–verb constructions. Not all children are working on all goals. During the activity the children will use various vehicles to drive, fly, or sail around a city made with blocks. The clinician will ask questions about which vehicle will go to which destination, and the children who are working on question forms will ask each other. Depending on their abilities the children will give instructions to each other or respond to clinician instructions using prepositions. Since responses have been anticipated by the clinician, it is possible to use a simple checklist system to monitor each child's success on the goals that pertain to him.

Several means of dealing with the prob-

Table 2. Response chart for interactive language activity

| | | I | C | S | Respond to Wh questions | | | | | |
					Who			What		
John	Label car train plane bus boat	I	C	S	I	C	S	I	C	S

		I	C	S	Formulate Wh questions	I	C	S
Mary	Production Prepositions in on under over through behind	I	C	S	Where	I	C	S
					What	I	C	S
					Who	I	C	S

		I	C	S	Production of subject and verb constructions	I	C	S
Mike	Production Prepositions in on under over through	I	C	S		I	C	S
					is going			
					is flying			
					is swimming			
					is walking			
					is running			

Anticipated responses for each child are listed. A column is provided to indicate if the production was imitated (I), Cued (C), or Spontaneous (S).

lems of response tallying have been presented. Often a combination of several methods is most efficient. There is no right or wrong way to do it. The clinician must be willing to accept not having data collected on each child daily. She must also organize her data collection so all children are charted frequently enough to provide information about their progress toward each goal.

• • •

Clinicians are currently attempting to implement pragmatic language intervention. The major goal of such a program is to recognize that the social use of language gives rise to form and meaning. The literature provides limited information to help in clinical application of theory. The role of the clinician in a pragmatically based intervention process is difficult and complex. Two problems that interfere with the clinician's ability to successfully carry through a competence-building interactive intervention program have been discussed, and possible solutions have been offered. There is a need to share ideas among clinicians and to collect empirical data to support or challenge the effectiveness of intervention procedures. The question of *what* to do in pragmatic intervention has become clear. There is a need now to explore *how* to do it.

REFERENCES

Bates, E. (1976). Pragmatics and sociolinguistics in child language. In D. Moorehead & A. Moorehead (Eds.), *Language deficiency in children: Selected readings.* Baltimore, MD: University Park Press.

Blank, M., Rose, S., & Berlin, F. (1978). *The language of learning.* New York: Grune & Stratton.

Bloom, L., & Lahey, M. (1978). *Language development and language disorders.* New York: Wiley.

Bowerman, M. (1976). Semantic factors in the acquisition of rules for word use and sentence construction. In A. Moorhead & D. Moorhead (Eds.), *Normal and deficient child language.* Baltimore, MD: University Park Press.

Brown, R. (1973). *A first language: The early stages.* Cambridge, MA: Harvard University Press.

Brown, R. (1977). In C. Snow & C. Ferguson (Eds.), *Talking to children: Language input and acquisition* (Introduction). Cambridge: Cambridge University Press.

Cardoso-Martins, C., & Mervis, C. (1981, March). *Maternal speech to prelinguistic Down's syndrome children.* Paper presented at the Gatling Conference for Research in Mental Retardation/Developmental Disabilities, Gatlinburg, Tennessee.

Constable, C. (1983). Creating communicative context. In H. Winitz (Ed.), *Treating language disorders.* Baltimore, MD: University Park Press.

Conti-Ramsden, G., & Friel-Patti, S. (1983). Mothers discourse adjustments to language-impaired children. *Journal of Speech and Hearing Disorders, 48,* 360–367.

Conti-Ramsden, G., & Friel-Patti, S. (1984a, July). Context and characteristics of mother-child conversations. Paper presented at Third International Congress for the Study of Child Language, Austin, Texas.

Conti-Ramsden, G., & Friel-Patti, S. (1984b). Mother-child dialogues: A comparison of normal and language impaired children. *Journal of Communication Disorders, 17,* 19–35.

Corsaro, W. (1981). The development of social cognition in preschool children: Implications for language learning. *Topics in Language Disorders, 1,* 77–95.

Craig, H. (1983). Applications of Pragmatic Language Models for Intervention. In T. Gallager & C. Prutting (Eds.), *Pragmatic Assessment and Intervention Issues in Language.* San Diego: College-Hill Press.

Cross, T. (1977). Mothers' speech adjustments: The control of selected child listener variables. In C. Snow & C. Ferguson (Eds.), *Talking to children: Language input and acquisition.* Cambridge: Cambridge University Press.

Cross, T (1978). Mothers' speech and its association with rate of linguistic development in young children. In N. Waterson & C. Snow (Eds.), *The development of communication.* New York: Wiley.

deVilliers, J., & deVilliers, P. (1978). *Language acquisition*. Cambridge, MA: Harvard University Press.

Friel-Patti, S. (1980). Aspects of mother-child interaction as related to the remediation process. *Annals of Otology, Rhinology, and Laryngology, 89,* 171–74.

Gleason, J., & Weintraub, S. (1978). Input language and the acquisition of communicative competence. In K. Nelson (Ed.), *Children's language Vol. 1.* New York: Gardner Press.

Grossfeld, C., & Heller, E. (1980). Follow the leader: Why a language impaired child can't be 'it.' *Working Papers in Experimental Speech Language Pathology and Audiology, 9.* New York: Department of Communication, Arts and Sciences, Queens College of the City of New York.

Halliday, M.A.K. (1975). *Learning how to mean: Explorations in the development of language.* London: Edward Arnold.

Kuczaj, S. (1982). On the nature of syntactic development. In S. Kuczaj (Ed.), *Language development: Vol. 1. Syntax and semantics.* Hillsdale, NJ: Erlbaum.

Kunze, L., Lockhart, S., Didow, S., & Caterson, M. (1983). Interactive model for the assessment and treatment of the young child. In H. Winitz (Ed.), *Treating language disorders.* Baltimore, MD: University Park Press, 1983.

Lucas, E. (1980). *Semantic and pragmatic language disorders: Assessment and remediation.* Rockville, MD: Aspen Systems.

MacNamara, J. (1972). Cognitive basis of language learning in infants. *Psychological Review, 79,* 1–13.

McCartney, K. (1984). Effect of quality of day care environment on children's language development. *Developmental Psychology, 20,* 244–260.

Moerk, E. (1983). A behavioral analysis of controversial topics in first language acquisition: Reinforcements, corrections, modeling, input frequencies, and the three-term contingency pattern. *Journal of Psycholinguistic Research, 12,* 129–55.

Muma, J. (1978). *Language handbook—Concepts, assessment, intervention.* Englewood Cliffs, NJ: Prentice-Hall.

Muma, J. (1983). Speech-language pathology: Emerging clinical expertise in language. In T. Gallagher & C. Prutting, (Eds.), *Pragmatic assessment and intervention issues in language.* San Diego: College-Hill.

Nelson, K. (1973). Structure and strategy in learning to talk. *Monographs of the Society for Research in Child Development, 38 (1-2, Serial No. 149).*

Nelson, K., & Gruendel, J. (1979). At morning it's lunchtime: A scriptal view of children's dialogue. *Discourse Processes, 2,* 73–94.

Newhoff, M., & Browning, J. (1983). Interaction variation: A view from the language-disordered child's world. *Topics in Language Disorders, 4,* 49–60.

Prutting, C. (1982). Pragmatics as social competence. *Journal of Speech and Hearing Disorders, 47,* 123–34.

Prutting, C., & Kirchner, D. (1983). Applied pragmatics. In T. Gallagher & C. Prutting (Eds.), *Pragmatic assessment and intervention issues in language.* San Diego: College-Hill Press.

Rees, N. (1978). Pragmatics of language: Applications to normal and disordered language development. In R.F. Schiefelbusch (Ed.), *Bases of language intervention.* Baltimore, MD: University Park Press.

Seibert, J.M., & Oller, D.K. (1981). Linguistics pragmatics and language intervention strategies. *Journal of Autism and Developmental Disorders, 11,* 75–88.

Snow, C. (1972). Mothers' speech to children learning language. *Child Development, 43,* 1–22.

Snow, C. (1977). Mothers' speech research: From input to interaction. In C. Snow & C. Ferguson (Eds.), *Talking to children: Language input and acquisition.* Cambridge, England: Cambridge University Press.

Snow, C., Midkiff-Borunda, S., Small, A., & Proctor, A. (1984). Therapy as social interaction: Analyzing the contexts of language remediation. *Topics in Language Disorders, 4,* 72–85.

Steckol, K. (1983). Are we training young language delayed children for future academic failure? In H. Winitz (Ed.), *Treating language disorders.* Baltimore, MD: University Park Press.

Strong, J. (1983). *Language facilitation.* Baltimore, MD: University Park Press.

Tiegerman, E., & Siperstein, M. (1984). Individual patterns of interaction in the mother-child dyad: Implications for parent intervention. *Topics in Language Disorders, 4,* 50–61.

Wilcox, M. (1984). Developmental language disorders: Preschoolers. In A. Holland (Ed.), *Language disorders in children.* San Diego: College-Hill Press.

Training parents to be language facilitators

Hiram L. McDade, PhD
Associate Professor and Graduate Director

Danielle R. Varnedoe MA
Clinical Instructor
Department of Communicative Disorders
University of South Carolina
Columbia, South Carolina

I T IS DIFFICULT to find a textbook on language intervention that does not devote a specific section to the training of parents and significant others. Its omission would render the book incomplete. What appears ironic, then, is the extent to which one much search to find clinicians actually engaged in such training.

This paradox became most evident from the data presented by Cartright and Ruscello (1979), who surveyed 198 clinics and training institutions in communicative disorders throughout the United States and Canada. Of the 115 respondents, 89 percent indicated that their facilities viewed parent involvement as an essential component of clinical services. However, only 51 percent of those who considered parent involvement to be essential indicated that their centers had actually organized such programs. And, of those who claimed to involve parents, 62 percent indicated that the approach most frequently utilized was to develop han-

Top Lang Disord, 1987, 7(3), 19–30
© 1987 Aspen Publishers, Inc.

douts, reading lists, and other written materials. While the importance of parent training is acknowledged, its practice remains the exception rather than the rule, even within university training programs. As Baker (1976) reports, parents, more often than not, assume the role of "uninformed spectators, receiving just enough information about the methods being employed to be accepting of them" (p. 694).

To many practicing clinicians, parent training is an appropriate subject for the classroom, but foreign to the clinic. Because students are products of their training programs, it should not be surprising that they are reluctant to involve parents in the intervention process. If professors and clinical supervisors do not make parent training a routine part of students' clinical practicum experience, new clinicians cannot be expected to develop and implement a therapeutic approach that they have never witnessed, much less practiced. As a result, clinician–parent interactions are often limited to occasional conferences and brief, impromptu interchanges following therapy.

MODEL PARENT TRAINING PROGRAMS

The failure to involve parents and significant others in the therapy process is certainly not due to a lack of model programs. Language intervention with hearing-impaired children has a long history of parent involvement (Fitzgerald & Fischer, this issue). In the 1960s, centers such as the Mama Lere Parent–Infant Program and the John Tracy Clinic pioneered the use of parents as primary change agents in the language behavior of their hearing-impaired children.

A decade later, the special education literature was filled with articles describing various home-based and center-based intervention programs, each of which advocated a different role for parents to play in their handicapped child's habilitation process. To illustrate, the 1970s witnessed the development of the Portage Project (Shearer & Shearer, 1972), the READ Project (Baker, Brightman, Heifetz, & Murphy, 1973), Parent Programs for Developmental Management (Denhoff & Hyman, 1977), Teach Your Child to Talk (Pushaw, 1976), Environmental Language Intervention (MacDonald, Blott, Gordon, Spiegel, & Hartmann, 1974), the Hanen Early Language Program (Manolson, 1979), the Birth to Three Curriculum (Bangs, 1979), and Modification of the Mother–Child Interchange in Language, Speech, and Hearing (Clezy, 1979).

EFFECTIVENESS OF PARENT TRAINING

Similarly, the paucity of parent training cannot be attributed to accountability or the lack of a scientific database. In fact, the literature is compelling in this regard. Simply put, programs that involve parents produce greater gains than those that do not (Baker, Heifetz, & Brightman, 1973; Baker, Murphy, Heifetz, & Brightman, 1975; Berkowitz & Graziano, 1972; Fudala, England, & Ganoung, 1972; Fredricks, Baldwin, & Grove, 1974; Johnson & Katz, 1973; Pascal, 1973; Risley & Wolf, 1966; Robinson & Filler, 1971; Schopler &

Reichler, 1971; Tizard & Rees, 1974; Watson & Bassinger, 1974). Schopler and Reichler (1971), for example, note that trained parents obtained better responsiveness from their autistic children than special education teachers. Tizard and Rees (1974) report that 2-year-old children with severe language deficits were able to "catch up" by age 4 when their home environment was made more conducive to normal development. Finally, Fredricks, Baldwin, and Grove (1974) observe that their parent-training program almost doubled the rate of acquisition of the skills being taught in school. In addition, studies have shown that parent training improves parents' adjustment to raising a handicapped child as well as their ability to cope with a child's unique set of problems (Baker, 1976; Baker, Heifetz, & Murphy, 1980; MacDonald, Blott, Gordon, Spiegel, & Hartmann, 1974).

THE NEED FOR PARENT TRAINING

A growing body of literature suggests that language-impaired children are exposed to a different linguistic environment than normal language learners (Bondurant, Romeo, & Kretschmer, 1983; Buium, Rynders, & Turnure, 1974; Clezy, 1979; Cohen, Beckwith, & Parmelee, 1978; Eheart, 1982; Lasky & Klopp, 1982; Newhoff & Browning, 1983; Petersen & Sherrod, 1982; Wulbert, Inglis, Kreigsmann, & Mills, 1975).

Buium, Rynders, and Turnure (1974) report that children with Down's syndrome were exposed to significantly more single-word responses, imperatives, and incomplete sentences than normal chil-

dren. Wulbert, Inglis, Kriegsmann, and Mills (1975) found language-impaired children received less verbal interaction and were involved in more parallel activities than children with normal language. Petersen and Sherrod (1982) report that mothers of language-impaired children used more asynchronous responses than mothers of children with normal language. Finally, Lasky and Klopp (1982) observe that mothers of language-impaired children used more gestures and commands when compared with mothers of normal language-learning children.

Cross (1984) presents an excellent review of this literature, and concludes, "The evidence for a strong effect of child impairment on parental language has been amply demonstrated" (p. 12). Given the deviant interactive patterns between parents and their language-impaired children, and evidence that children whose parents receive specialized training make greater progress in therapy than those whose parents do not, the question is no longer "Should parents become involved in the intervention process?" but rather, "*How* should parents become involved in the intervention process?"

THE PARENT IS THE CLIENT

Student clinicians are taught numerous approaches to intervention with handicapped clients, depending on the client's age, handicapping condition, and level of severity. Often, however, they are uncertain how to deal effectively with their clients' significant others (e.g., classroom teachers, resource teachers, Headstart or day-care personnel, parents), for these individuals are not the focus of traditional intervention. What should they be told? How should they be educated? What behaviors need to be modified? What role(s) should significant others play in the handicapped child's language habilitation process? How much time should clinicians spend with them? These are but a few of the issues that remain unresolved in the mind of the speech–language clinician, even after rigorous training at the graduate level.

Perhaps the most difficult aspect of implementing a program designed to train parents and significant others is recognizing who the client actually is. To most clinicians, regardless of whom they are training, the handicapped child is viewed as the client. Such an attitude is unfortunate because, more often than not, it gives parent training ancillary status. Simply put, the client is the individual whose behavior the professional is attempting to change. During child-directed therapy, the client is, of course, the child. In the case of parent training, however, the primary goal is to alter the parent's interactive behavior; thus the parent becomes the client. This approach to intervention is often difficult to conceptualize because it seems to contradict basic clinical and educational preparation. Speech–language clinicians typically see themselves as primary intervention agents for language-impaired children. Diverting attention to parents and significant others requires acknowledging two concepts: (a) that someone else is capable of functioning in the child's behalf as a primary change agent; and (b) that the child is not neglected or receiving less intervention as a result of this decision. It is unfortunate when the extent or intensity of intervention with language-impaired children is measured in terms of the amount of time that clinicians spend with each child. It is unfortunate because "language intervention" refers to a habilitative process. Who are or who should be the agents of this process is a matter to be determined by the clinician.

The speech–language clinician is but one of a number of individuals who is in a position to have a meaningful impact on a child's interactive language behavior. Rather than relying on the sophistication of a graduate education to become the sole provider of language therapy, clinicians should use their skills and talents to identify and train those individuals who are in a position to expand each child's interactive teaching environment.

THE PARENTS' ROLE

Once the critical change agents in a child's habilitative programming have been identified, the clinician must determine the roles these individuals will assume in the language-intervention process. To some extent, these will be determined by the type and severity of the child's language impairment. Some clinicians (Adler, 1983; King, 1976) advocate training parents to become paraprofessionals. They argue that traditional language therapy with severely and profoundly impaired children has not been demonstrated to be effective. Thus, these children must be exposed to a therapeutic process that involves repeated episodes of intensive intervention on a daily basis. Since this process is well beyond what most speech–language clinicians can provide, parents and significant others must

Once the critical change agents in a child's habilitative programming have been identified, the clinician must determine the roles these individuals will assume in the language-intervention process.

be trained to assume the role of the clinician.

The approach used in the Parent Training Program at the University of South Carolina (USC) differs from that advocated by Adler (1983) and King (1976) in a number of areas. First, the program was designed for the type of children typically seen in the USC Early Language Programs: $2^1/_2$–5 years of age, talking in one-to-three-word utterances. Second, the goal was not to train parents and significant others to be miniclinicians, but rather to be general language facilitators. And third, training was designed to be short term, ranging from 8 to 10 weeks in length. The language-impaired children involved in this program do not typically receive direct language therapy during the parent-training period. This is not by design, but primarily due to parents' time constraints. Once parent training is terminated, most children are enrolled in either individual or group therapy.

THE CONTENT OF PARENT TRAINING

Appropriate interactive styles

Establishing semantic contingency

Two basic approaches are available to clinicians in attempting to structure adults' interactions with language-learning children: (a) they can teach the adults the skills necessary for maintaining the child's attention so that it may be directed toward specific items and activities (generally, ones that interest the adult), or (b) they can train adults to follow the child's lead and attend to items that interest the child. In either instance, the joint reference must be established for optimal language-learning to take place (Bruner, 1975). In traditional child-directed therapy, clinicians commonly use the first, or what Fey (1986) terms the "trainer-oriented approach." Clinicians' therapy time is limited, and they have specific goals to accomplish within a particular session. Thus, any approach that fails to direct the child's attention to specific items is considered "unstructured." As Fey (1986) explains:

In trainer-oriented approaches, the trainer is in virtually complete control of the language learning situation. She has established notations about what the child should learn, how it should be learned, and where it should be learned. She controls the stimuli that the child must attend to, how the child must respond, and the specific contingencies that follow correct and incorrect responses. In at least some sense, the mechanisms of learning are placed in the hands of the trainer, not the child. (p. 191).

There are numerous advantages, however, to a child-centered approach. First, training parents to follow the child's lead, avoids task refusal and thus reduces behavior problems that often interfere with the learning process. Second, the approach guarantees joint reference; the parent simply shifts to whatever action or object the child is attending. Third, it enhances semantic contingency; conversely, fourth, it reduces the number of asynchronous responses, or topic shifts. According to Cross (1984):

In the literature on normal development, there are consistent findings that parental semantic contingency is positively associated with progress in a number of aspects of children's language development, particularly at the early stage when children first produce structured, multiword utterances. (p. 6).

Snow, Midkiff-Borunda, Small, and Proctor (1984) furthermore report that "language acquisition is impeded by a high frequency of adult utterances that change the topic or that do not relate to the child's focus of attention, ongoing activity, or previous utterance" (p. 74). Thus, the Parent Training Program teaches parents to be skilled observers who wait for the child to act and then "seize the present situation . . . to get in a bit of teaching" (Seegmiller, 1973, p. 7). In short, an utterance or action produced by the child represents a stimulus to which the parent is taught to respond.

Eliciting appropriate language

To facilitate a child's language development, parents and significant others must acquire an ability to elicit verbalizations in natural contexts. During the 3 years in which the Parent Training Program has been operational, the staff has had numerous opportunities to observe the interactions between parents and their children while they are seated in the waiting room prior to parent training. A striking feature of these interchanges is the constant interrogation that results from parents' well-intended, but misdirected, attempts to elicit speech from their children. Parents of language-impaired children appear concerned not only with the errors in their children's speech, but also with the limited amount of talking the children do. As a result, parents appear to expend a great deal of time and energy trying to get the child to talk more. *What is this, Johnny? What's that? Say 'tractor.' No, 'trac-tor'! What color is it? Say 'orange.' What are those over there? Say 'marbles.' How many are there?* And the interrogation goes on.

Such clinical observations appear to be consistent with the research findings of Marshall, Hegrenes, and Goldstein (1973), who report that parents of language-impaired children use more questions and directives to elicit speech than parents of normal language learners.

Clinicians experienced in the art of language sampling (Lee, 1974) realize that eliciting utterances through direct prodding or constant questioning has a number of undesirable consequences. First, talking becomes an unpleasant experience for the child, who is continually harassed to perform a difficult act. Second, as a result, the child is less likely to talk when pressured by parents. The scenario resembles a parent trying in vain to get the child to perform for a visiting relative. The more the parent tries, the less likely the child is to perform. Third, the interrogation process becomes a one-sided affair; the parent asks a question, a brief period of silence follows; the parents asks the same or a different question, more silence follows; the parent supplies the answer and demands an imitation. Pragmatically speaking, as long as the sender continues to generate messages, the other individual in the dyad remains the receiver. Switching roles (turn taking) requires more than sending an appropriate message (e.g., requesting a response). It requires that ample periods of silence be provided for that reply. Fourth, and perhaps most important, the utterances that parents do elicit using this approach generally will not reflect the child's true language capability. A single-word utterance, for example, is the appropriate response to all yes/no and most *wh*-questions.

The USC Parent Training Program teaches parents the art of generating language interactions that enable their children to use a variety of the more advanced structures available in their repertoires. Then, once the parent is able to elicit good language from the child, they are ready to learn various techniques to facilitate the elaboration of utterances. Thus, a parent's role is twofold—to get the child to use what language he or she has and then, to enhance this language base with various facilitative techniques.

Language facilitative techniques

Positive feedback

Furrow, Nelson, and Benedict (1979), Ellis and Wells (1980), Newport (1977), and Snow, Midkiff-Borunda, Small, and Proctor (1984) report that positive feedback (acknowledgment) is highly correlated with language improvement. According to Snow, Midkiff-Borunda, Small, and Proctor (1984), "most children, especially those with disordered language, need or at least benefit from some feedback as to the correctness and the communicative effectiveness of their utterances" (p. 74). Finally, Cross (1984) notes that "the literature on both normal and impaired children suggests that parental speech to impaired children could usefully be modified to more frequently support children's attempts at communication" (p. 7). Thus, parents are first taught to provide positive feedback for their child's verbalizations by acknowledging each communicative attempt. Such acknowledgment initially consists of praise and imitation of the child's utterances.

Expansions

Parents are next taught to expand all incomplete and grammatically incorrect utterances produced by the child. The rationale for using expansions is twofold. First, expansions have been shown to help facilitate grammatical development in young children (Maulof & Dodd, 1972; Nelson, 1977). Second, language-learning children are more likely to spontaneously imitate expanded utterances than any other form of adult verbalization (Folger & Chapman, 1978; Scherer & Olswang, 1984; Seitz & Stewart, 1975; Slobin, 1968).

Comments

Comments, sometimes termed models, expatiations, and semantic extensions, are utterances that provide new semantic information regarding a previous utterance. For example, were a child to say, *Daddy shoe*, the mother might respond, *Yes* (acknowledgment), *that's daddy's shoe* (expansion). *It's a big shoe, isn't it?* (comment). Of all the adult interactive behaviors, comments and expansions have been reported to be most closely linked to language growth (Barnes, Gutfreund, Satterly, & Wells, 1983; Cross, 1978). Generally, parents in the program are taught to provide appropriate comments following imitations or expansions of their children's utterances.

THE PROCESS OF PARENT TRAINING

Clinical procedures

Parents are trained individually during 30-minute weekly sessions for a period of 8–10 weeks. During the first and each subsequent session, the parent and child are videotaped while interacting freely for 15 minutes. During the week following the first session, the videotaped sample is analyzed to determine initial training goals and select sample target behaviors. Sample target behaviors are instances observed on the videotape in which the parent exhibits the desired behavior(s). When the parent returns for training the next week, the goals are presented, followed by the samples of the parent performing exactly as desired. Negative or undesirable interactions are neither discussed nor shown on the videotape. In this way, a positive and supportive atmosphere is developed and maintained throughout training. An example of instructions to the parent follows:

If you remember, Mrs. Ander, last week we videotaped you and Julie playing together. In going over the tape, we've noticed that there are a number of excellent things that you do that are helpful to Julie's language development. For instance, we noticed that you constantly shifted your attention to whatever *she* was interested in. Here on the videotape you can see an example of what we're talking about. There you are playing with Julie and

the clown puppet. Now watch what you do when Julie suddenly discovers the toy airplane on the chair. Notice that when Julie pointed and said "airpay" you said, "Yes, That's an airplane. Would you like to go get it?" Rather than trying to keep her interested in the puppet on your hand, you shifted your attention to an item that she was interested in. This is a very important technique that we like to see all of our parents do more often.

Also, Mrs. Anders, we noticed that when Julie said, "Airpay fly" you said, "Yes, the airplane flies." You took what Julie said and said it back to her in a more adultlike form by filling in the omitted words. This is what we call an *expansion*, and is a technique that will help Julie learn to make better sentences. Let's look at some other examples where you expanded Julie's speech. . . .

Finally, Mrs. Anders, we'd like to compliment you on the fact that you are responding to Julie's language rather than her pronunciation. We would like to encourage you to keep doing this. Her pronunciation will come in time, but like you, we are more concerned with the types of sentences that Julie makes when she talks.

Thus, parents are not taught a new set of interactive behaviors. Rather, the program's training goals focus on increasing the frequency of existing behaviors. Generally, no parent fails to exhibit the target behavior in question. In this way, the training centers around good parent–child interactions observed on the videotape, allowing a parent's own behavior to represent a model for change.

Parents are asked to keep a communication diary, listing the utterances the child produces during a 10-minute period each day. Beside each utterance, the parent is to indicate what was happening at the time as well as what the child meant by each utterance. When the parent returns the next week, the entries in the diary are discussed. The communication diary serves several important functions. First, the transcribed utterances can be compared with those produced by the child in the clinic, giving the clinicians insight into discrepancies that may exist. Second, the act of writing down utterances gives parents a brief but structured daily task and ensures that they will attend to their child's communicative skills outside the clinic. Third, it enables the parents to become more cognizant of their child's level of communicative functioning.

To summarize, odd-numbered training sessions (1, 3, 5, etc.) are spent videotaping the parent and child for 15 minutes, followed by review of the communication diary. Even-numbered sessions are devoted to observing the previous week's videotapes, with emphasis on viewing the interactions that exemplify the appropriate target behaviors. Each videotape serves as a means for assessing the parent's

> *Each videotape serves as a means for assessing the parent's progress with respect to goals presented the previous week as well as baseline data for goals for the coming week.*

progress with respect to goals presented the previous week as well as baseline data for goals for the coming week.

Dismissal from parent training

Parents are dismissed from parent training once they demonstrate that they can exhibit the target behaviors on a consistent basis (i.e., over two consecutive training sessions). Objective measurements of behavioral change are collected through the use of the observational scoring chart depicted in Figure 1. By comparing the scores from a parent's initial taped interaction with those of the most recent tap-

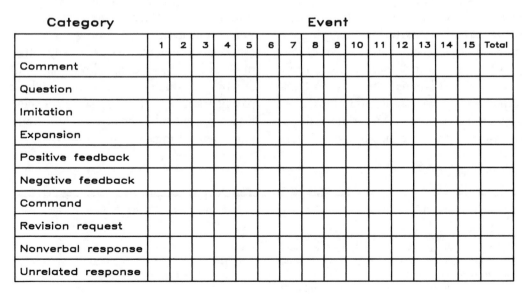

Category	Event															
	1	2	3	4	5	6	7	8	9	10	11	12	13	14	15	Total
Comment																
Question																
Imitation																
Expansion																
Positive feedback																
Negative feedback																
Command																
Revision request																
Nonverbal response																
Unrelated response																

Figure 1. Interactional analysis chart.

ing, clinicians are able to document improvement and, thus, have access to accountability data.

Since most of the children are enrolled in direct language therapy once parent training is discontinued, follow-up and continued consultation is relatively easy and, as a result, routine. Such follow-up may be more difficult in programs that do not provide comprehensive services or in instances in which the child receives direct therapy elsewhere. In such cases, there may be a tendency to lose contact with the families once parent training is completed.

Limitations of the program

All of the parents participating in the training program have been willing to discuss its strengths and weaknesses with the clinicians. Generally, the most frequently cited weakness is that the children tend to be more verbal at home than in the clinic. As a result, parents report feeling frustrated when their child produces fewer verbalizations during the taping sessions. When the child is less verbal, the parent has fewer opportunities to use newly learned language facilitative techniques such as expansion and imitation. As a result, the parent may use more directives in an attempt to encourage the child to talk more on camera (e.g., "Say _____" or "What's this?"). The communication diaries have been well received in light of this general concern. Parents appear to be willing to take the necessary time to maintain the diary as a means of documenting their descriptions of the child's verbal skills.

The program's use of videotaped parent–child interactions represents both a strength and limitation. The obvious benefit of replaying videotaped sessions is that parents are able to observe their own behavior as models for change. They need not depend solely on the clinician's verbal descriptions. However, the program is limited by several requirements. First, the clinician must have easy and routine access to video recording and playback equipment. Second, a quiet, self-contained room must be available for taping and training to take place. Third, the clinician must have ample time to review each taped session as well as train parents individually. While this model of parent training is ideal for students in clinical practicum, it has shortcomings in certain other environments. As with any other intervention approach, clinicians must carefully evaluate the various models of parent training available and select those that are acceptable or adaptable to their particular setting.

REFERENCES

Adler, S. (1973). *The non-verbal child* (3rd ed.). Springfield, IL: Charles C. Thomas.

Baker, B. (1976). Parent involvement in programming for developmentally disabled children. In L. Lloyd (Ed.), *Communication assessment and intervention strategies*. Baltimore: University Park Press.

Baker, B., Brightman, A., Heifetz, L., & Murphy, D. (1973). *Read project series: 10 instructional manuals for parents*. Cambridge: Behavioral Education Projects.

Baker, B., Heifetz, L., & Brightman, A. (1973). *Parents as teachers: Manuals for behavior modification of the retarded child*. Cambridge: Behavioral Education Projects.

Baker, B., Heifetz, L., & Murphy, D. (1980). Behavioral training for parents of mentally retarded children: One-year follow-up. *American Journal of Mental Deficiency, 85,* 31–38.

Baker, B., Murphy, D., Heifetz, L., & Brightman, A. (1975). Parents as teachers: Followup after 18 months. Cambridge: Behavioral Education Projects.

Bangs, T. (1979). *Birth to three: Developmental learning of the handicapped child.* Boston: Teaching Resources.

Barnes, S., Gutfreund, M., Satterly, D., & Wells, G. (1983). Characteristics of adult speech which predict children's language development. *Journal of Child Language, 10,* 57–65.

Berkowitz, B., & Graziano, A. (1972). Training parents as behavior therapists: A review. *Behavior Research Therapy, 10,* 291–317.

Bondurant, J., Romeo, D., & Kretschmer, R. (1983). Language behaviors of mothers of children with normal and delayed language. *Language, Speech, and Hearing Services in Schools, 14,* 233–242.

Bruner, J. (1975). The ontogenesis of speech acts. *Journal of Child Language, 2,* 1–19.

Buium, N., Rynders, J., & Turnure, J. (1974). The early maternal linguistic environment of normal and Down's syndrome language-impaired children. *American Journal of Mental Deficiency, 79,* 52–58.

Cartright, L., & Ruscello, D. (1979). A survey of parent involvement practices in the speech clinic. *Asha, 21,* 275–279.

Clezy, G. (1979). *Modification of the mother–child interchange in language, speech, and hearing.* Baltimore: University Park Press.

Cohen, S., Beckwith, L., & Parmelee, A. (1978). Receptive language development in preterm children as related to caregiver–child interaction. *Pediatrics, 61,* 16–20.

Cross, T. (1978). Mothers' speech and its association with rate of language acquisition in young children. In N. Waterson & C. Snow (Eds.), *The development of communication.* London: Wiley.

Cross, T. (1984). Habilitating the language-impaired child: Ideas from studies of parent–child interaction. *Topics in Language Disorders, 4,* 1–14.

Denhoff, M., Hyman, I. (1977). Parent programs for developmental management. In T. Tjossem (Ed.), *Intervention strategies for high risk infants and young children.* Baltimore: University Park Press.

Eheart, B. (1982). Mother–child interactions with nonretarded and mentally retarded preschoolers. *American Journal of Mental Deficiency, 87,* 20–25.

Ellis, R., & Wells, G. (1980). Enabling factors in adult–child discourse. *First Language, 1,* 46–82.

Fey, M. (1986). *Language intervention with young children.* San Diego, CA: College-Hill.

Folger, J., & Chapman, R. (1978). A pragmatic analysis of spontaneous imitations. *Journal of Child Language, 5,* 7–24.

Fredricks, H., Baldwin, D., & Grove, D. (1974). A home-center based parent-training model. In J. Grim (Ed.), *Training parents to teach: Four models.* Chapel Hill, NC: Technical Assistance Development Systems.

Fudala, J., England, G., & Ganoung, L. (1972). Utilization of parents in a speech correction program. *Exceptional Children, 39,* 407–412.

Furrow, D., Nelson, K., & Benedict, H. (1979). Mothers' speech to children and syntactic development: Some simple relationships. *Journal of Child Language, 6,* 423–442.

Johnson, C., & Katz, R. (1973). Using parents as change agents for their children: A review. *Journal of Child Psychology, Psychiatry, and Allied Disciplines, 14,* 181–200.

King, D. (1986). An innovative language habilitative program for preschool age children. In S. Adler (Ed.), *Early identification and intensive remediation of language retarded children.* Springfield, IL: Charles C. Thomas.

Lasky, E., & Klopp, K. (1982). Parent–child interactions in normal and language-disordered children. *Journal of Speech and Hearing Disorders, 47,* 7–18.

Lee, L. (1974). *Developmental sentence analysis.* Evanston: IL: Northwestern University Press.

MacDonald, J., Blott, J., Gordon, K., Spiegel, B., & Hartmann, M. (1974). An experimental parent training program for language delayed children. *Journal of Speech and Hearing Disorders, 39,* 395–415.

Maulof, R.,& Dodd, D. (1972). The role of exposure, imitation, and expansion in the acquisition of an artificial rule. *Developmental Psychology, 2,* 195–203.

Manolson, M. (1979). Parent training: A means of implementing pragmatics in early language remediation. *Human Communication, 4,* 275–281.

Marshall, N., Hegrenes, J., & Goldstein, S. (1973). Verbal interactions: Mothers and their retarded children vs mothers and their nonretarded children. *American Journal of Mental Deficiency, 77,* 415–419.

Nelson, K. (1973). Structure and strategy in learning to talk. *Monographs of the Society for Research in Child Development, 3* (149).

Nelson, K.E. (1977). Facilitating childrens' syntax acquisition. *Developmental Psychology, 13,* 101–107.

Newhoff, M., & Browning, J. (1983). Interaction variation: A view from the language-disordered child's world. *Topics in Language Disorders, 3,* 49–60.

Newport, E. (1977). Motherese: The speech of mothers to young children. In N.J. Castellan, D.B. Pisoni, & G.R. Potts (Eds.), *Cognitive Theory* (Vol. 2). Hillsdale, NJ: Erlbaum.

Pascal, C. (1973). Application of behavior modification by

parents for treatment of a brain damaged child. In B. Ashem & E. Posner (Eds.), *Adaptive learning: Behavior modification with children.* Elmsord, NY: Pergamon Press.

Petersen, G., & Sherrod, K. (1982). Relationship of maternal language to language development and language delay of children. *American Journal of Mental Deficiency, 86,* 391–398.

Pushaw, D. (1976). *Teach your child to talk.* New York: Dantree Press.

Risley, T., & Wolf, M. (1966). Experimental manipulation of autistic behaviors and generalization into the home. In R. Ulrich, T. Stachnik, & J. Mabry (Eds.), *Control of human behavior* (pp. 193–198). Glenview, IL: Scott & Foresman.

Robinson, C., & Filler, J. (1971). Maternal teaching style assessment scale. In S. Bricker & W. Bricker (Eds.) *Toddler research and intervention project report: Year I. IMRID Behavioral Science Monograph 20,* Nashville, TN: Institute on Mental Retardation and Intellectual Development, George Peabody College.

Scherer, N., & Olswang, L. (1984). Role of mothers' expansions in stimulating childrens' language production. *Journal of Speech and Hearing Research, 27,* 387–396.

Schopler, E., & Reichler, R. (1971). Parents as cotherapists in the treatment of psychotic children. *Journal of Autism and Childhood Schizophrenia, 1,* 87–102.

Seegmiller, B. (1973, March). *The norms and patterns of mother–child interaction in free play.* Paper presented to the biennial meeting of the Society for Research in Child Development, Philadelphia.

Seitz, M., & Stewart, C. (1975). Imitations and expansions: Some developmental aspects of mother–child communications. *Developmental Psychology, 11,* 763–769.

Shearer, M., & Shearer, D. (1972). The Portage Project: A model for early childhood education. *Exceptional Children, 36,* 210–217.

Slobin, D. (1968). Imitation and grammatical development in children. In N. Endler, L. Boulter, & H. Osser (Eds.), *Contemporary issues in developmental psychology.* New York: Holt, Rinehart, & Winston.

Snow, C., Midkiff-Borunda, S., Small, A., & Proctor, A. (1984). Therapy as social interaction: Analyzing the contexts for language remediation. *Topics in Language Disorders, 4,* 72–85.

Tizard, B., & Rees, J. (1974). A comparison of the effects of adoption, restoration to the natural mother, and continued institutionalization on the cognitive development of four year old children. *Child Development, 45,* 92–99.

Watson, L., & Bassinger, J. (1974). Parent training technology: A potential service delivery system. *Mental Retardation, 12,* 3–10.

Wulbert, M., Inglis, S., Kriegsmann, E., & Mills, B. (1975). Language delay associated with mother–child interactions. *Developmental Psychology, 11,* 61–70.

A parent-implemented language model for at-risk and developmentally delayed preschool children

Mary Trabue Fitzgerald, PhD
Language Development Consultant
Regional Intervention Program
Nashville, Tennessee

Dianne E. Karnes, MA
Language Consultant
Positive Education Program
Cleveland, Ohio

PERHAPS THE most debilitating characteristic of young at-risk and developmentally handicapped children is a lack of functional communication or a delay in the acquisition of early language skills. In recent years a plethora of language-based early-intervention programs for such children and their families have appeared (see Bricker, 1986, for a review). A majority of these intervention programs have involved some form of specific training for parents or significant others based on the premise that families can and should function as behavioral change agents for their own children (Carney, 1983; Cartwright, 1981).

Reviews of the parent training literature indicate that legal or advocacy (Turnbull & Turnbull, 1986), fiscal (Bruder & Bricker, 1985; Timm & Rule, 1981), and continuity or generalization rationales (Bricker & Casuso, 1979; Sanders & James, 1983) have been offered in support of parent involvement models. Many contemporary intervention programs,

Top Lang Disord, 1987, 7(3), 31–46
© 1987 Aspen Publishers, Inc.

whether derived from developmental (Bloom & Lahey, 1978; Bromwich, 1981; Dunst, 1981) or behavioral perspectives (Halle, Alpert, & Anderson, 1984; McCormick & Schiefelbusch, 1984; Rogers-Warren & Warren, 1984), have as a primary goal the training of significant others to facilitate language acquisition through the use of adult–child interaction strategies that presumably are used in functional exchanges in the home and preschool contexts.

Unfortunately, recent recognition of generalization and maintenance problems in behavioral programs (Cordisco & Strain, 1986; Sanders & James, 1983; Stokes & Baer, 1977; Warren, Rogers-Warren, Baer, & Guess, 1980), especially those focused on task-specific skills trained in highly structured one-on-one clinical settings, has forced language interventionists to reexamine training models. In addition, developmental language researchers have shifted their focus from the acquisition of specific language structures to a more global description of communicative exchanges in adult–child dyadic interactions. Naturalistic studies of the language acquisition process that have examined the interrelationships among social, cognitive, and linguistic domains (Bates, 1976; Dore, 1974; Halliday, 1975) have described adult strategies that support children's early communicative attempts in normally developing infants (Bruner, 1983; Moerk, 1983; Schachter, 1979) and in at-risk and handicapped children (Cross, 1984; Rogers-Warren & Warren, 1984). These changes in developmental perspectives, coupled with criticisms of traditional learning theory models, have

major significance for language specialists working with special-needs preschoolers (Friel-Patti & Lougeay-Mottinger, 1985; Snow, Midkiff-Borunda, Small, & Proctor, 1984).

The language intervention approach of the Regional Intervention Programs for Parents and Preschools (RIP) is responding to these changes in contemporary language theories. Drawing on both pragmatic and behavioral frameworks, RIP language intervention consultants have attempted to locate "overlapping and complementary principles and strategies" (McCormick, 1986, p. 123) within the naturalistic and operant models. An ecological approach to language intervention has begun to evolve that uses behavioral techniques to facilitate the acquisition of developmentally appropriate communication skills within the context of parent–child interactions in daily teaching and caregiving environments. The balancing of learning and developmental perspectives is not unique to the RIP model but has elements in common with several other ecological approaches (Mahoney & Weller, 1980) including: the Adult–Child Communication Project (MacDonald & Gillette, 1984), the Communication Model (Hayden, Morris, & Bailey, 1977), the Natural Environment Language Assessment and Intervention Model (Halle, Alpert, & Anderson, 1984), incidental or milieu teaching (Hart & Risley, 1975, 1980; Hart & Rogers-Warren, 1978; Rogers-Warren & Warren, 1980; Warren & Kaiser, 1986), and the Responsive Curriculum (McCormick & Noonan, 1984). The participation of parents and significant others in all phases of the RIP language intervention program represents a notable extension of the ecological approach. Using families as language trainers for other parents, as language interventionists in the classroom, and as collectors of assessment and evaluation data, in addition to their role as communicative interactants with their own children, constitutes a powerful modification of traditional language programs.

THE RIP SERVICE-DELIVERY SYSTEM

RIP began operation in 1969 as a pioneering effort in the treatment of families with young, at-risk and developmentally handicapped children within a noncategorical behavior-management framework. Despite extensive methodological refinements and structural adaptations to meet changing theoretical and service requirements, the essential elements of the original model remain evident in the current RIP network, which is composed of 22 certified programs sponsored by private organizations, governmental agencies, and public school systems in 16 communities throughout the United States, Canada, and Brazil (Timm, 1985). These basic components include extensive use of parents and classroom teachers, a parent-support network of professional consultants, a data-based clinical operation, and a modular service-delivery system.

Parental implementation is the central element of the RIP model. Parents serve as primary behavioral change agents for their own children, as case managers for fellow parents learning to perform the same functions, as implementers of the

service-delivery system's daily operation, and ultimately as evaluators of the program's strengths and shortcomings (Hester, 1977; Timm & Rule, 1981).

Parental participation is organized into two phases: active treatment and payback. During treatment, parents work individually with their own children both at the RIP site and at home. When not engaged in individual sessions with their own children or in training and feedback sessions with experienced parents following each session, the treatment parents assist in other program activities such as helping in the classrooms, collecting observational data, preparing materials, or supervising the sibling nursery. When a family's active treatment phase is completed, parents participate in a system of payback of time and skills to the program while their children continue to be enrolled in the project. During the payback phase, parents concentrate on support and training of newer parents by conducting intake interviews, managing individual therapeutic sessions, training data collectors, recording and analyzing coded data, and teaching in the classrooms.

Parental implementation in an RIP model does not take place in a vacuum, without benefit of professional expertise and guidance. The resource staff members include graduate-level individuals in developmental psychology, special education, early childhood education, and social work who devote full attention to the ongoing operation of the programs and research expansion projects. In addition, professional consultants in the areas of pediatrics, child psychiatry, clinical psychology, speech–language pathology and audiology, pediatric motor development, and educational assessment offer direct guidance to parents and staff members as needed.

Within the RIP model, the speech–language pathologist serves as a consultant and a team member responsible for the implementation of individual language programs for each child, as shown in Figure 1. As this figure clearly illustrates, the speech–language consultant provides professional expertise in evaluation and language program development, while significant others, in their roles as parents, classroom teachers, and case managers, serve as the adult interactants who implement the daily intervention. The consultant's primary duties are to conduct speech–language evaluations for diagnostic and educational placement purposes, to develop and monitor individual intervention programs derived from interac-

tion analyses and communication assessments, to offer inservice training for the staff regarding developmental language patterns and adult–child communication, to create parent-training materials, to design observational coding systems for adult and child behaviors, and to assist in research and expansion efforts.

The relationships between parents and the professional staff are illuminated by examining two other essential elements of the model: data-based clinical operation and modular format. The original behavioral orientation of the intervention methodology used in the RIP presupposes that all treatment activities and outcomes can be quantified and measured. The extent to which the data system is implemented by parents remains a significant aspect of the model (Hester, 1977). Each module of the intervention program is designed to address behavioral, cognitive, motor, or

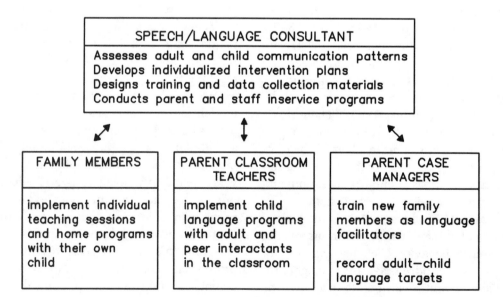

Figure 1. Roles and functions of staff and parents within the RIP language model.

communicative deficits and includes specification of the target skill, the antecedent and consequent events, and the child's responses, as well as a criterion measure for desired change. Observation data for each program phase are recorded daily during interactions between the adult and child and portrayed in graphic form for discussion and analysis by the parents themselves (Parrish & Hester, 1980).

The modular system developed at RIP (Timm & Rule, 1981) divides services into specific functions: referral and intake, generalization training, individual tutoring, preschool classrooms, liaison, media, and administration. Each module, with the exception of administration, is supervised by a resource staff member and coordinated by parents.

The referral and intake module accepts referrals from parents, professionals, or other agencies, schedules an intake interview, and enrolls the family in the direct service module appropriate to their needs.

The generalization training (GT) module is designed to teach parents to use differential reinforcement techniques to manage their children's behavior in a variety of structured play sessions and simultaneously implemented home programs (see Strain, Young, & Horowitz, 1981, for a complete description).

The individual tutoring (IT) module addresses the developmental needs of children exhibiting delays in speech and language, cognition, motor functioning, and self-help skills. IT sessions include assessment, specification of individual target behaviors, introduction of adult teaching strategies, practice sessions to attain skill mastery, and home programming to establish generalization of adults' techniques and children's skills (see Eller, Jordan, Parrish, & Elder, 1979, for a detailed description).

The classroom module is designed to develop child–child, adult–child, and child–material interactions that are developmentally appropriate and that facilitate effective functioning within a group instructional setting. Enrolled children and preschool siblings, who serve as models, participate in the classrooms where parents serve as lead teachers and assistants. Daily classroom observations of child and adult behaviors are made to help parents generalize basic interaction techniques and instructional strategies from individual IT and GT sessions to group settings. Classroom observations also serve to monitor children's behavior in a peer-group setting with a variety of adults other than their own parents or caregivers.

Classroom observations also serve to monitor children's behavior in a peer-group setting with a variety of adults other than their own parents or caregivers.

Finally, RIP classrooms serve as research settings for investigators concerned with the social behavior and language development of preschool children (Hester & Henderickson, 1977; Shores, Hester, & Strain, 1976; Strain & Timm, 1974; Strain & Wiegerink, 1975; Timm, Strain, & Eller, 1979).

THE RIP LANGUAGE CONSULTATION APPROACH

The language consultation model that is currently evolving in the RIP rests on basic assumptions that serve as a foundation for adapting pragmatic language assessment and intervention procedures to the RIP network of early intervention settings.

Assumptions

Two major assumptions provide the rationale for the RIP language approach. First, the natural context for language acquisition in young children, including those at risk for communicative disorders, is dyadic interactions with responsive, familiar adults. These facilitative exchanges provide the rich environmental database in terms of content, forms, and functions from which children learn their communicative system (Bloom & Lahey, 1978; Bruner, 1983; Cross, 1984; Lewis & Cherry, 1977; Lieven, 1984). The various types of reciprocal transactions that occur during daily child-care routines in homes and classrooms represent developmentally appropriate settings for learning a variety of interrelated motor, cognitive, social, and linguistic skills.

Second, the characteristics of these contexts, both the physical environments and the social cues available, can be systematically arranged to enhance the learning of functional linguistic skills. For example, the contingency of natural consequences can be modified; opportunities to exhibit language behaviors can be increased; and expectations within the communicative interchange can be varied. Particularly for children at risk for developmental delays or those with identified disabilities, these modifications in natural environments can enhance language acquisition.

On the basis of such balancing of social interaction and learning perspectives, the RIP language training approach facilitates the development of functional, spontaneous, appropriate communicative skills in children through the use of adult-mediated antecedents and consequences that are natural and response specific. Parents are trained to reinforce and expand their children's initial communicative repertoires toward more socially appropriate responses and more advanced linguistic forms and functions in the naturalistic contexts of adult–child play, group classroom activities, and home child-care routines. Through systematic modeling, children learn that their communication has predictable and consistent effects on their environment.

Intervention principles and procedures

The ABC assessment and intervention framework

To select child communication targets for intervention and to determine appropriate adult facilitation strategies and environmental antecedents and consequences, RIP uses the ABC analysis model depicted in Figure 2. This conceptual framework is presented to new parents through group and individual learning opportunities, which address general principles of differential reinforcement through adult attention and feedback and adult mediation of environmental events. Parents' knowledge of these techniques is measured through written assessments.

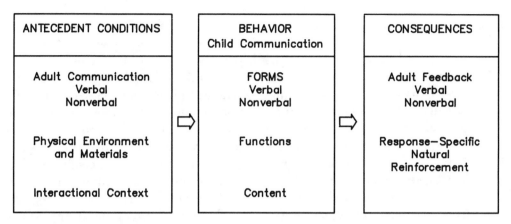

Figure 2. The ABC (antecedent–behavior–consequences) assessment intervention framework.

The subsequent application of this simplified, clearly defined interaction model for both assessment and interventions across all aspects of the RIP program ensures effective implementation by parents and significant others. The speech–language consultant helps staff members and families use the ABC framework to record and then analyze adult–child interaction patterns in dyadic play situations and in classroom activities with parent–teachers and peers. These occasions are used for baseline assessments of current communicative functioning. These observations, which are recorded using simplified forms by parent case managers, as well as communication samples and discourse analyses completed by the speech–language consultant, profile both adult and child behaviors. Baseline frequency counts and rates of verbal and nonverbal communicative behaviors are obtained. The resulting interaction patterns are then discussed with the significant others to assist them in becoming aware of how their communication affects their children's language and behavior.

Because parent–child communication is often distorted with the emotionally and behaviorally disordered preschoolers who comprise a significant portion of the RIP population, particular attention is directed to the analysis of adult conversational behaviors and interactional cues that may encourage deviant child behavior or communication. Situational features that contribute to breakdowns in parent–child communication are also specified. Certain antecedent variables, such as the rate of questioning by the adult or the structural complexity of the adults' requests, are manipulated to determine how they affect the child's responses. Similarly, the rate of parental expansions of children's single-word utterances, natural reinforcement of children's prelinguistic vocalizations, and compliance with children's requests made by pointing to preferred objects are varied to determine effects on children's communication and behavior. Within the ABC framework, parents are able to understand that receptive and expressive language skills represent one aspect of a total behavior pattern, and they learn how adult language can influence child behavior in daily social contexts.

Following the assessment phase, the ABC framework is used to specify intervention programs for children exhibiting specific language delays or deficits. Individual communication objectives derived from developmental sequences (B, the child's initiating and responding behaviors) are targeted, and adult-mediated environmental situations and cues (A, antecedents) and feedback sequences (C, consequences) that enhance the acquisition of these targets are defined. The significance of these "communicative matches" (Rogers-Warren & Warren, 1983, p. 77) between child targets and adult behaviors is emphasized by the ABC model, which focuses on the interactive nature of communication training and the importance of significant others as facilitators.

Training of significant others as communication facilitators

Significant others are specifically trained during IT sessions to apply the ABC model as a communication intervention procedure for increasing the frequency of appropriate responding and initiating behaviors and decreasing inappropriate behaviors. The IT module provides training sessions for parents and children to develop language interaction skills that will be generalized into the classroom and home settings.

After observing parent–child interactions and analyzing baseline and probe data to develop communication targets, the language consultant or case managers model specific techniques for the parents.

The case managers and parents practice each new strategy together before the parents use it with their child. For example, initially a parent might learn to arrange the environment to create a situation in which the child will need to communicate during play and then to reinforce any communicative response from the child with attention, confirming feedback, or compliance with the child's communicative intention. Another parent might practice prompting an approximate response, expanding *dolly eat* into *the dolly is hungry*, or remodeling an incorrect linguistic form. As a parent demonstrates mastery, each technique is practiced with the child, and the consultant and case manager provide feedback regarding its use and result. Subsequent sessions are used to measure parent–child language interactions relative to the newly acquired adult facilitation strategy and the child's response.

Training procedures that appear to be particularly effective in enabling families to use these behavioral techniques with their children include direct instruction, review of written procedural outlines, observation of videotaped examples of other parent–child interactions, role plays, demonstration by case managers and resource personnel, and written or verbal performance feedback. Parent-training guidelines have been developed for specifically targeted child communication behaviors that clearly define effective antecedent events and verbal cues or prompts, types of child response, and adult feedback sequences. Model–action–feedback flowcharts and "if–then" formats specifying adult antecedent and consequation strategies help parents apply general language facilitation strategies in a variety of communicative interchanges. The case managers and resource personnel also help families select content that is appropriate to each child's interests and other developmental needs as contexts for encouraging targeted language forms and pragmatic functions.

The systematic use of language expansions of children's spontaneous initiations (McLean & Vincent, 1984) and the mand-model procedures of verbal prompting and modeling to elicit requests for material (Rogers-Warren & Warren, 1980) that are taught in the RIP model have been delineated in several ecological language approaches. Similarly, the shaping and cueing sequences (Cavallaro, 1983; McCormick, 1986), the contingent delivery of natural reinforcers as consequences (Hart & Risley, 1975), the manipulation of environmental events (Klein, 1985), and time delay procedures (Halle, Alpert, & Anderson, 1984) share commonalities with other language-training curricula.

These techniques, which are congruent with natural adult–child interactions (Rogers-Warren & Warren, 1983), have also been found effective in several research studies with moderately and severely handicapped children (Alpert & Rogers-Warren, 1983; Halle, Marshall, & Spradlin, 1979; Halle, Alpert, & Anderson, 1984). Equally important, evidence has supported the feasibility of parents of at-risk toddlers serving as trainers of other parents and demonstrated the effectiveness of parent-trained significant others in using appropriate antecedent and consequation techniques with their own children (Bruder & Bricker, 1985).

Generalization of communication skills

Generalization of newly acquired skills—both children's communicative responses and adults' facilitation strategies—is enhanced by targeting behaviors across a variety of naturally occurring and planned instructional opportunities (free play, snack time, motor activities, cognitive/preacademic tasks, and family interactions). In addition, variations in physical settings (e.g., individual IT or GT sessions, classroom, home, and community facilities) and different communication partners (parents, siblings, peers, classroom parent teachers, and resource staff) are systematically introduced into the individual language plans. Figure 3 illustrates the RIP program for generalizing targeted language skills.

In the classroom, the parent teacher reinforces previously learned language targets and attempts to generate class-specific, untrained language responses in a group context using adult and peer interactions. Unique to the RIP model is the fact that parents who are the teachers in the classroom are responsible for providing input and making programming suggestions. The lead teacher is a parent staff member who coordinates the daily activities and monitors the intervention objectives for each child. The language consultant frequently assists the lead classroom teacher in designing or integrating language activities and other developmental objectives into the regular classroom routine. New parents observe the classroom, learn to count adult and child language behaviors, and gain skills in recording and graphing the resulting data. As individual communication programs are discussed,

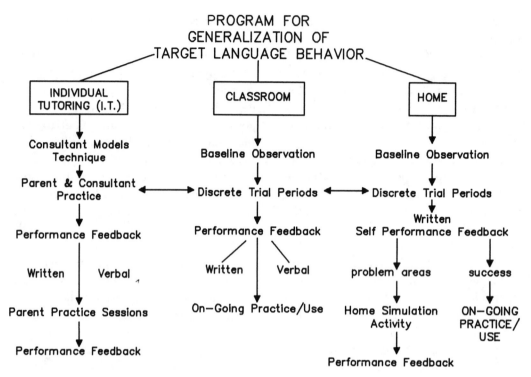

Figure 3. RIP program for generalization of target language behavior.

language facilitation strategies and intervention procedures are explained to the new families. As the parents apply the newly introduced teaching principles, they receive written and verbal feedback from the lead parent teacher regarding their classroom interactions with the children. Through active participation and practice in the various classrooms, parents become skilled at manipulating environmental events and providing reinforcing consequences to elicit targeted language behaviors.

As new parents demonstrate consistent use of language interaction techniques in the classroom and as the children's language responses generalize from the IT session to the classroom, the families are given a variety of home assignments to ensure broad generalization of skills. Significant others are encouraged to arrange the home environment (e.g., the location of preferred toys), and to examine everyday routines such as bedtime reading, when spontaneous communication can be elicited or language targets can be modeled. Consequently, these incidental teaching opportunities (Hart & Risley,

> *As the parents apply the newly introduced teaching principles, they receive written and verbal feedback from the lead parent teacher regarding their classroom interactions with the children.*

1975) that may be unique to the individual adult–child interaction are often the most effective contexts for practicing new skills or facilitating emerging behaviors.

After collecting baseline observational data for several activities and times when child-initiated communication is needed, the parents and other family members engage in specific language facilitation techniques with their child in the home setting. Written self-performance feedback is collected and shared with the parent case managers to determine whether the strategies are useful or need revision. If the techniques are successful, progress is charted over several days in different activities and at various times during the day to measure generalization.

By providing varied contexts and multiple interactants during the training phase of the program and by focusing on language behaviors that are defined by form and function but allow for variety in content individualized to the child's interests, the generalization shortcomings associated with traditional models are reduced (Cordisco & Strain, 1986). Similarly, the generalization and maintenance of parents' language-training techniques and incidental teaching strategies is enhanced by using the ABC model across different RIP modules, by emphasizing interactive techniques that are general rather than task-specific, and by focusing on having the adult apply these principles in a variety of settings and with many different youngsters including their own child.

Data-based documentation of language interventions

In keeping with the RIP emphasis on precise measurement, the implementation of the language program is carefully monitored by parent case managers and raters, who collect direct observational data on the children's language behaviors and the adults' facilitation techniques during individual sessions and during indirect teaching activities in the classroom. Parents then record these observations on simple forms that allow them to calculate both percentages and rates of specific adult antecedent and consequent behaviors and the child's correct and incorrect responses across diverse activities and varying partners. Case managers and resource personnel help parents and significant others to display the language data in graphic form to facilitate ongoing analysis and modification of individual intervention programs. Specific criterion mastery levels are set for all adult and child language behaviors to determine when communication goals have been achieved and new targets can be developed.

While behavioral data derived from the ABC model and the communication analyses form the basis of the assessment–intervention process, traditional standardized instruments may be administered at the request of the family or staff to establish the language functioning of individual children compared with their age peers. These data can be used to determine the need for specific language training in IT sessions, to document changes in formal linguistic skills during the RIP treatment phase, or to provide normative data for referral to other agencies when the family leaves the RIP project.

A CASE EXAMPLE

Bobby (not his real name), a 3; 9-year-old boy, was referred to the RIP project with a diagnosis of developmental delays in cognitive, motor, and language skills complicated by severe behavioral problems. Although his reported mean length of utterance was 1.6 morphemes per utterance, his phonology was marked by numerous omissions and his vocabulary consisted of approximately 100 words. His expressive language productions were characterized by frequent adjacent repetitions of adult utterances with little communicative intent.

Initial sessions consisted of obtaining baseline data on mother–child interaction patterns during 10-minute play sessions. Analyses revealed that Bobby's mother engaged in a directive communication style characterized by 65 percent use of questions and 25 percent use of declarative statements or commands. The mother-to-child turn ratios averaged 20 adult to 2 child turns per session. Bobby imitated 90 percent of his mother's single-word utterances, with only 10 spontaneous utterances per session. He maintained eye contact with his mother in 20 percent of the coded intervals and displayed frequent oppositional behavior (six occurrences per session).

Initial feedback was provided to the mother, and objectives for intervention were jointly determined by the language consultant, the special education resource teacher, and the parent. Two objectives were identified for immediate intervention: first, to decrease the mother's frequent use of questions and a dominant communicative style from a mother-to-child turn ratio of 20:2 with 7 questions per minute to a mother-to-child turn ratio of 10:10 with 1 adult question per minute; and second, to expand the utterance length and semantic complexity of the child's language.

Demonstration sessions were conducted to train Bobby's mother to use indirect language stimulation techniques and to reduce the frequency of questioning. The consultant initially modeled these strategies through role playing, and then the mother was encouraged to interact with Bobby, applying the new interaction pattern of asking only one question per minute, while the consultant and the case manager recorded her language behavior. Verbal and written performance feedback was then provided, and practice sessions were charted until criterion mastery was reached.

After the mother was comfortable and reliable with a more indirect interaction style, sessions involving the training of early sentence rules and turn taking were introduced. The Agent–Action structure (e.g., *mommy throw, Bobby throw*) was chosen because it is one of the earliest occurring sentence rules and because Bobby enjoyed playing with a ball. The mother was trained to use the procedure through role-playing Agent–Action sequences with the language consultant, who modeled a motor action and required a verbal response. After the mother was comfortable with the technique, both adult and child data were charted by the

After the mother was comfortable and reliable with a more indirect interaction style, sessions involving the training of early sentence rules and turn taking were introduced.

case manager during individual parent-implemented training sessions with Bobby. Data were obtained on the mother's production of the Agent–Action sequence as well as praising, remodeling or prompting the child's responses, which were coded as correct, incorrect, or nonresponsive, until both mother and child reached 80 percent criterion mastery.

While Bobby was learning to imitate and initiate new language targets in the IT session, a baseline classroom observation of his verbal and nonverbal interactions was conducted. These data were analyzed by the consultant with the classroom teacher as a basis for incorporating the new language objectives into everyday classroom activities, such as snack time, toileting, fine motor or art activities, and free play. Bobby's teacher initially targeted snack time for discrete trial periods to train Agent–Action sequences, where she included other peers who could provide additional modeling of the targeted language responses. Performance feedback was given to the teacher, as well as ideas for generalizing the language targets to a variety of classroom interactions.

Following the classroom training sessions, Bobby's mother and trainers discussed his progress and developed a home training program. During this generalization phase, the mother was taught to select discrete times of the day and discrete activites that were representative of Bobby's interests and communication needs at home for parallel training on Agent–Action sequences. By transferring training to the home setting, Bobby's mother was encouraged to apply appropriate language intervention strategies in casual, everyday routine involving new content.

The success of this intervention approach was documented by changes in both child and adult communicative behaviors within 10 IT sessions. Bobby maintained eye contact with his mother during 50 percent of the intervals in a 10-minute session following training, while his spontaneous speech increased from 10 to 30 utterances per session. His oppositional behavior, measured in terms of occurrences per session, decreased from 6 to 1, and his classroom behavior showed more appropriate peer interaction. However, the major success was observed in the mother's increased use of turn-taking strategies (i.e., a mother-to-child turn ratio of 9:11) and by her responses to Bobby's communicative attempts using imitation and expansion techniques (60 percent) with a corresponding decrease in the use of questions (20 percent) and commands (10 percent).

•   •   •

The language consultation approach of the RIP network regards functional communication rather than linguistic forms as the essential feature of language intervention. By having parents and significant others serve as primary change agents for their at-risk and handicapped preschoolers, and by focusing on interchanges in daily play sessions, classroom activities, and home routines during which language skills are immediately functional, the model effectively addresses the generalization and maintenance problems of traditional systems. The RIP consultation approach uses experienced parents to train new families in behavioral language intervention procedures through precise measurement of interaction patterns in the

ABC assessment and treatment framework. Significant others are taught to create environmental events and use social cues that elicit child responses, and then to provide natural consequation and feedback techniques to reinforce children's progressively elaborated communication attempts.

Despite the strengths of this approach, some caution is appropriate in expanding the RIP language model to other early intervention settings. First, it is important to note that not all parents wish to be trained as teachers for their children (Turnbull & Turnbull, 1982), nor do all parents wish to be taught by, or to teach, other parents. Certainly, the intensive involvement of families that characterizes all phases of the RIP system requires that significant others make a substantial commitment of time and effort.

While the RIP language approach has been used successfully with children exhibiting a range of communication impairments (including youngsters with identified developmental delays, mild or fluctuating hearing deficits, neurologically based language problems, and behavioral and emotional disturbances), this type of parent-implemented program may not be sufficient for children with severe speech or language disorders who may require additional intensive professional therapy. Accordingly, special educational personnel, day care providers, and public school teachers who attempt to implement this parent-training program must have access to a resource network of professionals in related disciplines who can provide the requisite administrative support and consultative skills. In addition, the RIP model requires a data-based evaluation design to efficiently monitor the modular management system and assess program efficacy.

Finally, the RIP ecological language intervention approach can be applied in public school or private agency programs serving the special-needs preschool population because it focuses on the functional language skills of children in any environment where natural communication occurs. Thus, a new and different role emerges for the language specialist because direct clinical intervention is replaced with professional consultation. When parents or teachers actually serve as language facilitators and trainers, the speech–language pathologist offers supportive services to these interactants as they implement language programs. While this consultative role is in keeping with recent shifts in clinical practice derived from pragmatic and sociolinguistic theories of language acquisition (Snow, Midkiff-Borunda, Small, & Proctor, 1984), many clinicians will require additional training to develop the necessary consultative skills to function effectively in this ecological intervention system.

REFERENCES

Alpert, C.L., & Rogers-Warren, A.K. (1983, March). Mothers as incidental language trainers of their language-disordered children. Paper presented at the Gatlinburg Conference on Mental Retardation, Gatlinburg, TN.

Bates, E. (1976). *Language and content: The acquisition of pragmatics.* New York: Academic Press.

Bloom, L., Lahey, M. (1978). *Language development and language disorders.* New York: Wiley.

Bricker, D.D. (1986). *Early education of at-risk and*

handicapped infants, toddlers, and preschool children. Glenview, IL: Scott, Foresman.

Bricker, D., & Casuso, V. (1979). Family involvement: A critical component of early intervention. *Exceptional Children, 46,* 108–116.

Bromwich, R. (1981). *Working with parents and infants: An interactional approach.* Baltimore: University Park Press.

Bruder, M., & Bricker, D. (1985). Parents as teachers of their children and other parents. *Journal of the Division for Early Childhood, 9,* 136–150.

Bruner, J.S. (1983). *Child's talk—Learning to use language.* New York: W. W. Norton.

Carney, I. (1983). Services for families of young handicapped children: Assumptions and implications. *Journal of the Division for Early Childhood, 7,* 78–85.

Cartwright, C. (1981). Effective programs for parents of young handicapped children. *Topics in Early Childhood Special Education, 7,* 1–9.

Cavallaro, C.C. (1983). Language interventions in natural settings. *Teaching Exceptional Children, 16*(1), 65–70.

Cordisco, L.K., & Strain, P.S. (1986). Assessment of generalization and maintenance in a multicomponent parent training program. *Journal of the Division for Early Childhood, 10,* 10–24.

Cross, T.G. (1984). Habilitating the language-impaired child: Ideas from studies of parent–child interaction. *Topics in Language Disorders, 4*(3), 1–14.

Dore, J. (1974). A pragmatic description of early language development. *Journal of Psycholinguistic Research, 3,* 343–350.

Dunst, C.J. (1981). *Infant learning: A cognitive–linguistic intervention strategy.* Hingham, MA: Teaching Resources.

Eller, P., Jordan, H., Parish, A., & Elder, P. (1979). Professional qualification: Mother. In R.L. York & E. Edgar (Eds.), *Teaching the handicapped* (Vol. 4). Seattle, WA: American Association for the Education of the Severely/Profoundly Handicapped.

Friel-Patti, S., & Lougeay-Mottinger, J. (1985). Preschool language intervention: Some key concerns. *Topics in Language Disorders, 5*(2), 46–57.

Halle, J.W., Alpert, C.L., & Anderson, S.R. (1984). Natural environment language assessment and intervention with severely impaired preschoolers. *Topics in Early Childhood Special Education, 4*(2), 36–56.

Halle, J.W., Marshall, A., & Spradlin, J. (1979). Time delay: A technique to increase language and facilitate generalization in retarded children. *Journal of Applied Behavior Analysis, 12,* 431–439.

Halliday, M.A.K. (1975). *Learning how to mean.* New York: Elsevier.

Hart, B., & Risley, T.R. (1975). Incidental teaching of language in the preschool. *Journal of Applied Behavior Analysis, 8,* 411–420.

Hart, B., & Risley, T.R. (1980). In vivo language intervention: Unanticipated general effects. *Journal of Applied Behavior Analysis, 12,* 407–432.

Hart, B., & Rogers-Warren, A. (1978). A milieu approach to teaching language. In R.L. Schiefelbusch (Ed.), *Language intervention strategies.* Baltimore: University Park Press.

Hayden, A.H., Morris, K.J., Bailey, D.D. (1977). *Effectiveness of early education for handicapped children.* (ERIC Document Reproduction Service No. ED 163 691).

Hester, P. (1977). Evaluation and accountability in a parent-implemented early intervention service. *Community Mental Health Journal, 13,* 261–267.

Hester, P., & Henderickson, J. (1977). Training functional expressive language: The acquisition and generalization of five-element syntactical responses. *Journal of Applied Behavior Analysis, 10,* 316.

Klein, D. (April, 1985). *Teaching severely handicapped preschoolers to use non-verbal functional requests.* Paper presented at the annual meeting of the Council for Exceptional Children, Anaheim, CA.

Lewis, M., & Cherry, L. (1977). Social behavior and language acquisition. In M. Lewis & L. Rosenblum (Eds.), *Interaction, conversation, and development of language.* New York: Wiley.

Lieven, E.V.M. (1984). Intervention style and children's language learning. *Topics in Language Disorders, 4*(4), 15–23.

MacDonald, J.D., & Gillette, Y. (1984). *Ecomaps: A manual for assessing language through conversation* (Adult–Child Communication Project, The Nisonger Center.). Columbus, OH: Ohio State University Research Foundation.

Mahoney, G., & Weller, E. (1980). An ecological approach to language intervention. *New Directions for Exceptional Children, 2,* 17–32.

McCormick, L.P. (1986). Keeping up with language intervention trends. *Teaching Exceptional Children, 18*(2), 123–129.

McCormick, L., & Noonan, M.J. (1984). A responsive curriculum for severely handicapped preschoolers. *Topics in Early Childhood Special Education, 4*(3), 79–96.

McCormick, L., & Schiefelbusch, R.L. (1984). *Early language intervention.* Columbus, OH: Charles E. Merrill.

McLean, M., & Vincent, L. (1984). The use of expansions as language intervention technique in the natural environment. *Journal for the Division for Early Childhood, 9*(1), 57–66.

Moerk, E.L. (1983). *The mother of Eve as a first language teacher.* Norwood, NJ: Ablex.

Parrish, V., & Hester, P. (1980). Controlling behavior

techniques in an early intervention program. *Community Mental Health Journal, 16,* 169–175.

Rogers-Warren, A., & Warren, S. (1980). Mands for verbalization: Facilitating the display of newly trained language in children. *Behavior Modification, 4,* 361–382.

Rogers-Warren, A.K., & Warren, S. (1983). Facilitating early language and social development: Parents as teachers. In E.M. Goetz & A.E. Allen (Eds.), *Early childhood education: Special environmental, policy, and legal-considerations.* Rockville, MD: Aspen Systems Corp.

Rogers-Warren, A.K., & Warren, S. (1984). The social basis of language and communication in severely handicapped preschoolers. *Topics in Early Childhood Special Education, 4*(2), 57–72.

Schachter, F.F. (1979). *Everyday mother talk to toddlers: Early intervention.* New York: Academic Press.

Sanders, M., & James, J. (1983). The modification of parent behavior: A review of generalization and maintenance. *Behavior Modification, 7,* 3–27.

Shores, R., Hester, P., & Strain, P. (1976). The effects of amount and type of teacher–child interaction on child–child interaction. *Psychology in the Schools, 13,* 171–175.

Snow, C., Midkiff-Borunda, S., Small, A., & Proctor, A. (1984). Therapy as social interaction: Analyzing the contexts for language remediation. *Topics in Language Disorders, 4*(4), 72–85.

Stokes, T.F., & Baer, D.M. (1977). An implicit technology of generalization. *Journal of Applied Behavior Analysis, 10,* 349–367.

Strain, P., & Timm, M.A. (1974). An experimental analysis of social interaction between a behaviorally disordered preschool child and her classroom peers. *Journal of Applied Behavior Analysis, 7,* 583–590.

Strain, P., & Wiegerink, R. (1975). The social play of two behaviorally disordered children during four activities: A multiple baseline study. *Journal of Abnormal Child Psychology, 3,* 61–69.

Strain, P., Young, C., & Horowitz, J. (1981). An examination of child and family demographic variables related to generalized behavior change during oppositional child training. *Behavior Modification, 5,* 15–26.

Timm, M. (November, 1985). RIP: *A parent-implemented treatment model for families with behaviorally disordered and/or developmentally delayed young children.* Paper presented for the National Strategy Conference, President's Committee on Mental Retardation, Washington, DC.

Timm, M.A., & Rule, S. (1981). RIP: A cost effective parent-implemented program for young handicapped children. *Early Development and Care, 7,* 147–163.

Timm, M.A., Strain, P., & Eller, P. (1979). The effects of systematic, response-dependent fading and thinning procedures on the maintenance of child–child interaction. *Journal of Applied Behavior Analysis, 12,* 142.

Turnbull, A.P., & Turnbull, H.R. (1986). *Families, professionals, and exceptionality: A special partnership.* Columbus, OH: Charles E. Merrill.

Turnbull, A., & Turnbull, H. (1982). Parent involvement in the education of handicapped children: A critique. *Mental Retardation, 20,* 115–122.

Warren, S.F., & Kaiser, A.P. (1986). Incidental language teaching: A critical review. *Journal of Speech and Hearing Disorders, 51,* 291–299.

Warren, S.F., Rogers-Warren, A., Baer, D.M., & Guess, D. (1980). Assessment and facilitation of language generalization. In W. Sailor, B. Wilcox, & L. Brown (Eds.), *Methods of instruction for severely handicapped students.* Baltimore: Paul H. Brookes.

Working with families of handicapped infants and toddlers

Michael Trout, MA
Director, The Infant–Parent Institute
Champaign, Illinois

Gilbert Foley, EdD
Director, Psychological Services Center
Albright College
Clinical Instructor in Pediatrics
Medical College of Pennsylvania
Philadelphia, Pennsylvania

Twenty-three-year-old Tommy Lee Halper works the afternoon shift at the pallet mill and cuts pulpwood and firewood in the mornings. He's also the father of a 3-week-old premature son who doesn't quite have a name yet but does have some kind of lung disease. The infant must be very sick, because he's been at the neonatal intensive care unit 70 miles away ever since the day he was born. Tommy Lee doesn't think of himself as the kind who gets upset easily, but that's exactly what happened after he had looked for only a couple of minutes at his little boy—tiny, scrawny, red, and all wired up to beeping machines. Tommy Lee's throbbing head and the waves of nausea coming over him as he ran down the hall of the hospital to find a bathroom led him to swear that he wouldn't come back to that place. He would just wait until his boy was well enough to come home.

The young speech–language pathologist has her hand on the doorknob and is eager to get to her next home visit after an hour spent with 18-year-old Caroline Tyler and her handicapped 2-year-old child. The words come out of the young mother's mouth in an artless, straightforward fashion: "I don't know. Sometimes I look down at her and I say to myself, 'Who *is* she? Where did she *come* from?'"

Top Lang Disord, 1989,10(1),57–67
© 1989 Aspen Publishers, Inc.

The usual rules of decorum and civility had certainly broken down at this Individual Family Service Plan meeting on an otherwise lovely fall day. Mrs. Frieda Sayles had just bolted out of her chair and begun to scream at the gathered members of the special education team, alleging that none of them understood her handicapped child's problem, that they treated her child as merely the latest in an endless line of retarded kids, and that they didn't understand that she had other children to take care of—including the healthy twin of the dying, multiply handicapped child who was the focus of today's meeting. The team psychologist was sputtering in disbelief—he knew, after all, that he had had several meetings with this mother to explain the results of the team's evaluation—when Mrs. Sayles topped off her outburst with the allegation that no one had even told her what was wrong with her child yet.

WHAT COULD BE the matter with these parents? Is there evidence of psychopathology in their apparent inability to "come to terms" with the handicapped child in their families? Are these parents unable to realize that their sick, handicapped, or dying child is relatively helpless without them? Do these parents not want their children to benefit from our carefully conceived therapeutic programs?

Why, indeed, do families keep "distracting" us from our roles as language specialists or special educators with their endless questions, complaints, and stories about the recently born healthy children of neighbors or siblings; with unsettling descriptions of marital strife; and with expressions of hopelessness or helplessness? Why are these parents unable to "accept" the illness or handicapping condition? Why do they overestimate or underestimate their children's condition? Why do they claim to want help and then fail to "cooperate" with us, or even appear to sabotage our plans by failing to show up for appointments or to carry out homework assignments? And why must there be so much guilt (in spite of our protestations that there is nothing to feel guilty about), not to mention the rage, defensiveness, and sorrow?

Perhaps the question ought to be asked in a new way: When are we, as professionals, going to stop being surprised when human beings have human reactions to that which is, for some, the most overwhelming, power-robbing, guilt-producing, isolating, and psychologically challenging event of their lives?

It is not a new idea that those who care for children must also care for their families. It is argued in this article, however, that caring for families should not be considered as an "extra" in an early intervention program—the sort of activity that one adds when there are surplus program resources, staff time, or energy. Instead, the authors contend that the family is at the very heart of the child's life and that the family, which is the handicapped child's ecological system, is critical to the child's optimal development.

THE FAMILY AS ECOSYSTEM

During the ecologically aware 1980s more people have come to understand that changes in any part of a system affect the whole system, that adjustments imposed by outsiders on any part of a system also affect the whole, and that ignoring the ecosystem in order to focus on one of its parts is hazardous. The handicapped child is part of an ecosystem, and it is folly to presume that we can pluck the child out of it to do our evaluations and interventions, then return him or her to it when we are finished. Apart from the issue of the respect that parents deserve from professionals, both clinical rigor and good science require us to assume that we do not know a child unless we know his or her family.

It may be, then, that proper assessment of handicapped infants and toddlers, as well as the likelihood that goals for their improvement will be achieved, are dependent on our willingness to attend to the psychology of their families. This may require a profound shift in attitudes and in evaluation and intervention methods, so that we are never again satisfied with a comfortable, one-on-one relationship with the child but feel impelled to ask the parent(s) in the room, "How is all of this for you?" Only then will a true alliance be possible with those who also want the best possible medical and developmental outcome for their child. Professionals must become students of the family, eager to learn from their perceptions of the child, their discoveries about what works and what does not, and their subjective realities. (The best teachers always earn their jobs by being excellent students first.) It is important to believe that listening attentively to parents' communications will facilitate their responsiveness to the communications of their children.

THE WORLD OF THE HANDICAPPED CHILD

What is the world of the handicapped infant that professionals have chosen to enter, eyes and ears attuned, ready to provide not only the specialized assistance that the infant requires but also the sup-

port, encouragement, training, and sensitivity that the family requires? Do we need advanced degrees in clinical psychology in order to intervene therapeutically in families' struggles?

Parental confusion

Many sick and handicapped infants and toddlers live in a world where parents are disappointed, angry, confused, and lonely. Perhaps even more striking, however, is the fact that parents of such children often do not know why they feel this way, and some are not aware that they feel this way at all. They may have a vague sense that some basic pleasure in infant–parent interaction is missing; that "It just doesn't feel the same to pick up this baby" as it felt when they picked up their earlier, healthy newborns; that there is a sense of emptiness when the infant cannot look at them, will not nuzzle, arches stiffly, or screams .when touched. Successful and supportive interactions between infant and caregiver occur when both parent and infant are maximally available, emotionally and physically, and when a pattern of contingent, attuned responsiveness is developed that helps them to "fit" together. Handicapped infants may not be available in these ways, and the fit does not come easily. From the parents' point of view, it may be simply that it is not pleasant to go to Johnny's crib, that it is immensely frustrating to try to put on his snowsuit, to feed him, or to carry out the home assignment delivered by that well-meaning specialist from the early intervention program.

Such parenting responses, although far from optimal, do not necessarily indicate either psychopathology or inadequate parenting. They may simply represent the parents' attempt to register that something is wrong. A language specialist who is well trained in the nature of human attachments and the course of normal infant–parent interaction may be uniquely capable of helping parents to articulate their feelings and of supporting their eventual efforts to "fit" better with their own child. Such training is critical if we are to take care of handicapped children, which means taking care of their families as well.

Parental losses

The world of the handicapped infant can be one in which the parents are struggling with a host of losses, including the loss of self-esteem, of control over their life, of a future unencumbered by the possibility of a fully grown and fully dependent retarded adult, and of even the semblance of stability and routine in daily life. Parents even feel grief at the loss of delight on the faces of people at the laundromat and at the grocery store, and at the loss of the healthy infant of their shared and separate fantasies. Of course, there is another child who has lived, but not the child to whom the parents had already become attached.

Is this kind of mourning and "chronic sorrow" (Olshansky, 1962) evidence of psychopathology, of a refusal to accept reality? Shall we once again call in the clinical psychologist, while keeping our specialized attention focused on the infant who is both a cause and a victim of all this sadness? Mourning is not a psychiatric illness, and it may be that early interventionists are in a unique position to understand parents' peculiar losses and the un-

resolved, natural grief that often follows them.

Mourning is not a psychiatric illness, and it may be that early interventionists are in a unique position to understand parents' peculiar losses and the unresolved, natural grief that often follows them.

Parental guilt

The world of the handicapped infant is one in which parents may be plagued by guilt. Specialists are often annoyed and frustrated by such guilt, since it seems to stand in the way of acceptance of the handicap and to prevent the mature movement forward that is desired for the family.

It is not, in fact, at all surprising that a parent would feel guilty about hoping for the death of the handicapped infant or about having profoundly different attitudes toward the malformed twin and the healthy twin. The guilt that parents often experience about having created a handicapped child may actually have a functional side: By holding onto "inappropriate" guilt regarding causation a parent may be playing a temporary trick (albeit an unconscious one) to inject some sense of power into a situation that is characterized by powerlessness (Gardner, 1969; Oster, 1984). By virtue of both understanding and careful observation, early interventionists are uniquely qualified to appreciate the peculiar nature of parents' guilt and to recognize its formidable power in the family dynamic.

Informational overload

The parents of a handicapped child are engaged in a constant struggle to acquire and interpret information. It is hardly surprising that such parents sometimes resort to denial, combativeness, tuning out, "doctor-hopping," and insistence on trying measures that professionals believe to be futile. Nor is it surprising that parents become suspicious of professionals, some of whom seem to provide too much information, or to present it too technically, while others seem determined to minimize parental questions and concerns. Moreover, can professionals be trusted to care for one's child as they would care for their own? Kupfer (1984) refers to the barrier between parents and professionals in the information-seeking and information-using arena as a "free-floating anger that has to do, very simply, with our children not being whole, and there's really nothing you can do about that, about fixing them. So sometimes when parents are aggressive and upsetting, I don't think you should take it personally" (p. 24). Oster (1984) suggests that denial in the face of overwhelming information can be adaptive: "Denial gives us time to learn new ways of coping, and the energy and humor to fight the facts in ways that sometimes generate new services and better futures for our children" (p. 29). Professionals should be able to empathize with parents when they feel adrift on a sea of diagnostic and treatment information.

Impaired family dynamics

Finally, the world of the handicapped infant is sometimes one in which healthy siblings both indulge and resent their sick or delayed new member; in which the infant is too much the center of the family; and in which other children in the family find themselves unable to confide their ambivalent feelings to anyone. It may also be a world in which parents are denied the normal, happy social exchanges with the healthy children in the family that could do so much to reassure them that they are doing a good job and that not everything they touch is blighted. It may be a world in which subsequent pregnancies are met with great ambivalence, and parents experience extraordinary anxiety until their new infant can be confidently pronounced to be normal. Thus it should be clear why early interventionists must spend hours with a family in their home, observing what the introduction of a handicapped infant has meant to each family member in order to work most effectively with the infant, and within the family system.

BECOMING FAMILY-CENTERED

It is worth reiterating that any reasonable intervention with a handicapped child involves an entrance into—and, to some extent, a manipulation of—a family system. The rules of scientific rigor, competent clinical practice, and common sense dictate that professionals should make very few moves inside this family system without trying to understand it, that the system's needs must be a central consideration of interventions with the child. When a blind child fails to develop language because he or she lacks the object constancy necessary to suggest the existence of objects "out there" that might be labeled, it may well be that the child is not saying "Mama." To go about the job of language development with such a child without attending to how it feels to the mother not to be named may well invite failure, not only in the area of language work, but also with respect to establishing bonds that are essential to both the child's and mother's development.

Each family's specific needs and circumstances differ as do the capacities of team members to address such difficult issues. Most of the time, however, families' affective and behavioral responses to crises such as the birth of a sick, dying, or handicapped infant are no more psychopathological than would be the professional's own response to the same situation. If the family's responses arise solely from the overpowering challenge of a handicapped infant in their midst, then early interventionists should be well qualified to help both with their infant's specialized needs and their own situation-specific feelings and struggles. The language specialist might well be the one professional in their world who accepts whatever they say on a particular day, who pays attention to everyone in the family, and who helps family members to find words for their questions and feelings.

Admittedly, however, the prospect of trying to address the powerful, even frightening, forces within a highly stressed family can be daunting to someone who was trained primarily in language development. Thus it is encouraging to note that teams can learn to function and to think in

family-centered ways. Teams can even work as families, themselves—teaching one another their disciplines, sharing burdens, challenging and supporting one another. Greenspan points out a danger: "Just as a caregiver may become 'mechanical' with and emotionally distanced from her chaotic and disorganized infant, the individual clinician or treatment team may become mechanical to avoid the intrusive, overanxious, disorganized caregiver or family" (Greenspan, 1988, p. 15). A family-centered approach can help to prevent the mechanical provision of specialized services.

FAMILY-CENTERED EARLY INTERVENTION TEAMS

To offer behavioral prescriptions for the professionals on the team would miss the point of this article, which is that disciplined, systematic immersion in the family system will teach one how the family works and, consequently, what should be done. However, an ecologically attuned early intervention team should possess the characteristics described in the sections that follow.

A family-centered team approach acknowledges the complex and transactional nature of development

The lines of development (i.e., motoric, linguistic, cognitive) are inextricably interlaced, each contributing to the whole. In the dynamic thrust of development there are innumerable promoting and inhibiting cross-over effects in both linear and nonlinear directions (Sameroff & Chandler,

1975). For example, the attainment of sitting balance liberates the hands, allowing more complex object interactions and thus the elaboration of cognitive schemes and language associations. Consequently, any single substrate of development is best understood in relation to all others and to the whole. The sphere of individual development is embedded within the family matrix, so that each developmental gain or loss affects the family, whose reactions (e.g., delight, sorrow, withdrawal, praise) in turn affect the child, in a continuous loop.

Acknowledgment of the complex and transactional nature of development via a family-centered approach is not inconsistent with the notion of a transdisciplinary team. However, this model (Foley, in press) demands a deliberate pooling and exchange of knowledge and skill across traditional disciplinary boundaries. Assessment is conducted in arena fashion, with intervention provided, to the degree possible, through a primary clinician or case manager. Role release among clinicians of several disciplines enables the team to deliver comprehensive, integrated services with cross-disciplinary contributions, all through the primary clinician. This approach reduces multiple handling of the child and acknowledges the centrality of the family–child relationship.

A family-centered approach respects diversity and the developmental nature of parenthood

The capacity to parent competently does not, unfortunately, occur as suddenly as does the capacity to reproduce. It develops over time and requires experience, empathy, and practice. In families with a handicapped child, parental development is further complicated by the unexpected, the unknown, and the tragic (Bernheimer, Young, & Winton, 1983; Murphy, 1982; Provence & Naylor, 1983; Trout, 1983).

Respect for the developmental nature of parenthood translates clinically into "beginning where the family is." This principle is given much lip service but too little practice, often because of professionals' own anxieties or rescue fantasies (Trout, 1988).

As they develop, families take on a wide range of configurations, styles, and psychosocial colorings. Because family diversity must be respected, professionals must make every effort to distinguish between deviance and difference and to remember that a family may be developmentally and functionally different at different times.

In normal development, for example, attachment–separation–individuation and the attainment of object permanence appear to be central themes. The particular form, rate, emphasis, and style with which they are mastered, however, may vary widely without manifest pathology, depending on cultural values, family history and character, and individual traits of temperament (Korchin, 1976). The expression of attachment and separation in one culture may emphasize closeness and proximity to the extended family, while in another, autonomy and nuclear organization are more important. The child-rearing patterns of the former culture may feature extended breast feeding and ample contact comfort; in the latter culture, rigorous promotion of independent behavior and a high tolerance for knocks and falls may be of greater consequence.

Similar variations in style will also be observed in the rearing of the handicapped infant. The aim of early intervention, then, is to facilitate mastery of essential developmental tasks while preserving cultural and familial diversity of means and style. To accomplish this, clinicians need a thorough understanding of normal development, of cultural patterns and norms, and of individual family histories. Because of increased risk for developmental fixation and deviance in delayed infants, family patterns may have to be modified in order to compensate. In such cases intervention may be directed at amplifying, augmenting, or reframing rather than changing the family style.

In any event, the early interventionist must enjoy, respect, and struggle to understand family uniqueness and diversity, while guarding against even the unconscious urge to "normalize" families.

A family-centered approach respects the decision making and autonomy of each family

Early intervention should never be tyrannical in style or engage in unacknowledged behavioral or social engineering. Instead it should strive toward a supportive partnership of learning, growth, and adaptation in which the entire family is encouraged to participate (Barnard, 1984). Commitment to this principle means that families have a right to shape the content and goals of intervention as well as to participate in determining the kind, level, and schedule of services that they receive. They also have a right to obtain second

opinions and to investigate alternative treatments. In other words, they have a right to set limits and to say "no." Parents "must be allowed the normal options of focusing on the needs of other family members or on the family unit as a whole without being blamed or punished by professionals" (Moroz, 1989, p. 116).

A family-centered approach is enabling

An enabling approach to early intervention promotes the self-sufficiency and self-esteem of families through the building of competence in parenting their children. This approach permits professionals to act with rather than on the family. It focuses on guided discovery rather than on direct instruction and is responsive, interactive, and naturalistic.

Responsive intervention builds on successful behaviors that are already a part of the parent–infant repertoire, and it reacts to behaviors initiated by the parent or infant in situ. This requires careful observation of what parents and infants do spontaneously and then seizing the therapeutic moment during each encounter. Responsive intervention is dynamic and vital, not static or staged.

For example, during a session the infant needs to be diapered. The language specialist or other primary clinician notices that the mother is adept at engaging the infant and stimulating reciprocity. The clinician unobtrusively suggests and demonstrates ways to heighten the interaction by increasing vocal output making vocal feedback more contingent. When suggesting or reshaping, the clinician is clear but sufficiently open-ended to allow parents to implement suggestions according to their own style. The teaching style is one of suggestion, demonstration, practice, and coaching.

Enabling intervention is interactive and relationship-centered (Bromwich, 1981), enhancing pleasurable reciprocity between parents and infants, which, in turn, promotes secure attachment. Clinically this implies that the process is as important as the outcome and that affective development is as important as moving, talking, and thinking.

For example, when promoting a block play activity with mother and infant the clinician or teacher should encourage the mutual process of play (not the construction of the tower) by reinforcing face-to-face gazing, turn taking, spontaneity, and the expression of surprise and delight. This kind of interactive intervention cannot easily be conceptualized or reduced to a set of goals on an individual family service plan; such intervention is not a series of static activities or tableaux but rather a dynamic sequence of reciprocal experiences in which multiple goals are embedded (Foley, 1986a).

Naturalistic intervention employs play, physical care of the infant, and the activities of daily living as its medium. It is not procedural but experiential, enabling families to parent their handicapped infant with pleasure and success.

By extension, enabling moves beyond the parent–child sphere. It focuses inward by supporting families in the exploration and activation of their psychological resources, both as individuals and as systems. It also extends outward by empowering families to use the political system, social service resources, relevant methods of ad-vocacy, and the collective support of networking families.

A family-centered approach recognizes the central role of relationships and the inner life in promoting optimal development

Early intervention has the potential to be an even more efficacious therapeutic force by merging the traditionally separate mental health and developmental streams and by integrating the psychological with the technical and didactic. The focus of intervention is expanded to include the inner life of families, the latent as well as manifest conflicts that arise from rearing a handicapped child, and the status of relationships among all family members (Fraiberg, 1980; Foley, 1986b). Families must be in charge of any such expansion, of course. Moroz (1989) emphasizes that families of handicapped children, "while under extraordinary stress, are not intrinsically different from families of nonhandicapped children and should not have psychotherapy foisted on them by well-intentioned social workers or other professionals" (p. 116). Instead, early intervention services should be provided in the context of a supportive, growth-promoting relationship between the clinician and the family. Each professional on the intervention team, regardless of discipline, must know the fundamentals of building and sustaining a supportive relationship that is characterized by consistency, predictability, warmth, positive regard, and empathy. There must be openness on the part of the professional, resulting in partial and temporary identification with the client, although optimal distance and a permeable therapeutic membrane must also be maintained lest overidentification interfere with judgment, limit setting, reality testing, and the stimulation of optimal stress when needed to promote movement (Foley, 1982).

As professionals move toward a more affectively attuned approach, self-insight and reflection become increasingly important. Our own psychological history colors what we see, how we see it, and the ways in which we respond (Trout, 1988). Self-knowledge reduces projective error by acting as a cognitive censor and heightening our sensitivity to feelings and responses that arise from our own psychodynamics, thus permitting us to substitute more thoughtful and therapeutic responses.

The aim, then, is to promote the optimal development of the child by partly supporting emotionally available relationships among all family members.

•   •   •

Families have a great deal to teach professionals about how they can best do their jobs. Although multidisciplinary teams and their members' specialized capabilities are by no means useless relics of the past, the unselfish sharing of functions by expanding roles that were once narrowly defined will be necessary to help early intervention teams to become transdisciplinary units that can assist families with handicapped infants and toddlers on their own turf.

REFERENCES

Barnard, K. (1984). Toward an era of family partnership. In *Equals in this partnership: Parents of disabled and at-risk infants and toddlers speak to professionals* (pp. 4–5). Washington, DC: National Center for Clinical Infant Programs.

Bernheimer, L., Young, M., & Winton, P. (1983). Stress over time: Parents with young handicapped children. *Journal of Developmental and Behavioral Pediatrics*, 4(3), 177–181.

Bromwich, R. (1981). *Working with parents and infants: An interactional approach*. Baltimore: University Park Press.

Foley, G.N. (1982). The principles of observation. *Journal of Children in Contemporary Society*, 14(4), 13–17.

Foley, G.N. (1986a). Emotional development of children with handicaps. *Journal of Children in Contemporary Society*, 17(4), 57–73.

Foley, G.N. (1986b). Family development planning: An intervention model for working with parents of handicapped children. In J. Levy, P. Levy, & B. Niven (Eds.), *Model programs and new technologies for people with disabilities*. New York: Young Adult Institute.

Foley, G.N. (In press). Portrait of the arena evaluation: Assessment in the transdisciplinary approach. In B. Gibbs & D. Teti (Eds.), *Interdisciplinary assessment of infants: A guide for early intervention professionals*. Baltimore: Paul H. Brookes Publishing.

Fraiberg, S. (1980). *Clinical studies in infant mental health*. New York: Basic Books.

Gardner, R. (1969). The guilt reaction of parents of children with severe physical disease. *American Journal of Psychiatry*, 126, 636–644.

Greenspan, S. (1988). Fostering emotional and social development in infants with disabilities. *Zero to Three: Bulletin of the National Center for Clinical Infant Programs*, 9(1), 8–18.

Korchin, S. (1976). *Modern clinical psychology*. New York: Basic Books.

Kupfer, F. (1984). Severely and/or multiply disabled children. In *Equals in this partnership: Parents of disabled and at-risk infants and toddlers speak to professionals* (pp. 18–25). Washington, DC: National Center for Clinical Infant Programs.

Moroz, K. (1989). Educating autistic children and youths: A school–family–community partnership. *Social Work in Education*, 11(2), 107–122.

Murphy, M. (1982). The family with a handicapped child: A review of the literature. *Journal of Developmental and Behavioral Pediatrics*, 3(2), 73–81.

Olshansky, S. (1962). Chronic sorrow: A response to having a mentally defective child. *Social Casework*, 43, 190–193.

Oster, A. (1984). Keynote address of the conference "Comprehensive Approaches to Disabled and At-Risk

Infants, Toddlers and Their Families," December 1984, Washington, DC. Reprinted in *Equals in this partnership: Parents of disabled and at-risk infants and toddlers speak to professionals* (pp. 26–32). Washington, DC: National Center for Clinical Infant Programs.

Provence, S., & Naylor, A. (1983). *Working with disadvantaged parents and their children.* New Haven, CT: Yale University Press.

Sameroff, A., & Chandler, M. (1975). Reproductive risk and the continuum of caretaking casualty. In F. Horowitz (Ed.), *Review of child development research, Vol. 4.* Chicago: University of Chicago Press.

Trout, M. (1983). Birth of a sick or handicapped infant: Impact on the family. *Child Welfare, 62*(4), 337–348.

Trout, M. (1988). Infant mental health: Monitoring our movement into the twenty-first century. *Infant Mental Health Journal, 9*(3), 191–200.

Assessment and intervention with at-risk infants and toddlers: Guidelines for the speech–language pathologist

Shirley N. Sparks, MS
Associate Professor of Speech Pathology
  and Audiology
Western Michigan University
Kalamazoo, Michigan

CURRENT research suggests that an infant should be assessed as part of a family system (Comfort, 1988) and as an interactive partner in a dyad when evaluating communicative function (Coggins, Olswang, & Guthrie, 1987; Wetherby, Cain, Yonclas, & Walker, 1988). Treatment programs for infants that attempt to modify caregiver–infant interaction are purportedly more effective than those that focus on infant behavior alone (Fitzgerald & Fischer, 1987; Mahoney, Finger, & Powell, 1985; Rocissano & Yatchmink, 1983; Snow, 1984). Moreover, Public Law 99-457 (1986) requires that planning intervention and charting progress involve the infant's family. Thus, speech–language pathologists (SLPs) must now garner education and experience in the assessment and treatment of children from birth onward as well as of their families. This article addresses risks to communication development in infants and toddlers and suggests basic guidelines for assessment of and

Top Lang Disord, 1989,10(1),43–56
© 1989 Aspen Publishers, Inc.

intervention with the infant, the interaction, and the caregiver.

RISKS TO COMMUNICATION DEVELOPMENT IN INFANTS AND TODDLERS

Some circumstances are presumed to decrease the chance that an infant will develop communication skills normally. In this issue of TLD Clark outlines birth defects and difficult medical and physiological circumstances that may complicate the development of communication skills. SLPs are particularly concerned with those conditions that interfere with the earliest interactions and that serve as warning signs of interrupted communication development. As Foley (1985) notes, interactional risk factors include:

- *Reduced or altered cuing ability.* The normal newborn has patterns of action and reaction that serve as a powerful preverbal communicative system. This "language" includes changes in posture and muscle tone, facial expression, rhythmic movements, and eye contact. Caregivers use these cues to guide them in their interactions. In handicapped infants these cues may be subtle, ambiguous, idiosyncratic, or absent. The absence of clear signals may result in the caregiver's withdrawal from the interaction, in varying degrees.
- *Delayed locomotion.* Infants may be deterred by limited motor abilities from exploring and learning. In turn, caregivers may interpret the lack of locomotion as a sign of helplessness

and respond as if the infant were at a cognitively younger stage.
- *Disturbances of state and temperment.* Infants who display hyperirritability, exaggerated reflexes, and unpredictable sleep/wake cycles are more difficult to care for, which may result in problems of bonding with caregivers.
- *High incidence of illness.* Illness and/or hospitalization may result in separation from caregivers and may thus impair both attachment and associated normal language development.
- *General developmental delay.* An infant who lacks curiosity about the world may also lack the impetus to develop language for describing and interacting with the world. At the same time, the caregiver may find it difficult to estimate what the infant can do and thus to react appropriately.

Family circumstances may also interfere with parents' ability to deal with infants in a nurturing manner (e.g., poverty, stress, teenage parents) and lead to inappropriate caregiving, which has consequences for communication development (Sameroff & Chandler, 1975). Moreover, biological and caregiving risk factors are not mutually exclusive; an infant's biologic difficulties may precipitate familial conditions that disrupt caregiving, and stressed family circumstances may contribute to biologic difficulties. The majority of infants who are presumed to be at risk for unsatisfactory communication development are at risk due to both factors (Clark & Sparks, 1988). Assessment and intervention, therefore, must consider both the biological and the environmental status of the infant.

ASSESSMENT GUIDELINES

Infant assessments should not be used to predict later behavior

Because most infants are born in hospitals, the idea of identifying all children at risk for abnormal development with an assessment during the first few days of life may seem reasonable. However, no instruments are available that can predict which newborns, even among those with seemingly overwhelming birth complications, will exhibit developmental delays (Horowitz, 1982; Rossetti, 1986). The majority of neonatal intensive care survivors do not suffer from severe or moderate handicaps (McCormick, 1989). Furthermore, an infant's development in one area may be arrested while development in another area advances perceptibly (e.g., motor skills versus language).

Assessment should be serial

Infant behavior changes strikingly, especially during the first 18 months of life. These changes depend to a considerable extent on the nature of the environment; research indicates that children with neonatal problems do less well when their parents are disadvantaged than do those children who, although equally ill during the neonatal period, enjoy better environmental circumstances (Escalona, 1982; Fisch, Belek, Miller, & Engel, 1975; Hunt, Cooper, & Tooley, 1988). The use of regular observations over time allows the examiner to observe developmental patterns, to chart rates of catch-up development, and to recognize new problems that occur.

Assessment must address the infant, the primary caregivers, and their interaction

An infant may be at risk for either biological or caregiving reasons. After a careful history has been taken and a hearing evaluation performed, the clinician will typically make decisions on the basis of the assessment procedures that are discussed in the sections that follow.

ASSESSMENT OF THE INFANT

Infant screening

For some children (e.g., those with identified birth defects) it is virtually certain that communication skills will be delayed or limited. For other children who are presumed to be at risk, delayed or limited skills are a possibility, not a certainty. For these children a screening test, such as the Early Language Milestone (ELM) Scale (Coplan, 1984), may be used; the ELM surveys a variety of communicative behaviors (i.e., auditory-receptive, expressive, visual) that occur with some reliability in children from birth to 36 months of age. Failure in any of the three areas calls for further assessment. The criteria for passing the screening are liberal, and so failure should be taken seriously. The ELM Scale may be administered by any health care professional. Chronological age must be corrected to allow for gestational age if the infant was premature (Clarke & Sparks, 1988). Those children with a reasonable risk of developing a communication disorder should have serial screenings, which should not be substituted, however, for the hearing screening of at-risk infants ("Audiologic Screening," 1989).

Infant in-depth assessment

Once an infant is identified as a candidate for in-depth assessment, information may be gathered in a number of areas: prelinguistic behaviors; verbalizations; cognition; gross and fine motor skills; oral–motor skills; self-help skills; and personal/social skills. The question is not what test should be used for all infants but what information is needed for this infant? Before assessment procedures are chosen, the particular objectives for that assessment should be specified, and each procedure evaluated critically (Johnson, 1982). The instruments suggested here are intended to serve as examples only.

Neonatal assessment

Just as the medical specialty of neonatology was unknown just a few years ago, so too was the assessment of an at-risk newborn by a SLP. Four general principles guide assessment of the neonate in an intensive care unit (NICU), or of the hospitalized infant by the SLP or language specialist.

Research the prenatal and perinatal history

What is the condition that puts this child at risk? What is known about communication development associated with that condition (Nelson, in press; Sparks, 1984)? Of primary importance is assessing the risks for secondary disorders that specifically affect communication (e.g., sensory deficits).

Evaluate the infant's ability to maintain homeostasis (i.e., physiologic organization)

Every aspect of the premature infant's physiologic functioning is immature. The very low birth weight infant (i.e., less than 1,500 g) will almost always require support for respiration, thermoregulation, and nutrition. The immaturity of such infants is evident in their irregular respiratory efforts, labile color changes, and visceral instability. They may be either quite jittery or flaccid and display very disorganized state of alertness patterns (Lawhon, 1986). Each preterm infant must be carefully evaluated to determine the current level of organization, as well as individual behavioral capacities and coping strategies, before any developmental interventions are offered (VandenBerg, 1985).

The Neonatal Behavioral Assessment Scale (Brazelton, 1984) provides a system of assessing organization in the full-term infant; however, its use with small–for–gestational age and premature infants has made clear that such infants are less well organized than full-term infants. Thus the

---

Each preterm infant must be carefully evaluated to determine the current level of organization, as well as individual behavioral capacities and coping strategies, before any developmental interventions are offered.

Assessment of Preterm Infant Behavior, or APIB (Als, Lester, Tronick, & Brazelton, 1982), was developed to meet the needs of the low birth weight infant. The infant's level of functioning is observed as well as his or her threshold for disorganization. The APIB is a comprehensive tool for evaluating the preterm infant's autonomic, motor, self-regulatory, attentional, and interactional abilities. It assesses behavioral capacities and organizational level from approximately 28 to 40 weeks of gestational age and is designed to answer the following questions:

- When, and with what help, does the infant function smoothly?
- How much and what kinds of stress and frustration are seen in the infant?
- How much energy does the infant have available for smooth functioning?
- How much handling can the infant tolerate before losing control?
- Is the infant's homeostatic balance easily disrupted?
- What strategies does the infant exhibit to avoid losing control?
- What support is necessary to help the infant to maintain self-control?

Evaluate oral-motor behavior

The contribution of the SLP may be crucial in this area. As Jaffe points out in this issue of TLD, aberrant oral–motor behavior is never part of normal development.

Evaluate the infant's hospital environment

The medical needs of the infant are necessarily the first priority of the hospital and staff. Nevertheless, evaluation of the types and amount of stimulation (including ambient noise) and of the availability of communication opportunities should be undertaken in the hospital as part of the overall assessment of the infant.

ASSESSMENT OF INTERACTIONS

An infant's communication development takes place via recurring interactions with caregivers; therefore, assessment must include observations of such interactions. Many clinicians have made the videotaping of caregiver–infant free play a standard part of their assessment procedure; the tape is then used to observe the interactive behavior. This has been termed "low-structured observation" (Coggins et al., 1987). Indeed, several new and exciting instruments for observing interaction are emerging from current research.

The measurement of specific behaviors as they occur, either through frequency counts or through duration recording, is termed "event sampling" (Bailey & Wolery, 1984). Building on the work of Bates (1979), Coggins et al. (1987), and Bruner (1981), Wetherby et al. (1988) studied communicative functions from the prelinguistic to the multiword stage of normal children in interaction with a clinician. Analysis indicated that virtually all subjects displayed some acts for the purposes of regulating adult behavior, engaging in social interaction (e.g., calling attention to self), and focusing attention on an object concurrently with the caregiver at all language stages. Based on that research, Wetherby and Prizant (1989) are presently developing the Communication and

Symbolic Behavior Scale for children from 9 to 24 months of age. The clinician presents a number of temptations to the child in order to elicit communication (e.g., eating a desired food item in front of the child without offering any to the child; activating a wind-up toy, permitting it to deactivate, and then handing it to the child). He or she also observes the child during structured and free play. Responses are recorded on 20 scales, and a profile of the child's strengths and weaknesses is the result. Other event-sampling instruments involve play behavior. For example, Lifter, Edwards, Avery, Anderson, and Sulzer-Azaroff (1988) and Westby (1980) have devised scales in which interpersonal behaviors and language markers are recorded during play with specified materials.

Another more highly structured technique is a "running record," which documents everything that occurs within a given time period. A running record familiar to clinicians is the language sample used with verbal children. When used to assess prelinguistic behavior, however, a running record includes all of the behaviors that a child uses for interaction. This technique permits the coding and analysis of caregiver behavior as well. Examples of the running record are the videotape analysis procedures of McCollum and Stayton (1985) and Cole and St. Clair-Stokes (1984), which was designed to measure communicative interactions between hearing-impaired infants and caregivers. Analysis of running records is quite time-consuming, because the clinician must convert disparate information into a meaningful form.

ASSESSMENT OF CAREGIVERS

This discussion is confined to the knowledge, skills, and attitudes that may affect how a caregiver approaches and responds to the infant. Caregivers vary in their degree of knowledge about infants; they may or may not be able to translate their knowledge into action when dealing with their own infants. They may be emotionally invested in their caregiving situation in helpful or harmful ways. Mahoney et al. (1985) identified three communicative styles that mothers use with their mentally retarded children: (1) Mothers may be responsive to their children's communication; (2) they may be didactic (i.e., oriented to instructing their children while communicating); or (3) they may fail to engage in reciprocal communication with their children. When Mahoney et al. studied the children's rate of communication development in relation to these maternal styles, they found that the children of "communicatively responsive" mothers developed more rapidly than children whose mothers used the other communicative styles. In this regard, four questions require particular attention:

1. Do the caregivers make themselves available, physically and emotionally, for interaction with the infant?
2. What are the caregivers' expectations about the infant's eventual attainment? They may expect an unrealistically positive outcome, or they may unfairly disregard the infant's potential.
3. How do the caregivers view interaction with the infant? Caregivers of a handicapped child may be expected

to make some accommodations to their child's individual ways of responding.

4. Are the caregivers highly directive in attempting to interact with the infant or, on the other hand, are they responsive to the infant's communicative signals (Clark & Sparks, 1988)?

It is important to remember that positive caregiver attributes occur in all socioeconomic and ethnic groups; the assessor must take particular care that his or her own cultural values do not form the only standard of acceptable caregiving.

A number of observation instruments are available to guide the clinician in assessing caregiver attributes. Typically observations are recorded on a checklist by the clinician while observing the caregiver in interaction with the infant or through direct caregiver interviewing. One instrument that uses both observation and interview is the Parent Behavior Progression, or PBP (Bromwich, 1981). The PBP allows the clinician to characterize the caregiver's attitude toward the infant, the caregiver's ability to observe and interpret the infant's behavior, and the caregiver's knowledge about the infant's abilities and needs.

A scale that was developed as part of a project to help low socioeconomic, mostly minority mothers to develop interactions that foster speech and language is the Observation of Communicative Interaction (Klein & Briggs, 1987). A list of 10 behaviors of the caregiver in interaction with the infant guides observation (e.g., mother smiles contingently at infant, mother encourages "conversation").

ASSESSMENT OF FAMILIAL STRENGTHS AND NEEDS

It should be noted that the instruments mentioned in the preceding section do not fulfill the mandate of Public Law 99-457, which calls for an assessment of family strengths and needs as part of the individual family service plan (IFSP). In that assessment, which is intended to individualized treatment, the family must participate by identifying their perceptions of their own strengths and needs. Guidelines for family assessment may be found in Bailey and Simeonsson (1988); their Family Needs Survey is highly recommended. Another widely used instrument is the Home Observation for Measurement of the Environment (Caldwell & Bradley, 1984). The authors studied the family dynamics, the objects (e.g., toys, books), and the experiences that were common to the homes of children who did well academically, and they constructed a scale of those items. As they freely admit, the scale is culture-bound and is most useful with families that are comparable with the sample used for standardization (i.e., white, middle-class Americans).

It may be necessary to compose two lists: a list of strengths and needs as defined by the family and a comparable list based on the judgment of professionals. Designing goals for intervention will clearly be smoother if there is considerable overlap between the two lists. However, if they are divergent, the needs identified by the family must be the first priority for intervention. When families are not only empowered to be full participants in decision making but are viewed as the most important participants, then the intent of the legislation is fulfilled and goals for intervention can be formulated.

INTERVENTION GUIDELINES

It is beyond the scope of this article to discuss intervention strategies in depth. However, some guidelines and resources for intervention with infants at various linguistic stages and their families will be suggested.

Put infants and caregivers in touch with one another while facilitating the infants' communicative competence

Both infants and caregivers have immediate and powerful needs to establish communication, even if traditional communicative modes are not viable. The clinician who helps caregivers to interpret infant cues (e.g., a tantrum is a communication born of frustration when there is no other avenue of communication), and who gives the infant even one gesture with which to shape caregiver behavior in a positive way, has put them in touch. Keeping them in touch is an ongoing process that is enhanced as the clinician works to facilitate the infant's language development.

Based on assessment data, the target for intervention may be the infant, the caregiver, the interaction, or a combination of all three

Traditional intervention models have focused primarily on developmental change in children, with little attention directed to the adaptive characteristics of their families. Virtually no attention has been paid to ongoing interactions despite general recognition that development is a transactional process between a child and his or her family (Shonkoff, Hauser-Cram, Krauss, & Upshur, 1988). The infant and caregiver(s) compose the critical unit; in fact, the younger the child, the more important it is for intervention to focus on the infant in interaction with the caregiver(s) rather than with the clinician. Instead of deciding on a single approach to therapy (i.e., How does this infant learn best?), clinicians must also make decisions about intervention approaches for the caregiver or family, being sensitive to personal, cultural, and stylistic differences among caregivers.

Goals and objectives should reflect the focus on caregiver and interaction as well as on infant behavior

At this point there may be an assumption that intervention with infants and toddlers is completely unstructured and that the only role for the clinician is to act as a coach who points out ways for the caregiver to interact appropriately with the infant. Although less structure and more flexibility are certainly called for than in traditional therapy, goals and objectives are as appropriate for early intervention as they are for traditional treatment. The difference is that they may be formulated for the unit of infant and caregiver (e.g., mother and infant will engage in interactive play with equal turns). This is not to say that some handicapped infants will not have goals for specific skill areas, such as those derived from the criterion-referenced tests. However, in the context of the IFSP, priority should always be given to those goals that are especially important to the family; for example, saying or signing "mama" or the elimination of whining might be much more important than the next objective on the program list. Recognizing, therefore, that considerable overlap between intervention for the infant and intervention for infant–caregiver interaction is both inevitable and desirable, the following discussion addresses how intervention goals may be implemented the primary focus of which is the infant or the caregiver–infant interaction.

Intervention with focus on the infant

Intervention with the Infant

Duchan and Weitzner-Lin (1987) surveyed the literature and concluded that intervention through nurturant–naturalistic interactions, in which the infant takes the lead in contexts that are likely to be encountered in everyday life, are preferable to didactic methods with infants and toddlers. The authors suggest changes in current ways of planning lessons and tracking progress. Nurturant–naturalistic situations are created in which the caregiver or clinician has opportunities to supply or add information (Manolson, 1985). Strategies include labeling and describing that which has the child's attention, imitating and expanding verbalizations, talking about what is happening in short sentences, and repeating often. Two examples may illustrate these strategies: (1) A caregiver says an oft-repeated rhyme, stops before the last word, looks in anticipation at the child, and waits for an attempt; the infant's attempt is then imitated by the caregiver and repeated or expanded. (2) A child points to the refrigerator; the caregiver, at eye level, says "Want juice?" and pours a small amount (so that the situation may be repeated), this time saying only "Want?" and waiting for the child to supply the missing word.

Intervention with the High-Risk Neonate

The initial goal with the very low birth weight infant is not the achievement of developmental milestones or the development of skills appropriate for full-term infants, but rather stabilization and homeostasis (Gorski, 1983; VandenBerg, 1985). However, for those multihandicapped but stable infants who must stay in the hospital for a protracted period of time, intervention is appropriate. A program for direct intervention is Education for Multihandicapped Infants (Wallen, Elder, & Hastings, 1982).

Another goal for clinicians is to prevent or minimize secondary disorders associated with biological and environmental conditions. Infants who are cared for in the NICU are at risk for hearing loss from high noise levels and from ototoxic drugs, with secondary risk for language delay associated with hearing loss. Another risk is for laryngeal damage from endotracheal tubes, with associated voice disorder (Sparks, 1984). Certainly low language stimulation and sensory overstimulation from constant light and sound are cause for concern. Clinicians who have earned credibility and respect in the NICU may reduce these risks through their work with nurses.

*Intervention with focus on the
caregiver-infant interaction*

Interaction of Infants and Caregivers

Most parent–child interaction goals define the parent as the target of intervention, because the parent is the more competent partner in the dyad. It is assumed that a change in the parent's behavior will elicit a change in the infant's behavior. Some caregivers may need only a brief period of developmental guidance (e.g., information about expected infant development), while other caregivers' knowledge and skills may be grossly insufficient, requiring extensive help. Comfort (1988) groups intervention strategies into direct and indirect techniques. Direct intervention strategies typically include discussing parent and child characteristics and behaviors, modeling, and teaching. For example, the clinician and parent select a target skill; the clinician explains the techniques required to teach the skill; the clinician models the technique, observes the parent using the technique, and gives feedback. Teaching strategies may be preferred by highly motivated, well-educated caregivers who are eager to have information.

Girolametto, Greenberg, and Manolson (1985), MacDonald and Gillette (1984), and Mahoney and Powell (1984) have used direct teaching for an interaction approach that is child-centered. They help parents to observe what the child is doing, wait with anticipation, listen as if every sound or action is a communication, and react appropriately. Included in the basic principles of all three programs are

- Follow the child's lead as to what interests him or her. The caregiver adapts to the child.

- Take turns: first, by waiting for the child to request that the caregiver continue an activity by any demonstrable gesture or sound; later, through social games and routines (e.g., peek-a-boo); and, still later, with objects. Turns may be prompted verbally or physically.

Other caregivers may learn best in an environment that responds to them as individuals and nurtures personal relationships over an extended period of time (see the article by Trout & Foley in this issue of TLD). For them, indirect approaches to child-centered interaction should be considered, such as counseling, viewing videotapes of themselves, and peer modeling. Klein, Briggs, and Huffman (1987) discuss videotape strategies for use in individual and group sessions with low-socioeconomic-status mothers and their infants, the goals of which are to convey information and to enhance and encourage caregivers' use of positive communicative interactions with their infants. A particular segment can be replayed so that the clinician can carefully point out the elements of the strategy being used by the mother and its effect on the infant. A useful technique for clinicians is to attribute intention on the part of the mother when, perhaps, none truly exists; a desirable behavior is reinforced when the mother hears it described as positive. When pointing out errors, it is important that a staff member instead of a mother be identified as interacting in a counterproductive way. In addition, peer modeling is possible in group situations, with one member of the group assuming the role of authority figure or advisor (perhaps a mother who has several children). The other mothers may emulate her interactions as shown on videotape during the group session.

Interaction in the NICU

Promotion of appropriate communication and interaction between neonate and caregivers is the primary goal. When visiting the neonate in the NICU with the parents, the clinician may facilitate parents' enjoyment of their infant as they observe him or her together; this is also an excellent opportunity to point out the physiologic changes in heart beat, temperature, color, and breathing rate as communicative cues as well as signs of the infant's present state of alertness. Parents who learn to recognize when the infant is in an alert state, and thus ready for interaction, are rewarded by their infant's response. On the other hand, signs of stress may also be pointed out, such as spreading the fingers, grunting, averting the gaze, and arching the back (Kavalhuna, 1988). As the infant achieves homeostasis and is prepared to go home, the clinician may counsel the parents concerning the cues and responses of their infant, which may include atypical communications. For example, the infant may still have difficulty maintaining eye contact without losing homeostasis and, consequently, look away frequently. The parent may react by following the infant's gaze and trying to reengage, which interrupts the infant's attempts to become organized. Parents may be counseled to allow the infant "time out" and to interact only when he or she turns back to them. Videotapes of the newborn in the NICU are useful when parents return for follow-up visits; as they look back in time at their fragile newborn,

they are helped to appreciate their accomplishments as caregivers.

Maintaining a relationship with the family and the timing of intervention are important to intervention outcome

There is little empirical evidence as to which early intervention approaches produce the best results. However, Heinicke, Beckwith, and Thompson (1988) compared evaluations of family change in 20 early intervention programs with those of control families who did not experience intervention. They found that intervention contacts had to be of a certain frequency and duration before their effects differentiated the experimental group significantly from a nonintervention group. The best results were found when intervention began shortly after birth. The minimum number of intervention contacts was found to be 11, and the intervention had to last for at least 3 months, strongly suggesting that a trusted and sustained relationship with a clinician early in the child's life is important to the intervention process. It also has implications for continuity of treatment, which leads to the last guideline.

As a member of a team of professionals, clinicians can work toward integrating communication with all other aspects of intervention

The intervention guidelines presented thus far have been based on the assumption that the SLP is the direct intervenor. In fact, the SLP may be a part of a transdisciplinary team of which the case manager is the sole intervenor, assisted by advice from the other team members. The guidelines in this article can be readily adapted to fit a team model in which the SLP functions as a consultant. In that case, it is the SLP's responsibility to incorporate communication goals for the infant, caregiver, and interaction into the goals of the other professionals. For example, communication goals may be integrated into feeding interventions (e.g., turn taking, face-to-face positioning, caregiver talking and enjoyment, waiting for the infant to initiate food intake). Motor activities are also excellent opportunities for communication (e.g., distal communication by caregiver as the child moves away, communication games during motor activities, imitation of the infant and waiting for a response, and interaction during naturalistic play situations). Integrating communication with all other goals may seem too ambitious, but it is difficult to imagine a goal that would not involve some form of communication.

• • •

The discussion by Bailey and Simeonsson (1988) of barriers to effective family assessment has relevance for SLPs striving to provide the best possible service to infants and their families. First, many barriers are self-imposed. To a large degree, the training and experience of SLPs has prepared them to work with small children, but in traditional ways. Different skills are required to change adult behavior, and family counseling requires additional expertise. Second, institutional programs have traditional criteria for assessment and intervention that seem to be inflexible. Third, the families themselves may resist service delivery that they perceive to be intrusive. Fourth, meaningful measures of the efficacy of intervention programs are unavailable. Nevertheless, SLPs are gaining new competencies, working in new delivery systems, assessing and intervening in innovative ways, and building an empirical base in support of their contention that early intervention is effective. Certainly SLPs can do no less.

REFERENCES

Als, H., Lester, B.M., Tronick, E., & Brazelton, T.B. (1982). Toward a research instrument for the assessment of preterm infants' behavior (APIB). In H.E. Fitzgerald, B.M. Lester, & M.W. Yogman (Eds.), *Theory and research in behavioral pediatrics, Vol. 1* (pp. 35–132). New York: Plenum Press.

Audiologic screening of newborn infants who are at risk for hearing impairment. (1989). *Asha 21*(3), 26–29.

Bailey, D.B., & Simeonsson, R.J. (1988). *Family assessment in early intervention.* Columbus, OH: Charles E. Merrill.

Bailey, D.B., & Wolery, M. (1984). *Teaching infants and preschoolers with handicaps.* Columbus, OH: Charles E. Merrill.

Bates, E. (1979). *The emergence of symbols: Cognition and communication in infancy.* New York: Academic Press.

Brazelton, T.B. (1984). *Neonatal behavior assessment scale.* Philadelphia: Lippincott.

Bromwich, R.M. (1981). *Working with parents and infants: An interactional approach.* Baltimore: University Park Press.

Bruner, J. (1981). The social context of language acquisition. *Language and Communication, 1,* 155–178.

Caldwell, B.M., & Bradley, R.H. (1984). *Home observation for measurement of the environment* (Revised ed.). Little Rock, AR: University of Arkansas.

Clark, M.J., & Sparks, S. (1988). Evaluation of the at-risk infant. In D. Yoder & R. Kent (Eds.), *Decision making in speech–language pathology* (pp. 178–179). Toronto: B.C. Decker.

Coggins, T., Olswang, L., & Guthrie, J. (1987). Assessing communicative intents in young children: Low structured observation or elicitation tasks? *Journal of Speech and Hearing Disorders, 52*, 44–49.

Cole, E., & St. Clair-Stokes, J. (1984). Caregiver-child interactive behavior: A videotape analysis procedure. *Volta Review, 86*, 200–217.

Comfort, M. (1988). Assessing parent–child interactions. In D.B. Bailey, & R.J. Simeonsson (Eds.), *Family assessment in early intervention* (pp. 65–94). Columbus, OH: Charles E. Merrill.

Coplan, J. (1983). *The Early Language Milestone Scale.* Tulsa, OK: Modern Education Corporation.

Duchan, J.F., & Weitzner-Lin, B. (1987). Nurturant–naturalistic intervention for language-impaired children: Implications for planning lessons and tracking progress. *Asha, 29*(7), 45–49.

Escalona, S.K. (1982). Babies' double hazard: Early development of infants at biologic and social risk. *Pediatrics, 70*, 670–676.

Fisch, R.O., Belek, M.D., Miller, L.D., & Engel, R.R. (1975). Physical and mental states at 4 years of age of survivors of respiratory distress syndrome. *Journal of Pediatrics, 86*, 497–503.

Fitzgerald, M.T., & Fischer, R.M. (1987). A family involvement model for hearing-impaired infants' language facilitation: The role of parents and others. *Topics in Language Disorders, 7*(3), 1–18.

Foley, G.M. (1985). Emotional development of children with handicaps. *Journal of Children in Contemporary Society, 17*(4), 57–72.

Girolametto, L.E., Greenberg, J., & Manolson, H.A. (1986). Developing dialogue skills: The Hanen early language parent program. *Seminars in Speech and Language.*

Gorski, P.A. (1983). Premature infant behavioral/physiological responses to caregiving intervention in the NICU. In J.D. Call, E. Galenson, & R.I. Tyson (Eds.), *Frontiers in infant psychiatry.* New York: Basic Books.

Hedrick, D.L., Prather, E.M., & Tobin, A.R. (1984). *Sequenced inventory of communication development.* Seattle: University of Washington Press.

Heinicke, C.M., Beckwith, L., & Thompson, A. (1988). Early intervention in the family system: A framework and review. *Infant Mental Health Journal, 9*(2), 111–141.

Horowitz, F.D. (1982). Methods of assessment for high-risk and handicapped infants. In C.T. Ramey & P.L. Trohanis (Eds.), *Finding and educating high-risk and handicapped infants* (pp. 101–118). Baltimore: University Park Press.

House of Representatives Report #99-860, P.L. 99-457. (1986). *Education of the handicapped act amendments of 1986.* Washington, DC: Author.

Hunt, J.V., Cooper, B.A.B., & Tooley, W.H. (1988). Very low birth weight infants at 8 and 11 years of age: Role of neonatal illness and family status. *Pediatrics, 82*, 596–602.

Johnson, N.M. (1982). Assessment paradigms and atypical infants: An interventionist's perspective. In D. Bricker (Ed.), *Intervention with at-risk and handicapped infants.* Baltimore: University Park Press.

Kavalhuna, R. (1988). Service delivery to infants at risk for communication disorders. Paper presented at the Van Riper Lectures, Western Michigan University, Kalamazoo, MI, October 14, 1988.

Klein, M.D., & Briggs, M.H. (1987). Facilitating mother–infant communicative interactions in mothers of high-risk infants. *Journal of Childhood Communication Disorders, 10*(2), 95–106.

Klein, M.D., Briggs, M.H., & Huffman, P.A. (1987). *Facilitating caregiver–infant communication.* Los Angeles: California State University at Los Angeles, Division of Special Education.

Lawhon, G. (1986). Management of stress in premature infants. In D.J. Angelini, C.M. Whelan Knapp, & R.M. Gibes (Eds.), *Perinatal/neonatal nursing: A clinical handbook* (pp. 41–49). Boston: Blackwell Scientific Publications.

Lifter, K., Edwards, G., Avery, D., Anderson, S.R., & Sulzer-Azaroff, B. (1988). Developmental assessment of children's play: Implications for intervention. Paper presented at the annual convention of the American Speech–Language–Hearing Association, Boston. (Play Scale is available from K. Lifter, 203 Lake Hall, Northeastern University, Boston, MA 02115.)

MacDonald, J., & Gillette, Y. (1984). *Ecological communication system.* Columbus, OH: The Nisonger Center, Ohio State University.

Mahoney, G.J., Finger, I., & Powell, A. (1985). The relationship between maternal behavior style and the developmental status of mentally retarded infants. *American Journal of Mental Deficiency, 90*, 296–302.

Mahoney, G., & Powell, A. (1984). *Transactional intervention program: A demonstration early intervention project for birth through three-year-old handicapped infants.* Woodhaven, MI: Woodhaven School District.

Manolson, A. (1985). *It takes two to talk.* Toronto: Hanen Early Language Resource Centre.

McCollum, J.A. & Stayton V.D. (1985). Social interaction assessment/intervention. *Journal of the Division for Early Childhood, 9*, 125–135.

McCormick, M.C. (1989). Long-term follow-up of infants discharged from neonatal intensive care units. *Journal of the American Medical Association, 261*, 1767–1772.

Nelson, S. (In press). NICU assessment. In S.N. Sparks, M.J. Clark, D. Oas, & R.L. Erickson (Eds.), *Infants at risk for communication disorders: Professional's role with the newborn.* Tucson, AZ: Communication Skill Builders.

Rocissano, L., & Yatchmink, Y. (1983). Language skill and interactive patterns in prematurely born toddlers. *Child Development, 53*, 1229–1241.

Rossetti, L. (1986). *High-risk infants: Identification, assessment, and intervention*. Boston: College-Hill Press.

Sameroff, A., & Chandler, M. (1975). Reproductive risk and the continuum of caretaking causality. In F.D. Horowitz (Ed.), *Review of child development research, Vol. 4*. Chicago: University of Chicago Press.

Shonkoff, J.P., Hauser-Cram, P., Krauss, M.W., & Upshur, C.C. (1988). A community of commitment: Parents, programs and the early intervention collaborative study. *Zero to Three, 8*(5), 1–7.

Snow, C.E. (1984). Social interaction and language acquisition. In P.S. Dale & D. Ingram (Eds.), *Language—An international perspective: Selected papers from the first international congress for the study of child language* (pp. 195–214). Baltimore: University Park Press.

Sparks, S.N. (1984). *Birth defects and speech–language disorders*. Boston: College-Hill Press.

VandenBerg, K.A. (1985). Revising the traditional model: An individualized approach to developmental interventions in the intensive care nursery. *Neonatal Network, 4*, 32–56.

Wallen, P.B., Elder, W.B., & Hastings, S.N. (1982). *Education for multihandicapped infants*. Charlottesville, VA: Department of Pediatrics, University of Virginia Medical Center.

Westby, C.E. (1980). Assessment of cognitive and language abilities through play. *Language, Speech and Hearing Services in Schools, 23*(2), 89–99.

Wetherby, A.M., Cain, D., Yonclas, D., & Walker, V. (1988). Analysis of intentional communication of normal children from the prelinguistic to the multi-word stage. *Journal of Speech and Hearing Research, 31*, 240–252.

Wetherby, A.M., & Prizant, B. (1989). *Communicative and symbolic behavior scale*. San Antonio: Special Press.

The first three years: Special education perspectives on assessment and intervention

Gail L. Ensher, EdD
Associate Professor of Special Education
Syracuse University
Syracuse, New York

IN A forward-looking article published in the *Journal of the Division for Early Childhood*, Odom and Warren (1988) project early childhood special education ahead to the year 2000. Many issues will change; some will undoubtedly remain the same. Already, however, several new factors are appearing on the horizon, and these will clearly affect how we, as teachers and clinicians, will work with young children. For example, delivering services within the least restrictive environments is not a new idea, but it will be mandatory in the future, as interpreted by guidelines of Public Law 99-457. This movement will surely create greater incentives to offer services within the context of typical classroom settings—a trend already evident in some public school early education programs and day care centers. In addition, special educators, language specialists, and other clinical personnel will have to become much more conversant with typical early education efforts (Forman & Hill, 1984; Hohmann, Banet,

Top Lang Disord, 1989,10(1),80–90
© 1989 Aspen Publishers, Inc.

& Weikart, 1979; Peterson & Felton-Collins, 1986) in order to foster optimal environments for children. A second change that can be confidently predicted is the increasing focus on family involvement and family services (Bailey & Simeonsson, 1988a; Odom & Warren, 1988). The importance of the "ecology of human development" (Bronfenbrenner, 1979) has long been recognized by early childhood specialists, and yet most assessment and intervention services have remained largely child-centered. The new requirements of Public Law 99-457 for individual family service plans (IFSPs) will necessarily broaden our views of planning and programming. Third, although the past decade has witnessed great interest in the fields of early childhood special education, demands for services in the future are likely to increase (Ensher & Clark, 1986), causing a proportionate need for new program models. The medical technologies of neonatal intensive care nurseries have markedly improved the survival rates of the tiniest of infants at 24 to 28 weeks of gestation. These newborns typically require long hospital stays of at least 3 to 4 months and are often discharged home with technology dependencies, such as oxygen requirements (Report of the Task Force on Technology-Dependent Children, 1988). In addition, the near epidemic of acquired immunodeficiency syndrome (AIDS) in the United States has become a significant concern of families and schools (Odom & Warren, 1988) and placed substantial demands on the public sector. As a result, requirements for assessment and intervention will be increasingly extended beyond the confines of the school to hospital and home settings. If professionals have been reluctant to work together in the past, such will not be an option in the future. In the fullest sense, teams will become transdisciplinary. Concomitantly, educators and clinicians alike will have to become adept at evaluating, in the earliest months, such factors as infant state, behavioral organization, and temperament, which may well be related to both the medical and developmental needs of handicapped and at-risk infants and young children.

EARLY LANGUAGE DEVELOPMENT DELAY WITHIN HIGH-RISK AND HANDICAPPED POPULATIONS

It is clear that various events and conditions decrease the likelihood that some infants will develop typical patterns of communication, cognition, movement, and other skills. Numerous birth defects and difficult medical and physiologic circumstances have been associated with adverse developmental outcomes, which predictably complicate the acquisition of speech, language, and hearing abilities. Similarly, the infant's and toddler's cognitive and social/emotional development are inseparable from, and almost totally dependent on, the environment and psychosocial–communicative interaction with primary caregivers. Families may fail to act in nurturing ways toward their infants, thus creating inappropriate or maladaptive caregiving environments (Cicchetti & Toth, 1987). In addition, biological difficulties may precipitate familial reactions that disrupt the normal course of parent–child interaction. Today most specialists in early childhood special education recognize that high-risk and handicapped populations are vulnerable as a result of clusters of factors (Clark & Sparks, 1988; Tjossem, 1976). A prime example is the high incidence of child abuse and neglect that is widely reported to occur among preterm and/or young handicapped populations.

Language specialists and early childhood special educators are especially concerned about situations and conditions that interfere with the earliest childhood interactions and thus constitute warning signs of problematic psychological and communicative development. Teachers and clinicians must always be alert to such signs—not to the extreme; on the other hand, they must be vigilant, not naively to ignore genuine areas of concern. Distinguishing between an expectable delay (e.g., several weeks of prematurity) and the need for intervention is an elusive problem that often tests the most highly developed clinical acumen.

FOCUSING ON INFANTS, TODDLERS, AND THEIR FAMILIES IN ASSESSMENT

Screening and diagnosis: Some general guidelines

Assessing infants and toddlers is a challenge for even the most experienced teacher and clinician. Irrespective of professional discipline or the specific methodologies used, effective screening and diagnosis should follow certain basic guidelines to ensure valid and reliable results:

- Flexibility in terms of time, setting, materials, and administration (Bailey & Wolery, 1988). Infants and toddlers obviously have their own characteristics and idiosyncratic needs that may require altering schedules, evaluation plans, and the persons involved in a session. For example, between the ages of 6 to 9 months, when infants are especially anxious in the presence of strangers, it may be necessary to include family members in the assessment process.

- Use of multiple measures that sample information about the child, family, and overall home environment (Ensher & Clark, 1986). Most teachers and clinicians recognize this point; however, it deserves special emphasis in the context of very young children, who are egocentric and tend to be impulsive. Combinations of strategies (e.g., family interview, direct observation of family interaction in varied situations) in addition to developmental evaluation of the child will yield the most revealing information.

- Assessment by diverse teams of professionals. Typically, whenever infants or toddlers are referred for screening and diagnosis, the problems manifested are noteworthy in several behavioral, perceptual, language, and cognitive areas. As a result, assessment should be broadly based, representing several different disciplines (i.e., speech–language pathology, physical and occupational therapy, early childhood special education, psychology). It may also be important to involve medical personnel, depending on the nature of medical concerns.

- Ongoing assessment in its various phases of screening, diagnosis, and follow-up. Because change during the first three years of life is dramatic, the course of evaluation needs to be designed to sample behavior frequently in hospital, home, and school settings.

- Observation during the optimal state of alertness and behavior. Before the evaluation of any infant or toddler, time should be spent with the child and parent(s) or primary caretaker in order to determine patterns of sleeping and feeding, special preferences, and periods of optimal alertness (Ensher, Bobish, Michaels, Meller, Gardner, & Butler, in press). If children are irritable or inattentive, the evaluation should be discontinued and rescheduled.

Screening, diagnosis, and ongoing assessment: Prominent and emerging concepts

Assessment typically encompasses three broad phases: screening, diagnosis, and ongoing evaluation. Moreover, assessment (as distinguished from testing) involves the use of several measures and techniques that should serve at least four major purposes: (1) identifying those in need of intervention, (2) determining goals, (3) monitoring developmental progress, and (4) evaluating the effectiveness of intervention (Johnson, 1982). Invariably, each of these objectives becomes the focus of efforts during the course of evaluation processes. Furthermore, assessment procedures should be consistent with specified goals and provide the kinds of information that clinicians and teachers need in order to answer certain questions or hypotheses about behavior and performance.

Recognizing the wide range of capacities in infants and young children, professionals have long searched for valid and reliable assessment instruments (Gorski, Lewkowicz, & Huntington, 1987); however, such expectations in regard to language and developmental evaluation are bound to be disappointed. Although recent measures and observational techniques, which focus on families as well as children, are more closely aligned with intervention objectives, much of that which is done under the rubric of "testing" remains difficult to apply to educational practice.

Identifying children in need of intervention has been carried out most often via norm-referenced, standardized screening and diagnostic tools that yield either age-equivalency scores or scores that show the extent of deviation from mean performance at given ages. Most of these tests have been conceived in order to examine mental development, although many of the items (especially those for the earlier months of the first year) are more motor-oriented than language- or cognition-based. Such instruments have been standardized on populations of children that were deliberately selected so as to exclude youngsters with biological or other known handicapping conditions, in spite of which they have been widely employed to describe the performance of just such developmentally delayed groups. Unfortunately, these instruments do not allow for the careful "charting" of change and progress (Neisworth & Bagnato, 1988) that is essential to educational programming.

Criterion- and curriculum-referenced tests and scores evolved, in part, in response to the need for measures that are directly related to teaching. They identify skills in various domains that are useful in guiding the formulation of intervention goals, and they sometimes offer suggestions for correlated curriculum activities. Frequently they contain lists of hierarchically organized developmental skills and specific criteria defining the mastery of tasks. Commonly used measures include the Carolina Curriculum for Handicapped Infants and Infants at Risk (Johnson-Martin, Jens, & Attermeier, 1986), the Hawaii Early Learning Profile (HELP) (Furuno, Inatsuka, O'Reilly, Hosaka, Zeisloft, & Allman, 1984), and the Early Learning Accomplishment Profile (Glover, Preminger, & Sanford, 1978). In many instances, skills are categorized into six areas: cognition, language and communication, self-help and adaptation, social/emotional, fine motor, and gross motor. Such tools have been designed particularly for children with a variety of developmental problems and may be administered by paraprofessionals and parents as well as by specialists.

Unfortunately, criterion-referenced tests often include items taken directly from the standardized tests that they were designed to replace. In an attempt to construct profiles of strengths and weaknesses of handicapped children, researchers have often assigned age levels to skills on the basis of norm-referenced measures (and thus on the basis of mean ages at which typical children master those skills), so that children are once again described in terms of deviation from expected norms. Moreover, scores may be less reliable than those obtained from any one standardized test because, derived from several tests, they are based on different standardization samples (Johnson, 1982).

Several authors (Neisworth & Bagnato, 1988; Paget, 1988) have noted that the Battelle Developmental Inventory (Newborg, Stock, Wnek, Guidubaldi, & Svinicki, 1984) offers a desirable compromise between criterion-referenced and norm-referenced tests. Created for youngsters from birth to 8 years of age, the Inventory is a standardized measure that permits the examiner or clinician to gather information that is based on structured developmental evaluation, parent interviews, and observations in natural settings. An additional advantage is that the instrument provides alternative techniques for assessing children with various handicapping conditions.

Although teachers, clinicians, and other professionals who work with young populations have long recognized the inadequacies of prominent assessment measures, alternative paradigms have been used much less frequently than have standardized and/or formally structured instruments. Services provided from birth to the age of 3 years have aimed primarily at developmental change in children, with less attention directed to the adaptive characteristics of families. Moreover, little heed has been paid in programmatic evaluations to ongoing interactions at home, despite the general recognition that development is a transactional process between child and family (Barber, Turnbull, Behr, & Kerns, 1988; Shonkoff, Hauser-Cram, Krauss, & Upshur, 1988). A plausible solution to this problem has been offered by Bailey and Simeonsson (1988a). Consistent with the IFSP mandated by Public Law 99-457, their strategy requires that evaluations focus on the attainment of goals rather than on test scores for the child and that intervention be developed by a team of professionals and the family. Indeed, some practitioners have now adopted procedures for generating recommendations with the respective families. In essence the assessment process is becoming much more ecological in nature. As a result, it can be expected that all types of evaluation will take into account factors such as behavioral state and infant organization (Helm & Simeonsson, 1988); the behavior, temperament, and cognitive styles of young children; family interaction; social interaction and play; and diverse environmental influences.

FOCUSING ON INFANTS AND TODDLERS IN EARLY INTERVENTION

Greenspan and White (1985) wrote that

in future studies we would be well advised to employ a comprehensive methodology including comprehensive approaches to both intervention and evaluation. That overall efficacy has now been well established at program termination allows us to get to more difficult questions about what kinds of approaches work best with what kinds of children and with what kinds of effects. (p. 5)

Most recent intervention research in hospital, home, and school settings confirms this analysis. Moreover, contemporary studies in early childhood are beginning to isolate and study those variables affecting individual children that seem to bring about positive change in particular situations. In addition, emerging directions in assessment, as noted previously, should be extremely beneficial in defining new approaches.

Intervention in neonatal intensive care nurseries

Studies conducted during the past two decades in neonatal intensive care nurseries (NICNs) have often focused on tactile–kinesthetic, auditory–visual, and multimodal stimulation. In particular, researchers have been interested in such questions as the effect of nonnutritive sucking on behavioral states; the benefits of stroking, cud-

dling, and rocking; the effects of parental voice on behavioral state; and the impact of vestibular stimulation with waterbeds. As DeSocio and Ensher (1986) have pointed out, however, a number of questions yet remain unanswered. They suggest that

research in the future will have to address many issues about the appropriateness and timing of intervention with varying degrees of prematurity, the nature of specific interventions, sensitive measures of developmental change, the diversity of high risk infant populations, best individuals for program implementation, and the guidance that should be offered to parents relative to earlier and later stimulation. (p. 210)

Fortunately, studies that respond to some of the issues just noted are beginning to emerge.

Researchers and clinicians are now suggesting that interventions with infants in intensive care units should be contingent on the ability of individual infants to handle particular stimuli (Cole & Frappier, 1985; Linn, Horowitz, & Fox, 1985; Oehler, 1985). Als and her colleagues (Als, 1986; Als, Lawhon, Brown, Gibes, Duffy, McAnulty, & Brickman, 1986) have been pioneers in developing strategies for assessing behavioral state organization and determining, for example, how much handling an infant can tolerate before losing control, which techniques might be helpful in easing infant stress, and which kinds of support are necessary in order to maintain stability. Concomitantly, studies in the biomedical fields have increasingly offered evidence of the strong relationship between physiological factors and environmental conditions (Mastropaolo, 1988), suggesting that the proper handling and positioning of infants may reduce stress, which might, in turn, decrease oxygen and caloric requirements at particularly critical points. Likewise, providing parents with information about how to touch their critically ill infants and when to temper interaction in order to prevent withdrawal reactions could conceivably lead to more mutually satisfying child–family relationships. Such research is important given the many reports of excessive irritability and difficult temperament among preterm infants (Spungen & Farran, 1986) and the prevalence of child abuse and neglect.

Finally, recent preventive approaches in NICNs seem to support the wisdom of targeting both parent and child in the developmental intervention process. Resnick and his colleagues developed a multimodal intervention program, in-hospital and at home, for high-risk infants weighing less than 1,800 grams up to 12 months of adjusted age (Resnick, Armstrong, & Carter, 1988; Resnick, Eyler, Nelson, Eitzman, & Bucciarelli, 1987). Children in a contrast group received "traditional, remedially oriented care."

Although questions remained in terms of the relative importance of specific interventions, the authors concluded that

> Our findings convince us that treatment programs in neonatal intensive care units (NICUs) and their follow-up components must be parent-centered as well as infant-centered. Parents need to be integrated into the treatment program as soon as their baby is admitted to the NICU, as they were in our intervention protocol, so that they can learn to respond to the baby's cues and to stimulate the baby appropriately. In addition, a strong, ongoing relationship must be established between parents and the health professionals who are involved with the baby's developmental program. (Resnick et al., 1987, p. 77)

This study indicated that early parental involvement can have significant positive effects on infant mental development and on the quality of caregiver–infant interactions.

Family-focused, community-based interventions with infants and toddlers

Like the work conducted in intensive care nurseries, intervention in community settings—both home-based and center-based—is focusing on questions that are vastly different from those of the efficacy research of the 1960s and 1970s. Thus there is new promise that some of the numerous and complex variables that affect the analysis of change in children with handicapping conditions and their families will be understood. For in-depth coverage of the topic, the reader is referred to several excellent reviews and discussions (Dunst, 1985; Greenspan & White, 1985; Guralnick, 1988; Shonkoff & Hauser-Cram, 1987; Shonkoff et al., 1988; Warren & Kaiser, 1988).

FUTURE DIRECTIONS FOR RESEARCH AND INTERVENTION

As the 1990s approach, research and community-based early intervention alike will have to take into account rapidly changing times, new political and economic pressures, multiproblem families, and multiply involved infants and young children. In light of such inevitable demands, careful attention must be paid to:

• Descriptions must be provided of the populations of families and children involved in programming. Several authors (Bailey & Simeonsson, 1988b; Guralnick, 1988; Shonkoff et al., 1988) have noted the ambiguity that has plagued research on the effectiveness of early education as a result of the diversity of targeted populations. Guralnick (1988) in particular has suggested the alternative of organizing "efficacy analyses initially within disability samples themselves" (p. 78). In view of considerable individual differences within the various disabled groups, studies of change within such samples, aligned along certain dimensions, might be extremely helpful. Guralnick has described this strategy with respect to children. In light of the new emphasis on ecological approaches, researchers and educators should also assume the task of identifying particular dimensions of family functioning (e.g., income and educational levels, types of support, family structure, religious affiliations, locale of residence) that could be examined in relation to a continuum of positive changes.

• Descriptions must be provided of the types and intensity of program models (Guralnick, 1988) in relation to existing community resources, the context of the environment, and specific populations of children and families. This consideration is closely tied to the previous point and has already received limited investigation by researchers who have examined the benefits, for example, of home-based and center-based models of early intervention with low-income families and children as compared with the advantages of these models for more severely impaired youngsters in middle-and upper-income families (Bailey & Simeonsson, 1988b). Illustrating this point, Ramey, Bryant, Sparling, and Wasik (1985) carried out a study to look at the effectiveness of two early intervention approaches in the prevention of mental retardation. They concluded that the strategy of developmental day care plus family education was most effective in preventing the early decline of intellectual development. Factors in given communities that act to enhance or suppress the self-actualizing abilities of families and their children.

• The goals of intervention and the specific roles of parents. Until recently, achieving positive change in the child's development has taken precedence over family goals and priorities and other dimensions of living within a community (e.g., the degree of isolation of families). Moreover, curricular and programmatic efforts have been confined to narrowly defined developmental areas, without considering that the enhancement of interactions and relationships might have broader, longer-lasting, and more meaningful effects on child and family behavior. Indeed, the provisions of Public Law 99-457 will compel interventionists both to reorganize their priorities and to document their transactional processes that have been used to achieve intervention goals.

• Professional roles must be redefined within naturalistic settings.

As our priorities change in the decade ahead, the ways in which we accomplish objectives and measure them to determine their effectiveness will shift to new strategies for evaluation, new partnerships and collaborations (Shonkoff et al., 1988), and new educational paradigms within naturalistic settings. Toward a process of implementation, perhaps we should begin to

• establish baselines of data prior to and concomitant with implementation;
• carry out practice and research on a small scale, carefully documenting long-term changes in families, children, and communities;
• establish—on local, state, and federal levels—registers of best-practice pro-

gramming and descriptions of the milieus within which such interventions take place;

- establish "program support hotlines" at local and state levels for resolving critical issues and impediments to change;
- collect data on the effectiveness of working relationships within transdisciplinary teams;
- reexamine and modify personnel preparation programs in early childhood, special education, and communication disorders in light of new requirements (e.g., family-focused assessment and intervention); and
- develop proactive local task forces to examine and plan for problems and issues on the horizon (e.g., the education of children with AIDS).

In short, there is much that we must accomplish by the year 2000. We have the capacity to change. The question is: *How will we change?*

REFERENCES

Als, H. (1986). A synactive model of neonatal behavioral organization: Framework for the assessment and support of the neurobehavioral development of the premature infant and his parents in the environment of the neonatal intensive care unit. *Physical and Occupational Therapy in Pediatrics, 6,* 3–55.

Als, H., Lawhon, G., Brown, E., Gibes, R., Duffy, F., McAnulty, G., & Blickman, J. (1986). Individualized behavioral and environmental care for the very low birth weight preterm infant at high risk for bronchopulmonary dysplasia: Neonatal intensive care unit and developmental outcome. *Pediatrics, 78,* 1123–1132.

Bailey, D.B., Jr., & Simeonsson, R.J. (1988a). *Family assessment in early intervention.* Columbus, OH: Charles E. Merrill.

Bailey, D.B., Jr., & Simeonsson, R.J. (1988b). Home-based early intervention. In S.L. Odom & M.B. Karnes (Eds.), *Early intervention for infants and children with handicaps: An empirical base* (pp. 199–215). Baltimore: Paul H. Brookes.

Bailey, D.B., Jr., & Wolery, M. (Eds.). (1988). *Assessing infants and preschoolers with handicaps.* Columbus, OH: Charles E. Merrill.

Barber, P.A., Turnbull, A.P., Behr, S.K., & Kerns, G.M. (1988). A family systems perspective on early childhood special education. In S.L. Odom & M.B. Karnes (Eds.), *Early intervention for infants and children with handicaps: An empirical base* (pp. 179–198). Baltimore: Paul H. Brookes.

Bronfenbrenner, U. (1979). *The ecology of human development: Experiments by nature and design.* Cambridge: Harvard University Press.

Cicchetti, D., & Toth, S.L. (1987). The application of a transactional risk model to intervention with multi-risk maltreating families. *Zero to Three: Bulletin of the National Center for Clinical Infant Programs, 7*(5), 1–8.

Clark, M.J., & Sparks, S. (1988). Evaluation of the at-risk infant. In D. Yoder & R. Kent (Eds.), *Decision making in speech–language pathology* (pp. 178–179). Toronto: B.C. Decker.

Cole, J.G., & Frappier, P.A. (1985, November-December). Infant stimulation reassessed: A new approach. *Neonatal Network, 3*(5), 24–30.

Dunst, D.J. (1985). Rethinking early intervention. *Analysis and Intervention in Developmental Disabilities, 5,* 165–201.

Ensher, G.L., Bobish, T.P., Michaels, C.A., Meller, P., Gardner, E.F., & Butler, K.G. (In press). *Syracuse scales of infant development.* Syracuse: Syracuse University Press.

Ensher, G.L., & Clark, D.A. (Eds.). (1986). *Newborns at risk: Medical care and psychoeducational intervention.* Rockville, MD: Aspen Publishers.

Forman, G.E., & Hill, F. (1984). *Constructive play: Applying Piaget in the preschool* (rev. ed.). Menlo Park, CA: Addison-Wesley.

Furuno, S., Inatsuka, T.T., O'Reilly, K.A., Hosaka, C.M., Zeisloft, B., & Allman, T.L. (1984). *Hawaii early learning profile.* Palo Alto, CA: VORT.

Glover, M.E., Preminger, J.L., & Sanford, A.R. (1978). *Early learning accomplishment profile.* Winston-Salem, NC: Kaplan Press.

Gorski, P.A., Lewkowicz, D.J., & Huntington, L. (1987). Advances in neonatal and infant behavioral assessment: Toward a comprehensive evaluation of early patterns of development. *Developmental and Behavioral Pediatrics, 8,* 39–50.

Greenspan, S.I., & White, K.R. (1985). The efficacy of preventive intervention: A glass half full? *Zero to Three:*

Bulletin of the National Center for Clinical Infant Programs, 5, 1–5.

Guralnick, M.J. (1988). Efficacy research in early childhood intervention programs. In S.L. Odom & M.B. Karnes (Eds.), *Early intervention for infants and children with handicaps: An empirical base* (pp. 75–88). Baltimore: Paul H. Brookes.

Helm, J.M., & Simeonsson, R.J. (1988). Assessing behavioral state organization. In D.B. Bailey, Jr., & M. Wolery (Eds.), *Assessing infants and preschoolers with handicaps* (pp. 202–224). Columbus, OH: Charles E. Merrill.

Hohmann, M., Banet, B., & Weikart, D.P. (1979). *Young children in action.* Ypsilanti, MI: The High/Scope Press.

Johnson, N.M. (1982). Assessment paradigms and atypical infants: An interventionist's perspective. In D.D. Bricker (Ed.), *Intervention with at-risk and handicapped infants* (pp. 63–76). Baltimore: University Park Press.

Johnson-Martin, W., Jens, K.G., & Attermeier, S.M. (1986). *The Carolina curriculum for handicapped infants and infants at risk.* Baltimore: Paul H. Brookes.

Linn, P.L., Horowitz, F.D., & Fox, H.A. (1985). Stimulation in the NICU: Is more necessarily better? *Clinics in Perinatology, 12,* 407–422.

Mastropaolo, A. (1988, November). The role of the physical therapist in early intervention. Paper presented at the Margaret L. Williams Developmental Evaluation Center Conference, "Early Prevention, Early Intervention," Syracuse, New York.

Neisworth, J.T., & Bagnato, S.J. (1988). Assessment in early childhood special education. In S.L. Odom & M.B. Karnes (Eds.), *Early intervention for infants and children with handicaps: An empirical base* (pp. 23–49). Baltimore: Paul H. Brookes.

Newborg, J., Stock, J.R., Wnek, L., Guidubaldi, J., & Svinicki, J. (1984). *Battelle developmental inventory.* Allen, TX: Teaching Resource.

Odom, S.L., & Warren, S.F. (1988). Early childhood special education in the year 2000. *Journal of the Division for Early Childhood, 12,* 263–273.

Oehler, J.M. (1985). Examining the issue of tactile stimulation. *Neonatal Network, 4*(3), 25–33.

Paget, K.D. (1988). Assessment of cognitive skills in the preschool-aged child. In D.B. Bailey, Jr., & M. Wolery (Eds.), *Assessing infants and preschoolers with handicaps* (pp. 275–300). Columbus, OH: Charles E. Merrill.

Peterson, R., & Felton-Collins, V. (1986). *The Piaget handbook for teachers and parents: Children in the age of discovery, preschool–third grade.* New York: Teachers College Press.

Ramey, C.T., Bryant, D.M., Sparling, J.J., & Wasik, B.H. (1985). Preventive education for high-risk children: Cognitive consequences of the Carolina Abecedarian project. *American Journal of Mental Deficiency, 88,* 515–523.

Report of the Task Force on Technology-Dependent Children. (1988, April). *Fostering home and community-based care for technology-dependent children.* Washington, DC: U.S. Department of Health & Human Services.

Resnick, M.B., Armstrong, S.S., & Carter, R.L. (1988). Developmental intervention program for high-risk premature infants: Effects on development and parent–infant interactions. *Developmental and Behavioral Pediatrics, 9,* 73–78.

Resnick, M., Eyler, F., Nelson, R., Eitzman, D., & Bucciarelli, R. (1987). Developmental intervention for low birth weight infants: Improved early developmental outcome. *Pediatrics, 80,* 68–74.

Shonkoff, J.P., & Hauser-Cram, P. (1987). Early intervention for disabled infants and their families: A quantitative analysis. *Pediatrics, 80,* 650–658.

Shonkoff, J.P., Hauser-Cram, P., Krauss, M.W., & Upshur, C.C. (1988). A community of commitment: Parents, programs and the early intervention collaborative study. *Zero to Three: Bulletin of National Center for Clinical Infant Programs, 8*(5), 1–7.

Spungen, L.B., & Farran, A.C. (1986). Effect of intensive care unit exposure on temperament in low birth weight preterm infants. *Developmental and Behavioral Pediatrics, 7,* 288–292.

Tjossem, T. (Ed.). (1976). *Intervention strategies for high-risk and handicapped children.* Baltimore: University Park Press.

Warren, S.F., & Kaiser, A.P. (1988). Research in early language intervention. In S.L. Odom & M.B. Karnes (Eds.), *Early intervention for infants and children with handicaps: An empirical base* (pp. 89–108). Baltimore: Paul H. Brookes.

Index

trained, empiric research on, 111, 112
world of, 179–181
Hanen Early Language Program, 150
Hawaii Early Learning Profile (HELP), 206
Hearing-impaired children
  acquisition and, 126–129
  communication skills, 98
  interaction and, 126–129
  learning potential, 125
  preschool intervention plan, 124
Hearing loss
  early detection, 106
  neonatal risk, 196
HELP (Hawaii Early Learning Profile), 206
High-risk populations
  early language development delay, 203–204
  neonatal intervention, 196
Hollingshead Scale, 67
Home Observation for Measurement of the Environment, 194
Homeostasis, prematurity and, 191–192
Hospital environment, of infant, evaluation, 192
Hyperirritability, 189

I

IFSPs (individual family service plans), 194, 203, 206
Illinois Test of Psycholinguistic Abilities, 58
Illness incidence, interrupted communication development and, 189
Illocutions, 8, 10
Imperatives, in maternal speech, 86
Implementation process, future directions for, 209–210
Incidental teaching opportunities, 170–171
Individual family service plans (IFSPs), 194, 203, 206
Infant(s). *See also* Infant assessment
  caregiver-infant interaction approach, 188
  communication with caregiver, 195
  cues, 195, 198
  family-focused interventions for, 208
  as intervention focus, 196
  maltreatment, 54–58
Infant assessment
  family system and, 188
  guidelines, 190
  homeostatic evaluation, 191–192
  hospital environment evaluation, 192
  in-depth, 191
  of interactions, 192–193

oral-motor behavior evaluation, 192
  perinatal history, 191
  prenatal history, 191
  primary caregivers and, 190
  screening, 190–191
  serial, 190
Informant interviewing, 13
Information exchange, in Mama Lere Program, 95–96
Information mapping, 36–38
Informational overload, of parents of handicapped children, 181
Intake, vs. input, 141
Intelligence quotients (IQs), maltreatment and, 58, 60
Intent, as intervention focus, 130–131
Interaction. *See also specific types of interaction*
  generation, 154–155
  intervention and, 129–131
  language acquisition and, 125–126
  in neonatal intensive care unit, 198
  styles, for parent training, 153–155
Interrogation, in eliciting language, 154–155
Intervention. *See also* Early intervention programs
  with caregiver-infant interaction focus, 197–198
  framework, for RIP model, 166–168
  goals, 195–196
  guidelines, 195–199
  with high-risk neonate, 196
  with infant focus, 196
  integration guidelines, 198–199
  in Mama Lere Training Program, 101–104
  objectives, 195–196
  outcome, 198
  tasks with words, 44–48
Intervention specialists, for family involvement models, 106
Interventions
  data-based documentation, 171
Introspectionism, 5–6
IQs, maltreatment and, 58, 60

J

John Tracy Clinic, 150
Joint attentional intentions (comments), 70, 155–156
Joint focus of attention, 113
Joint reference, child-centered approach and, 153

K

Kaluli community, Papua New Guinea, 87
Keyword method, 47–48

Preschool children
  developmental effects of maltreatment, 58–60
  maltreatment, language deficits and, 57
Preschool curricula, sociodramatic play training and,
  117
Preschool language intervention
  clinical issues, 138–142
  play and, 140
Preschool Language Scale (PLS), 59
Preschool-period, 124
Productive syntactic level, 72
Program model descriptions, 209
Promoting requests, 113
Prompting
  requests, 113
  structured free play, 114–115
  teacher, peer strategies and, 116
Propositions
  hierarchy, 25, 26
  in topic maintenance, 24–25
Public Law 94-142
  implementation, 93
Public Law 99-457
  individual family service plan and, 188, 194, 203,
    206
  intervention goals and, 209
  least restrictive environment and, 202

Q

Question usage, parents of language-impaired
  children and, 154

R

Rationalism
  description, 4–6
  pragmatism and, 4–5
READ Project, 150
Reality-play distinction, 11
Receptive vocabulary
  tests, 39
  of toddlers, 66
Reciprocity measures, 130
Recording systems, 145
Recordkeeping, 145
Reflexes, exaggerated, 189
Regional Intervention Programs for Parents and
  Preschools (RIP). *See* RIP model
Regulatory intentions, 70
Reinforcement, peer strategies and, 116

Relationship function, of communication, 9
Repetitions, in word knowledge development, 34
Requestives, 145
Research
  clinical populations, 82–83
  empiric, on handicap training, 111, 112
  future directions for, 208–210
  longitudinal, on family-centered intervention, 107
  on maltreatment, 51, 60–62
  pragmatic, 8
  social interaction, 7
Resource personnel, 171
Response chart, for interactive language activity,
  146
Responsive communicative style, of mothers of
  mentally retarded children, 193
Responsive intervention, 184
RIP model
  active treatment phase, 163
  assumptions, 166
  case example, 171–173
  classroom module, 165
  data-based clinical operation, 164–165
  data-based documentation of language interven-
    tions, 171
  ecological language intervention, 174
  generalization of communication skills, 169–171
  generalization training module, 165
  individual tutoring module, 165
  intervention framework, 166–168
  intervention principles and procedures, 166–171
  language consultant and, 169
  language consultation approach, 166–173, 173–174
  language intervention approach, 162–163
  lead classroom teacher, 169
  lead parent teacher, 169–170
  limitations, 174
  modular system, 164–165
  parental participation, 163–164
  payback phase, 163
  referral and intake module, 165
  resource staff, 163–164
  service-delivery system, 163–165
  speech/language consultant, 164
  training of significant others, as communication
    facilitators, 168–169
Root-word strategy, 45
Routine, in topic maintenance, 26–27
Running records, 193